INTERCULTURAL MEDIATION
IN HEALTHCARE

INTERCULTURAL MEDIATION ᴵᴺ HEALTHCARE:

FROM THE PROFESSIONAL MEDICAL INTERPRETERS' PERSPECTIVE.

IZABEL E. T. DE V. SOUZA, PH.D.

To order additional copies of this book, contact:
Xlibris
1-888-795-4274
www.Xlibris.com
Orders@Xlibris.com
741016

CONTENTS

LIST OF ABBREVIATIONS

ASTM	American Society of Testing and Materials
CCHCP	The Cross Cultural Health Care Program
CCHI	The Certification Commission for Healthcare Interpreters
CLAS	National (US) Standards for Culturally and Linguistically Appropriate Services in Health Care
CHI	Certified Healthcare Interpreter
CMI	Certified Medical Interpreter
CMIE	Commission for Medical Interpreter Education, a Division of the IMIA
EDC	Education Development Center, Ltd.
FIT	International Federation of Translators
IMIA	International Medical Interpreters Association
ISO	International Standards Organization
JAMI	Japan Association of Medical Interpreters
JCI	Joint Commission International
NB	National Board of Certification for Medical Interpreters, IMIA Division
TJC	The Joint Commission (United States)
WASLI	World Association of Sign Language Interpreters

LIST OF TABLES

LIST OF FIGURES

DEDICATION

I dedicate this work to my parents; Angela Maria
Telles and Miguel Pedro de V. Souza,
for each one, in their own very special and unique way,
taught me the priceless value of research and continuous learning.

I thank my six children and Frank Cohen for
their encouragement and support.

SUMMARY

Cultural differences are a strong barrier to high-quality healthcare for culturally diverse patients. Providing culturally appropriate services eliminates health disparities, minimizes risk, and decreases culturally diverse patient safety incidents. Medical interpreters mediate language and culture, and supporting intercultural mediation is essential for healthcare organizations to provide culturally competent care to this vulnerable patient population.

This book is the result of a five-year project to study and explore the perspectives of professional medical interpreters. As practitioners in a complex healthcare environment, professional medical interpreters are the primary experts regarding their own practice of *interpreting culture*. The doctoral study described in this book utilized a mix of qualitative ($n= 35$) and quantitative ($n=423$) design, obtaining data from four hundred and fifty-eight (N=458) medical interpreters working in twenty-five countries. A critical review and analysis was conducted via verbal reporting methodology on four data collection sources (interview, survey, focus group, essay). Participants shared case studies, advantages, disadvantages, challenges, timing, stressors, effects, and the training related to their work as intercultural mediators. Results indicated their mediation work affects provider and institutional cultural competency, patient satisfaction, trust, compliance, and most importantly, the health outcomes of culturally diverse patients.

Medical interpreters are acting as intercultural mediators in ways beyond addressing miscommunication between patients and providers due to a cultural issue. This role includes intercultural tasks and interventions, taking place both within and outside interpreted-assisted communicative events, simultaneously or not to mediating language. Participants described decision-making processes unobservable to the parties involved in the triadic encounter, as well as observable behaviors as cultural agents. Data analysis indicates that some of their opinions about interpreting culture are strongly tied to the medical interpreter's healthcare objectives (work environment related), and a professional identity beyond the scope of linguistic conversion. This research developed new theoretical frameworks, by categorizing the data into three macro domains of professional scope of practice. These include: 1) healthcare professional, 2) intercultural communication professional, and 3) linguistic professional. For example, participants reported some activities and professional objectives that are healthcare related, vs. language related. These included goals such as providing culturally competent care, enhancing the patient-provider therapeutic rapport, acting as part of the healthcare team, improving patient health outcomes, and ensuring patient safety. The work described in this book is also characterized by a relatively high degree of facilitation skills and effort to reduce the complexity of the intercultural communication events. 99.56% of participants of the study challenge the linguistic-only paradigm of their work, reporting working as active participants with contributions far beyond accurate language mediation.

A model that recognizes intercultural mediation as an integral part of a medical interpreter's work, is more applicable to the highly contextualized patient and provider needs of the healthcare setting. They act as welcomers, integration agents, community agents, bilingual professionals, cultural informants, and educators, all within the context of intercultural mediation. Better institutional policies, professional standards, and education are needed for this subspecialty of healthcare interpreting. This cultural work needs to be recognized as essential in patient safety and the provision of culturally competent healthcare services.

INTRODUCTION

Ancient cultures interacted with different groups that did not speak their language and were not from their cultural background for several reasons, such as for trade or treaties. These interactions required the reliance on intermediaries in order to communicate. These intermediaries, in some cases called interpreters, or intercultural mediators, needed to be proficient in the languages in question and understand the cultural frameworks to be served, in order to mediate language and culture.

Since the 1960s, due to the rise of immigrants who do not speak the local language, in certain countries, healthcare organizations started relying on medical interpreters to enable healthcare providers to communicate with their patients and vice-versa. In the countries with higher immigrant populations, there has also been a movement to provide healthcare services in a culturally and linguistically competent manner in order to prevent negative health outcomes for these vulnerable populations. Healthcare policymakers have developed standards in these countries (United States, Canada, United Kingdom, Australia, Israel, and Europe) that now require hospitals to provide care in a manner that is understood by the patient, with the provision of medical interpreters, also called healthcare interpreters.

Medical interpreting, also referred to as healthcare interpreting, is a specialization of general interpreting, and requires, in addition to specialized medical terminology, specific knowledge and skills related to the complexity of delivering healthcare services to better understand and interpret healthcare discourse. These include healthcare protocols, goals, and objectives, in addition to those related to providing accurate linguistic interpretation. Providing culturally competent care or ensure patient safety are examples of working objectives that medical interpreters do not share with other specializations of interpreting. The Commission for Medical Interpreter Education (CMIE) in the United States, describes the knowledge and skills required of medical interpreters. How professionalized is the medical interpreting specialization?

In some countries, medical interpreters have undergone a professionalization process that underscores its unique specialized setting, cognizant of healthcare objectives and norms. These tend to be the countries with large immigrant populations and migrant friendly policies. The Unites States leads the world in medical interpreting. It is the country with the largest number of hospital based interpreter departments, and is the only country with several standards of practice and national certification schema specifically for healthcare interpreting. It includes CLAS guidelines that recommend employers confirm interpreter competency level that not only ensures accurate interpretation, but that ultimately guarantees patient health.

Other countries have groups of interpreters who work in multiple settings, such as healthcare, legal or educational, as community interpreters. These interpreters are trained and hired to work in all these areas, without the requirement to specialize in any specific one. The term community interpreting, also called public service interpreting, according to most studies and educational programs, is an umbrella grouping of interpreters, and not quite a specialization per se, but a group of specializations. In other countries, medical interpreting is still an emerging specialization, often not performed by professionals. In these latter countries, hospitals and other healthcare organizations are still mostly unaware of the need to hire professional interpreters. In their absence, assistance is requested of lay individuals or employees who are semi-bilingual, with no knowledge of the risks of miscommunication to the patient safety. Countries, such as Brazil (Queiroz, 2014) or the United Arab Emirates (Hannouna, 2012), without well-developed medical interpreter professional services, have started to recognize the need for interpreters to provide culturally competent care and the vital role of medical interpreters to the healthcare field.

The opportunities for education and certification for this specialization vary greatly worldwide, but on the other hand, healthcare interpreting is the specialization that is growing at the fastest rate, perhaps precisely due to its impact in patient safety.

Since medical interpreting a fairly young specialization of the interpreting profession, the literature specifically related to professional level medical interpreting practice is not vast. Research in interpreting has come mostly from linguists and the historical framework of conference interpreting (Pöchhacker, 1995), and often the participants were semi-professional or simply identified as those authorized to interpret for the healthcare organization. For example, there are some studies that do not differentiate between dedicated interpreters and the bilingual employees who occasionally interpret. More recently, healthcare providers, anthropologists, social scientists, educators, conference or legal interpreters have performed the majority of the academic research about medical interpreting.

Due to the limited academic programs in medical interpreting, few practicing professional healthcare interpreters have actually authored these research studies, as of the date of the publication of this book. Historical research has traditionally portrayed interpreters as linguistic conduits, and focused on the linguistic or cognitive processes of language interpreting, whereas more recent research has studied the non-linguistic aspects of an interpreter's work (Angelelli, 2004, Dysart-Gale, 2005; Hsieh, 2006; Kaufert, 1999; Solomon, 1997; Tracy, 2002. Medical interpreting is an area of growing interest and requires interdisciplinary understanding. This is why the study described in this book was housed in the Graduate School of Human Sciences of Osaka University, Japan: an interdisciplinary department that combines social psychology, social theory, medical anthropology, public health, and interpreting studies.

The study aimed to explore the intercultural aspect of the professional medical interpreter's work. What do medical interpreters have to say about mediating intercultural communication? Are interpreters actually mediating culture in addition to mediating language? If so, how are they doing it and what are the ethical values behind their decisions? These are just some of the questions that will be explored. This study was based on the premise that practitioners, in this case, medical interpreters, are the ultimate experts of their craft, not educators, researchers, managers, or policymakers. It was important to give interpreters a greater voice in academia, so that their perspectives would be taken into account. This study did not observe what interpreters did, but rather what interpreters think about their work. While this was a limitation of the study, it did provide unexplored areas of understanding related to the interpreters work, from the interpreters' point of view. Further study is needed to explore the views of healthcare providers and culturally and linguistically diverse patients. Most importantly, this study shed light into better ways to provide culturally and linguistically competent healthcare services. The book evolved out of the need to provide interpreters with an educational resource to better understand this subjectmatter.

The Introduction sets the stage for the context of this book. Chapter One describes the theoretical framework from which to work from in three parts: 1) The connection of language and culture, 2) the context of providing culturally competent healthcare services to culturally diverse patients, and 3) the essential work of medical interpreters in the delivery of such culturally competent services. This section also includes a small glossary. Since the profession of mediation is a separate profession from the profession of interpreting, this study refers to any intercultural mediation activity performed by medical interpreters as a set of activities related to intercultural mediation in healthcare. This set of skills and knowledge is also referred to as *mediating culture* and *interpreting culture* and lastly as *intercultural medical/healthcare interpreting,* a practice of interpreting that recognizes and addresses intercultural issues as an integral part of their specialization. This aims to avoid confusion and distinguish intercultural mediation in the interpreting field from other forms of mediation in other sectors. However, intercultural mediation is a set of activities that may be performed in a myriad of settings. In the healthcare setting it is performed by dedicated intercultural mediators, who may mediate between two parties in the local language, or by a healthcare interpreter who provides intercultural mediation while mediating language simultaneously.

Chapter Two comprises of the literature review for this work. A review of the relevant Professional Standards of Practice, published by professional associations of interpreters was needed. These standards were analyzed regarding the interpreter's role in mediating culture. Six standards and one guide were included. Of these, two are international, and the other four were published in the United States, Europe, Canada, and Australia. Interpreting studies were also analyzed and most have utilized the framework of interpreter roles to describe the work of interpreters in this area. This chapter discusses some of the intercultural roles described in academic research, and telephonic interpreting and the intercultural work of interpreters. Last, two current theoretical models, for intercultural intervention, were analyzed: 1) the Demand Control Schema, and 2) Jezewski's (1990) theoretical model for intercultural mediation.

Chapter Three discusses the research design and methodology: the mixed qualitative and quantitative design, and the self-reporting methodology as a means to gain insight into the thought processes and task analysis of participants. Research questions involved asking practitioners what they believed were the advantages, disadvantages, challenges, strategies, timing, and training in interpreting culture. As stated before some studies define interpreters as the individuals in a healthcare setting who interpret. This may include bilingual healthcare workers that were not trained in interpretation or mediation skills. Since this study is mostly interested in professional views, it was necessary to target only professionals. Therefore, the target population of participants was an important aspect of the study. This study required participants to be trained and practicing professional medical interpreters, and not bilingual individuals who were called upon to interpret, or other stakeholders of the healthcare interpreting profession.

Chapter Four includes the results of the study. This includes first the demographic area, followed by thematic views based on the research questions. This includes the analysis of thirty-two case studies, and thematic analysis of the research questions described above. The thematic analysis starts with the qualitative data from the eighteen interviews, followed by the qualitative data from the focus group, and the essay. Last, the quantitative data was analyzed. While the study included a comparative analysis of survey participants, this book does not include it, as results did not show significant variations.

Chapter Five provides a comparative analysis of survey participants, this book does not include it, as results did not show significant variations.

Chapter Six provides readers with a theoretical discussion based on the study data results, past research, and the analysis of professional standards. New theoretical models are proposed in this book that address some of the new findings on interpreting culture. These include models related to the collective space of intercultural communication, a new formulation of the incremental intervention model (Cross Cultural Healthcare Program, 1999) into macro domains of work that describe the activities of medical interpreters in a more realistic manner, given what we know now of the practice, incorporating observable and unobservable interpreter analyses and actions. Last, a discussion of the trends in interpreting theory sums the direction the field is moving into.

In Chapter Seven, research implications of this study are explored and recommendations are provided for the following stakeholders: educators, healthcare providers, professional medical interpreters, employers and the healthcare systems attempting to provide culturally and linguistically appropriate healthcare.

Chapter Eight concludes with a discussion of where some of the areas of greatest discovery and concern evolve. This chapter also addresses the importance of giving practitioners a voice, a professional standing that allows them to work effectively. The lessons learned from the professionals about their work, is emphasized.

How medical and healthcare interpreters are mediating culture has not been explored in depth. This book will appeal to the various readers who wish to see how intercultural mediation in healthcare relates to the medical interpreters' work. Moreover, how it affects patient safety or the provision of culturally competent healthcare is more relevant now than ever. Stakeholders in the field of medical interpreting can benefit from reading these pages in order to gain insight about the practice of intercultural interpreting. The aim of this book is for the reader to gain a new and broader understanding about the interpreters' intercultural work. For those who are interpreters in other areas such as legal, conference, or educational, this book demonstrates how specialization, setting, or context of the work the interpreters face may shape, define, and ultimately guide the future of the development of each specific specialization as they evolve.

Chapter One

THEORETICAL FRAMEWORK

1.1 Language and Culture

Language and culture are inseparable. Researchers have long studied the role of culture in the act of understanding and how this perception is communicated through language. The success of the communication exchanged is directly related to the participants' integration of language and culture.

Researchers have long investigated this connection. Sapir (1884-1939), an American anthropologist-linguist, promoted the idea that languages contained the key to understanding differing worldviews (Sapir, 1929). In his writings, he argued that because of the differences in the grammatical systems of languages, no two languages were ever similar enough to allow for a perfect translation between them. Sapir (1929) also thought that because language represented reality differently, it followed that the speakers of different languages would perceive that reality differently:

> No two languages are ever sufficiently similar to be considered as representing the same social reality. The worlds in which different societies live are distinct worlds, not merely the same world with different labels attached. (Sapir, 1929, p. 209)

Another linguist, Whorf (1897–1941), expanded upon this idea as an advocate that states because of linguistic differences in grammar and

1

usage, speakers of different languages conceptualize and experience the world differently. More than any other linguist, Whorf promoted the principle of linguistic relativity. He went beyond the assumption that language influences thought and behavior (Sapir, 1929). He studied Native American languages, and attempted to account for the ways in which differences in grammatical systems and language use affect the way their speakers perceived the world (Whorf, 1939).

In the healthcare field, differences in concepts related to health beliefs and practices may affect the vocabulary and the perceptions of health and disease of individuals of different cultures. In the field of medical interpreting, interpreters find themselves not only interpreting for patients and providers who do not share the same language, but who also do not share the same culture, or the same perceptions of framework of the health concepts and diseases. The standards for the profession state the following:

> At the technical level, the communication is explicit and the negotiation of meaning is minimal. However, at the semantic level, the intercultural communication of an interpreted encounter in healthcare is not explicit and negotiation of meaning is left to interpretation of all parties (International Medical Interpreters Association [IMIA] & Educational Development Center [EDC], 2007).

Not all agree that language and culture are intertwined. Steven Arthur Pinker's (1995) academic specializations are visual cognition and psycholinguistics. He promoted the idea that thought is independent of language, language is itself meaningless in any fundamental way to human thought, and human beings do not even think in natural language, i.e., any language that we actually communicate in. He explains that we think in a meta-language, preceding any natural language, called *mentalese* according to Pinker (1995).

However, this mentalese, embedded or expressed in a spoken or signed language, can be a cultural concept, idea, or belief, which does not exist in another culture or language. In the field of interpreting and translation, these are called *untranslatable words, terms,* or *expressions.* This is a misnomer as interpreters and translators do not translate or interpret *words* but *concepts* and *messages.* A word or term sometimes needs to be interpreted by using phrases and explanatory models in order for the other party to understand the concept behind the word. In reality, as Pinker expounded, it is the concept that is communicated, through the symbol of a word, term or expression. It is that specific concept, having its own meaning, that needs translation and/or interpretation into another language, and not the word or term itself. For example, often, there is no equivalent term in the other language. Therefore, the function of interpreting is not to provide literal word for word renditions. Literal renditions never make sense in the other language.

In healthcare, for example, when a Spanish speaker says he has *dolor de cabeza* it translates literally as "pain in the head." This is actually a different symptom to a doctor than a headache, which is what the patient actually would have meant in Spanish when stating *dolor de cabeza*. The challenge for the interpreter is to interpret the concept expressed in the source language (the language being spoken or signed by a speaker) in a manner that will be understood as if it had been spoken in the target language (the language used for the output of the interpretation by the interpreter). Interpreters use strategies such as expanding, explaining, describing, and paraphrasing in order to enable communication (Wadensjö, 1998). Some would say that this is not a cultural issue, but rather a linguistic issue, which is true. However, some cultures have concepts that others do not, such as *susto* (a culturally bound concept among some Latino communities, where illness is thought to be provoked by psychological trauma), and when these concepts are brought up, they need to be reinterpreted, brought to light, discussed, or explained to an individual who has no knowledge of the concept, or in other cases, has a completely different oppositional concept.

In intercultural encounters, each party, including the medical interpreter, may have a different knowledge or viewpoint about what causes a disease, established health practices, or what treatment will work. The assumption that a disease or a treatment has the same meaning to all parties is not realistic. Medical interpreters need to be highly proficient in at least two languages (spoken or signed) and also need a certain amount of knowledge about the cultural groups that that they serve in order to understand these cultural concepts when they are conveyed and require interpretation. In a healthcare encounter, the interpreter may be the only participant with knowledge of both cultures. Because of this, they are the only party that can actually identify or address a view. This would be required when one party's culturally based belief or practice may be unknown to the other party. It may also be necessary to address the reality of two differing cultural views.

Therefore, what are interpreters to do when they listen to a patient or a provider convey a cultural issue while interpreting? What if they cannot render these cultural differences in their linguistic output, gestures, and tone? How important is it for the interpreter to explore and address the cultural issue in question to the parties involved, for the delivery of culturally sensitive healthcare services? If a provider does not know the health practices patients are engaged in, the provider will not able to monitor or modify those practices as needed for the patient's adherence, compliance, and ultimate desired health outcome. Likewise, if a patient is not informed about a specific concept or reason for a specific treatment, she may insist on a practice that is culturally acceptable to her, even if it is different from what the provider advised or prescribed.

The medical community must consider the following question: How does a medical interpreter assist in the process of ensuring the culturally diverse patient's satisfaction, adherence, compliance, and trust in the healthcare system? This book describes the interpreters' specific views regarding addressing these cultural issues in their work. One of the goals in medical interpreting is accurate communication (the absence of miscommunication), and not necessarily just accurate interpretation (the absence of interpreting errors, omissions, additions or distortions). Healthcare interpreters have a fundamental communicative role in helping both parties understand each other's explanations on health and illness (Kaufert & Koolage, 1984; Kleinman, 1980; Kleinman, Eisenberg, & Good, 1978). The significance of what is proposed in this book is the emphasis on understanding the practitioner's perspective on interpreting culture and enabling a positive experience and outcome for the culturally diverse patient.

1.2 List of Definitions

The definitions below assist readers to understand terms within this study in a consistent manner.

Table 1
List of Definitions

Term	Definition
Acculturation	Degree of cultural modifications measured by values and practices from another culture. Different aspects of the original culture and new culture(s) are present.
Adaptation	The process of acculturation

Agency	In sociology and philosophy, agency is the capacity of an entity (a person or other entity) to act in any given environment. In interpreting, agency is the ability to act and speak for oneself.
Assimilation	Original culture is rejected or replaced with the new culture.
Cognitive Dissonance	the state of having inconsistent thoughts, beliefs, or attitudes, especially as relating to behavioral decisions and attitude change
Collective Communicative Space	The space where all communication converges in a communicative event with three or more persons. The space where semiotics occurs.
Cultural Advocate	Professionals (healthcare providers, interpreters, or other staff) who are culturally competent, and utilize their knowledge and skills to advocate and ensure cultural competence in the institutions they work in.
Cultural Awareness	Being knowledgeable, cognizant, observant, and conscious of similarities and differences among cultural groups.
Cultural Competence (also known as cultural responsiveness)	A set of knowledge, values, beliefs and principles that are demonstrated through behaviors, attitudes, and skills, that enables one to work effectively between cultures. Such skills include ability to conduct self and other party cultural assessments, manage the dynamics of cultural difference, knowledge of specific cultural beliefs and practices one works with, and the ability to adapt to the diversity of cultural contexts of the communities one serves (Cross, Bazron, Dennis, & Isaacs, 1989). Note: This term may be better used to describe organizations that have systems in place to address cultural issues, versus individuals who can not be competent in all circumstances.

Cultural Humility (also known as cultural sensitivity)	The ability to maintain an interpersonal stance that is other-oriented in relation to aspects of cultural identity that are most important to the individual (Hook, 2013). Note: Alternative term to cultural competence, which assumes that one can learn or know enough, that cultures are monolithic, and that one can actually reach a full understanding of a culture to which they do not belong.
Cultural Differences (also known as cultural dissonance/conflict)	Two or more sets of different concepts, beliefs, values, or practices, which may be unique to one of two cultures, different or in conflict between cultures.
Cultural Issue	In healthcare, a belief or practice of a particular culture that may affect an intercultural communication, provider-patient therapeutic rapport, or patient safety, satisfaction, or compliance.
Cultural Intervention	In interpreting, the practice of stopping the linguistic interpretation in order to address a cultural issue.
Cultural Liaison	Professionals in different fields who help individuals of different cultures to work together and communicate with each other.
Cultural Rephrasing (also known as cultural reformulation, or paraphrasing)	The act of reformulating the source message to include the cultural norms of the target culture, which may include adding and deleting information in the source language when interpreting into the target language. It also refers to re-stating the communication in a culturally appropriate manner to allow all parties to process the information before continuing. This can be done within an interpretation or as an intervention.

Cultural Sensitivity (also known as cultural humility)	The understanding of the needs and emotions of one's own culture and the culture of others and of institutions, such as the healthcare system in different cultures. Interest in the way other people construe culture and in the varying kinds of experience that accompany different constructions. This experience is termed *[inter]cultural sensitivity* (Bennett, 1993).
Ethnicity (also known as cultural background)	Of or relating to a group of people classified by a common racial, national, tribal, religious, linguistic, or cultural origin or background.
Intercultural Interpreter Mediator	an individual that is adequately trained and tested in both intercultural interpretation as well as intercultural mediation
Intercultural Interpreting	Linguistic interpreting that includes interpreting culture, requiring intercultural activities including, but not limited to, intercultural mediation.
Intercultural Mediation (also known as culture brokering)	The act of bridging, linking, or mediating between two persons with different cultural backgrounds, for the purpose of reducing conflict or misunderstandings (Jezewski, 1990). A healthcare intervention through which a professional uses cultural and health science knowledge and skills to negotiate with the client and healthcare system effectively, beneficial to the healthcare plan (Wenger, 1995).
Impartiality (See Neutrality)	Not taking sides. In interpreting, the premise that certain professions (interpreters, mediators, judges, etc.) need to be impartial to the parties they serve, not favoring one side over another, working objectively, controlling personal bias, claiming the trust of both parties to mediate effectively.

Integration (See Ethnorelativism)	Own experience broadened to include various cultural points of view as equally valid.
Invisibility Model	The state of being invisible. The absence of own voice, opinions, or agency. In interpreting, the belief that the goal of interpreters, under this paradigm, is to maintain a low profile (see neutrality), and act so that the parties forget that they are there.
Linguistic Rephrasing	The act of finding an equivalent expression in the target language, so that the receiver of the information receives it as if someone had said it in his/her language.
Multiculturalism (also known as Cultural plurality)	The presence of more than one cultural set of values, beliefs, or customs.
Neutrality (Impartiality)	The absence of taking sides, strong expression, or feelings.
Professional Medical/Healthcare Interpreter	An individual who has been professionally trained and tested and/or certified, and has the knowledge and skills to mediate language and culture to ensure accurate and meaningful communication between providers and patients in a clinical setting.
Semiosis	This involves any action or influence for communicating meaning by establishing relationships between signs which are to be interpreted.
Transparency	In interpreting, transparency means interpreting everything that is stated by all parties (including the interpreter's statements), so that each party has full knowledge of all discussions, including side discussions, with the goal of achieving communication transparency and the trust of both parties.

Visibility Model	The state of being visible. In interpreting it refers to being a participant of any interaction, maintaining an impartial professional profile, while having the agency and voice needed to make their professional views known, when required.
Working Language(s)	A working language is the term used in the language field to denote the language(s) for which a professional has high enough proficiency and oral fluency to work as an interpreter in that language.

1.3 Culturally and Linguistically Competent Services

Biomedicine refers to medicine based on the application of the principles of the natural sciences, especially biology and biochemistry. *Ethno-medicine* practitioners aim to understand the health related beliefs, knowledge, and practices of different cultural groups. In *humoral medicine*, also known as *traditional medicine*, practitioners conceive the universe as made of opposing qualities, such as wet and dry, hot and cold, or by body types, or other frameworks, and they see health as a balance between these opposites. When a patient and a provider do not share the same culture, health concepts and treatments may be divergent. During the 1960s, researchers began to use *intercultural mediation* as an activity in the healthcare delivery to diverse communities. Wenger (1995) defined intercultural mediation as a healthcare intervention through which the professional increasingly uses cultural and health science knowledge and skills to negotiate with the client and the healthcare system for an effective, beneficial healthcare plan. There are many reasons for the reliance on intercultural mediation in healthcare in the United States and other countries with growing immigrant populations:

(a) projected increase in the cultural and linguistic diversity of patients,
(b) diverse patients' lack of understanding of the local healthcare system,
(c) different beliefs and perceptions of illness and treatment, and
(d) the use of traditional remedies or health practices.

The provision of culturally and linguistically appropriate services has been one effective strategy to help eliminate the health disparities identified in the United States and a few other countries. In 2001, the U.S. Office of Minority Health published the first National Standards for Culturally and Linguistically Appropriate Services in Healthcare, also known as the CLAS Standards (U.S. Department of Health and Human Services, 2001). This document provided a framework for all healthcare organizations to best serve the United States' increasingly diverse communities. According to this document, health professionals can ensure more positive health outcomes for diverse populations when they identify and address a patient's cultural and linguistic preferences and needs. Healthcare services that are respectful of and responsive to different health beliefs, practices, and needs of patients from diverse cultures can help close the gap in healthcare outcomes.

The need for cultural and linguistic competence in healthcare delivery systems is emerging in other countries as a fundamental approach: to eliminate racial and ethnic disparities in health and protect patient safety by avoiding linguistic and culturally based miscommunication. The European project called migrant-friendly hospitals (MFH, MFH Project Group, 2004), sponsored by the European Commission and counting on the participation of 13 countries, has been highly successful in improving outcomes. Its 12 recommendations are listed in the *Amsterdam Declaration Towards Migrant Friendly Hospitals* (MFH Project Group, 2004) in an ethno-culturally diverse Europe. Specialized cultural competency trainings have been developed in several countries in response to such efforts. Often these trainings are geared towards physicians and nurses, and include a module on how to work with a medical interpreter. In Ireland, the National Intercultural Health Strategy (Health Service Executive, 2012) is another progressive initiative to increase cultural competency in healthcare in Ireland. In Israel, a document called *Cultural competence in healthcare organizations in Israel: A concise guide* (Jerusalem Intercultural Center Competence Team, 2007) has been instrumental in adopting policies that provide services for their population in a cultural and linguistically competent manner. Other countries have developed regional guides, such as Nova Scotia and Canada. The need for culturally competent services will continue to increase because of the interest in medical tourism in countries such as Japan, Malaysia, and Brazil, or due to the increase of immigration in countries such as the United States, Germany, and Australia. These national policies establish a global standard and a possible future trend of how healthcare services are going to be provided in the future to culturally diverse patients.

These initiatives are proliferating in the provision of global health and medical tourism as well, and have been instrumental in assisting healthcare organizations to become more welcoming to those coming from diverse cultural backgrounds. The concept of intercultural mediation may soon become an integral component to such a system of care. It is crucial to understand how medical interpreters fit into this paradigm of providing culturally and linguistically appropriate healthcare services.

1.4 The Medical Interpreter and Culturally Competent Care

This study will use the term *interpreter* to refer to professional dedicated medical or healthcare interpreters, and not to bilingual providers, assistants, family members, friends, volunteers, or other individuals who are not medically trained or proven to be technically competent to interpret medical terminology for patients. How does the interpreter fit into the provision of services that are culturally and linguistically appropriate? Is the interpreter the linchpin to bridge the cultural and linguistic gaps? In addition, doesn't the interpreter need to provide his own linguistic/cultural services in a culturally and linguistically competent manner?

Bennett introduced the developmental model of intercultural sensitivity (DMIS) as a way of exploring how "people construe cultural difference and in the varying kinds of experience that accompany different constructions. This experience is termed *intercultural sensitivity* (Bennett, 1993, p. 3). He defined this continuum of learning as one that moves an individual from an *ethno-centric worldview* (own culture seen as central and only world reality) into *an ethno-relative worldview* (own culture seen in the context of other cultures). Professional interpreters are at least bilingual, if not polyglots. They are often bicultural or multicultural by virtue of having lived abroad or by cultural heritage. They are trained to have an ethno-relative worldview. This enables them to work with cultural differences in order to bridge possible ethno-centric worldviews of the parties they interpret for.

1.4.1 The difficulties of communication with an interpreter.

Quality healthcare services depend in part on accurate communication between a patient and a healthcare provider. Most healthcare encounters are dyadic communicative events between two people: the provider and the patient. Communicating with the assistance of a medical interpreter is not easy or natural. When an interpreter is present, the encounter becomes a triadic communicative event, a working environment that involves three individuals or more, and may create an unfamiliar scenario for providers. Healthcare providers and patients are not used to relying on a third party to communicate. Direct communication is more straight forward, but when this is not possible, they have to communicate with the assistance of a professional medical interpreter.

This complicates the provider's work, especially if she has not been trained previously and properly on how to work with an interpreter in her interactions with patients. How does the medical interpreter communicate with his patient, yet speak or sign to another individual? It is not an intuitive behavior and actually requires practice and patience, as the speaking or signing parties have to wait for their utterances or signs to be interpreted and stated by the interpreter in another language that they do not understand. When the interpreter is speaking or signing, the receptive party is actively listening or viewing the signs, while the other party is simply waiting and listening to a language or viewing signs she cannot understand. The communicative event may be awkward for some individuals.

Listening to a foreign language or seeing signs that are not directed to oneself is uncomfortable. This may result in momentary disengagement, breaking one's train of thought, or confusing and distracting the non-engaged party, until he hears the interpreter again in his language. If something is not understood, then the interpreter may intervene and ask for a clarification, making this the communication between three individuals, and not two. The additional time needed for each utterance to be given in two languages doubles the time of communication, not counting clarifications or other discourse that occur in that communication space that were not initiated by the provider-patient. This is a considerable delay in time, which causes stress to the parties who have another patient to see (provider and interpreter), and limits the time with the patient. The space where all the ideas converge is called the collective communicative space. This space can be confusing and unknown, creating an innate lack of trust until the interpreter has interpreted each message. The space belongs to three or more speakers and participants, including the interpreter further compounding the difficulties, of what was expected to be a dialogue between two individuals and has become an interaction between three individuals or more.

1.4.2 Traditional public view of interpreters as conduits.

There is a tendency among healthcare professionals to see the interpreter solely as a conduit, or a channel for linguistic conversion. This is verbalized by some persons as speaking 'through' an interpreter. When a provider says "please repeat what I say," or "tell her this," the provider may be under the impression that interpreters, like robots, merely repeat the same words or terms in another language (Hsieh, 2008). They do not realize that complete understanding of the message, through active listening skills, is required. Reformulating the meaning of the message is also needed in order for the interpreter to reconstruct a new utterance to convey the exact intent and message of the original speaker. If the meaning of the words uttered is unclear, the interpreter will not be able to repeat it because repetition of words is not what she is doing in the first place. Since interpreters do not interpret words, but concepts between two cultures and languages, it may be more accurate to state that the interpreter mediates language and culture for mutual understanding. This is different from repeating or telling someone something you heard in another language. The concept of interpreters having a mediation role is rarely on the provider's mind.

Intercultural mediation intervention is typically initiated with a cultural identification and/or a request for cultural clarification. Providers do not always understand the complexity of the linguistic and cultural tasks of the medical interpreter (Kaufert, Kaufert, & Koolage 1986). Kaufert et al.'s (1986) observations of Aboriginal medical interpreters were the first to suggest that interpreters act as intermediaries, playing key roles in the process of restructuring knowledge. In negotiating mutually understandable models in the exchange between the patient and the provider, medical interpreters influence the flow and content of information between provider and patient. The interpreter therefore contributes to the collective communicative space with the reconstruction of shared explanatory models. In Kaufert et al.'s (1986) study, the medical interpreter usually checked back with the clinician to clarify and confirm the new explanation and ensure it is restated it in more basic language, before rendering the reformulated message to the patient. This form of interpreting is also called paraphrasing (Wadensjö, 1998). This does not mean the register of the language was changed (formal to informal or complex to simple), which is to be avoided as a professional practice according to the various standards of practice. However, when the target language does not have the complex register for a concept, then the only rendition possible will have to be in simpler language or a lower register. In that case, breaking down the information and rephrasing is a difficult task that that is unfamiliar to providers. Interpreting is the act of restructuring rephrasing information from one language into another language, so this skill tends to come more naturally to interpreters. Asking the provider to explain the complex concept in simpler terms can work sometimes, and it is the golden norm of practice. However, sometimes the provider simply does not know how to explain the concept in simple terms, and will request that the interpreter do so.

Kaufert et al.'s (1986) early research suggests that models of intercultural communication need to have the capacity to represent realistic situations where the interpreter plays a semi to autonomous role or what is called *agency* in the interaction and formulation of messages. These are situations where interpreters are not only relying solely on the provider and the patient's explanatory models, but may also introduce their own professional explanatory models during their interpretation reformulations, as described in the previous paragraph. Interpreters incorporate explanations that integrate biomedical knowledge and information about sociocultural and economic factors influencing the patient's response and compliance (Kaufert, 1999). The appropriate level of interpreter intervention is still a debated topic in the field of medical interpreting due to the dichotomy of the invisibility/visibility paradigms, to be explained further later. This is a controversial subject of contention for the interpreting profession, as on one end of the spectrum there are those who advocate for stricter conduit models for interpreters (Phelan 2010), where the interpreter has no agency, but achieves all goals within linguistic interpretation strategies. Others have observed medical interpreters as participants in the role of intercultural as well as linguistic agents (Angelelli, 2004; Kaufert, 1997; Kelly, 2000; Pöchhacker, 1998). Research on interpreting, from a linguistic perspective, has focused on the linguistic aspects of the difficult skills of interpreting technical language accurately from one language to the other. Research with ethnographic, sociolinguistic, medical, or anthropological perspectives have focused on other aspects of the medical interpreter practice such as social roles, power dynamics, intercultural communication as understanding, or healthcare outcomes. This book focuses on the intercultural practice of medical interpreting within the context of providing culturally competent healthcare, and working within the healthcare environment.

1.4.3 Intercultural mediation.

The concept of intercultural mediation is an ancient concept that can be traced to the earliest recorded encounters between cultures. The term *cultural broker/mediator* was first coined by anthropologists who observed that certain individuals acted as middlemen, mediators, negotiators, or brokers between individuals of varying cultures, either due to international trade or when colonial governments and the societies they ruled interacted, among other scenarios. Mediation has become an activity in the legal setting where 'mediators' mediate conflict between parties, as an alternative to the justice system. Intercultural mediation has not been formalized into a distinct profession in most countries, and remains mainly as an activity practiced by many different professionals that work with different cultures, such as diplomats, international negotiators, interpreters, among others. Different definitions of intercultural mediation have evolved over time. One broadly accepted definition states that, "intercultural mediation is the act of bridging, linking, or mediating between groups or persons of different cultural backgrounds for the purpose of reducing conflict or producing change" (Jezewski, 1990). This definition will be compared to what interpreters say they do when they are addressing cultural issues. Some researchers in the field may argue that they do not have in their scope of work to reduce conflict, as sometimes conflict is inevitable. The *Medical Interpreting Standards of Practice* (IMIA & EDC, 2007) speaks of interpreters "managing conflict" but not necessarily reducing it. However, reducing cultural miscommunications or managing cultural dissonance may be viewed as reducing intercultural conflict to provide culturally sensitive services.

1.4.4 The importance of accurate communication in healthcare.

Studies have shown that errors in communication due to incorrect interpretation can lead to negative health outcomes and a degree of liability to the healthcare provider and organization (Flores et al., 2003). The most famous case of the outcome of an error was the case of a young man in Florida, Willie Ramirez, who became quadriplegic due to inappropriate care resulting from an error of the translation of the term *intoxicado* in Spanish, which was incorrectly literally interpreted as *intoxicated* in English. The semantic meaning of *intoxicado* in Spanish is different from that of *intoxicated* in English, and, due to the literal interpretation of the word, versus the concept, the patient was ill-treated and became a quadriplegic. The hospital was found negligent for not obtaining a professional interpreter, and ordered to pay $71 million dollars to the family of the victim (Price-Wise, 2015).

In other language access lawsuits, the U.S. Department of Justice has sided against states such as Hawaii (Kelleher, 2014). The National Health Law Program, published a document entitled *The high costs of language barriers in medical malpractice.* This study analyzed and described 35 cases and groups them by theme related to the provision of language services. In a seminal case, failure to provide competent interpreter services resulted in death. The patient, a 9-year old Vietnamese girl, died from a reaction to the drug Reglan.

These grave situations showcase the importance of accurate communication in healthcare. Communication can only occur when the recipient of the information understands the sender's message (Rao & Sridhar, 2007). Ultimately, the provision of culturally and linguistically competent care is imperative in order for a healthcare system to provide services that protect patient safety and avoid the miscommunications that can cause hard and adverse outcomes to patients. To conclude, providing culturally competent care is not a matter of simply being sensitive to a patient. Identifying and addressing the patient's cultural and linguistic needs for accurate and clear communication is key for patient safety. Accurate communication cannot occur without addressing the understanding of underlying cultural concepts so both parties can truly understand each other. Healthcare professionals depend on communication to understand the symptomology that will lead to an eventual diagnosis. Without accurate communication, the provider may not understand the symptoms described to properly diagnose the patient, and the patient may not understand well the best treatment option to select, the risks of a particular procedure, etc.

There is another well known real case that has been video recorded and is utilized in cultural sensitivity training (Haslett & Grainger-Monsen, 2003). It shows the healthcare struggle of Mohammad Kochi, a devout Muslim from Afghanistan. He underwent surgery for stomach cancer, but refused the chemotherapy recommended by his physician. Due to the continuous misinterpretation of the concept or term of *chemotherapy* as *catheter treatment* by a well-educated bilingual family friend with a Ph.D., the patient erroneously believed that he would have an intravenous device attached to him as the only option for chemotherapy. The practice of having a hanging device in his body while in daily prayer is against his religion, so he continuously denied chemotherapy, based on how chemotherapy was being rendered in his language. The cultural/religious reason, if alerted to the provider by the interpreter, could have been easily resolved by adapting the treatment to the patient's cultural needs, as there are many forms of chemotherapy. Unfortunately, the friend interpreting did not know this and actually thought chemotherapy treatment needed to be given by catheter. By the time the doctor found out about the misinterpretation, the cancer had spread beyond repair. In this case, there was a linguistic and a cultural breakdown in communication. If a professional interpreter had been hired for this case, the provider and patient would have resolved the issue and appropriate treatment would have been administered before it was too late. This documentary showcases vividly how addressing cultural barriers appropriately may prevent even the most grievous of negative healthcare outcomes: death.

Patient safety training programs have been developed to address cultural minority patients. One such program is TeamSTEPPS: Strategies and Tools to Enhance Performance and Patient Safety. The U.S. Agency for Healthcare Research and Quality (U.S. AHRQ, 2015) developed it, and it is an evidence-based teamwork system aimed at optimizing patient care by improving communication and teamwork skills among healthcare professionals, including frontline staff. It includes a comprehensive set of ready-to-use materials and a training curriculum to successfully integrate teamwork principles into a variety of settings. It also includes a module specifically to enhance the safety of patients with limited English. This specific module trains professional care teams to work together in hospital units to acquire the knowledge, attitudes, and team behaviors needed to reduce the number and severity of patient safety events affecting culturally diverse patients in their unit. According to TeamSTEPPS (emphasis by author), "Participants (doctors, nurses, technicians, front desk staff, and *interpreters*) will be able to do the following:

1. Understand patient safety risks to culturally diverse patients,
2. Assemble the most appropriate and effective care team in their hospital, and
3. Identify and raise patient communication issues" (U.S. AHRQ, 2015, p. 31).

As seen above, some hospitals using this model are training interpreters to identify and raise patient communication issues as a patient safety issue, in addition to interpreting, by virtue of their role as part of the professional care teams. In the United States, in particular, the patient safety paradigm has shifted from it being a responsibility solely of the doctors to becoming a responsibility of all the healthcare workers who are in contact with patients, including medical interpreters.

Chapter Two

LITERATURE REVIEW

2.1 Introduction

This chapter reviews the literature in the field from several perspectives. First, the various existing standards of practice for medical interpreters will be reviewed, but only as they specifically relate to interpreting culture. In addition, different models for possible intercultural mediation will be explored. The first includes the first intercultural mediation model for medical interpreters, first published in 1996 by the *Medical interpreting standards of practice* (IMIA & EDC, 2007, p. 41). Jezewski's theoretical model for intercultural mediation will also be reviewed, and, finally, the Control-Demand (C-D) Schema, a practitioner intervention model produced by and for the Sign language interpreting community and widely adopted in the United States and abroad (Dean & Pollard, 2001), will be presented. Specific research, published in medical journals, about medical interpreters addressing culture, will be reviewed. These publications focus on the healthcare outcomes of such activities. Finally, the literature published in sociolinguistic journals will be reviewed and analyzed in relation to interpreting culture. These publications focus on the sociolinguistic outcomes of such activities.

2.2 Standards of Practice and Interpreting Culture

Some medical interpreters and other professionals behave and conform to guidelines and rules of conduct that are more specific than a code of ethics. These standards of practice are not common in most countries (Bancroft, 2005). For the purposes of this study, standards of practice referring to medical interpreting will be reviewed, as well as those for community and general interpreting, which include the medical interpreting specialization in their scope.

The *Medical Interpreting Standards of Practice* (IMIA & EDC, 2007), is the only and oldest standard (first version published in 1996), written specifically for medical interpreters, translated and adopted in several countries. There are two other standards from the United States: 1) from the National Council of Interpreting in Healthcare [NCIHC], and 2) the California Healthcare Interpreting Association [CHIA]). The national standards in Canada for community interpreters will also be reviewed. It is important to note that the Canadian standards that do not limit themselves to medical interpreting may be less specific in their language, as the practices are for interpreters working in many sectors, such as the healthcare, legal, and educational sectors, all with similar yet also very different needs and approaches. Published in 2014, the International Organization for Standardization (ISO) published the first international *Standard for Community Interpreting* (ISO-13611). ISO is working on another international standard for general interpreting, but as of 2016, ASTM International provides the only current published international standard on general interpreting (ASTM-2089), so it is hereby included as well. Finally, the New South Whales (NSW) *Guidelines for Healthcare Interpreters* (Australia) (2014) is included, even though this is not a standards of practice document, in order to have a broader geographic representation of practice norms for medical interpreting, appropriate for an international study.

2.2.1 IMIA & EDC Standards (International).

The first published standards for the profession remain the only standard of practice with international reach to address the practice of medical or healthcare interpreting as a specialization. It was developed in 1992 by the organization then called the Massachusetts Medical Interpreting Association (MMIA), now the International Medical Interpreters Association (IMIA) and the Educational Development Center (EDC), using the DACUM curriculum development process, a well-known and validated method of occupational analysis for professional and technical jobs. It was published in 1996, with the explicitly published objective of being the foundation work for future medical interpreter certification in the United States. It was adopted at a national level in the United States at the 4th National Working Group conference in Seattle, WA, in 1998. These standards (IMIA & EDC, 2007) have since been translated and utilized internationally in the following languages: Spanish, Italian, Hebrew, Japanese, and Portuguese. The standards of practice are organized into three major task areas: (a) interpretation, (b) cultural interface, and (c) ethical behavior.

What does the standard of practice say about the cultural aspect of the medical interpreter's professional practice? The standard defines medical interpreting as the series of tasks of understanding, analyzing, and reinterpreting a spoken or signed message into another language faithfully and accurately, taking into account the biomedical objectives, as well as the sociolinguistic and cultural context of the message, in such a way as to elicit the same response as if it had been stated originally in the target language (IMIA, 2013, p. 25). If all that the provider and patient need to achieve the goals of the clinical encounter is linguistic conversion, then simply providing such a conversion fulfills the interpreter's role. The standard, however, goes beyond the skills of conversion and recognize the complexities of interpretation within the clinical interview.

The medical encounter is a highly interactive process in which the provider uses language (the provider's and the patient's) as a powerful pool to understand, evaluate, and diagnose symptoms (Woloshin, Bickell, Schwartz, Gany, & Welch, 1995), and to mutually inform and instruct. The interpreter, therefore, cannot simply be a "black box converter" but must know how to engage both provider and patient effectively and efficiently in accessing the nuances and hidden sociocultural assumptions embedded in each other's language, which could lead to dangerous consequences if left unexplored (IMIA & EDC, 2007, pg. 12). General public perception may view the interpreter as a linguistic converter. However, the IMIA stipulated, in the original standard of practice published for the first time in 1996, that the work, knowledge, skills, and responsibilities of the medical interpreter went beyond linguistic conversion in order for the work to be accomplished in a culturally competent manner within the healthcare field.

The standard (IMIA & EDC, 2007) explains this ethical and practical responsibility further, with specific guidelines on how interpreters are to proceed. According to the standard, interpreters have the task of identifying occasions when unshared cultural assumptions create barriers to understanding or message equivalence. Their role in such situations is not to "give the answer" but rather to help both provider and patient to investigate the intercultural interface that may be creating the communication problem. Interpreters must keep in mind that no matter how much "factual" information they have about the beliefs, values, norms, and customs of a particular culture, they have no way of knowing whether the individual facing them in that specific situation stands along a continuum from close adherence to the norms of a culture to acculturation into a new culture. Cultural patterns, after all, are generalized abstractions that do not define the individual nor predict what an individual believes or does. They are simply hypotheses that may be more likely to occur to a member of that culture than in someone who is not a member (Avery, 2001; IMIA & EDC, 2007).

In the section of the Standard B-2 (culture interface) these specific tasks are clearly delineated, forming the first intercultural mediation model available for medical interpreters:

1. Pays attention to verbal and nonverbal cues that may indicate implicit cultural content or culturally based miscommunication (e.g., responses that do not fit the transmitted message; display of discomfort or distress when certain topics are brought up).

2. Assess the urgency/centrality of the issue, at that point in time in that particular exchange, to the goals and outcomes of the encounter: Assess the best time and method by which to raise the issue. Interject and makes explicit to both parties what the problem may be. Prompt the provider and patient to search for clarity.

3. Share cultural information with both parties that may be relevant and may help clarify the problem (e.g., says "It's possible this is what is happening, because often people from ... believe that ...").

4. In cases where "untranslatable" terms are used, assist the speaker in developing an explanation that can be understood by the listener (IMIA & EDC, 2007, p. 41).

The standard also describes, for each of the parameter above, indicators of lack of mastery. As described, while these standards of practice give ample information about the specifics of a medical interpreter's work whereas it relates to cultural issues, it never actually states that medical interpreters are to act as cultural brokers or mediators. However, it does point to the task of sharing cultural information with both parties that may be relevant and may help clarify a communication problem. According to this standard, the culture interface tasks are to be used when and only when implicit cultural content may cause miscommunication. The IMIA & EDC standard does not address interpreters' activities within the framework of roles.

2.2.2 NCIHC Standards (United States)

The National Council on Interpreting in Healthcare (NCIHC) published the National Standards of Practice for Healthcare Interpreters (NCIHC, 2005), which contains 32 standards grouped under nine headings. The headings show the relationship between the standards of practice to the nine ethical principles published in the NCIHC National Code of Ethics. One of the sections of the standards of practice is on cultural awareness. According to NCIHC (2005), standards of practice are a set of guidelines that define what an interpreter does in the performance of his or her role: that is, the tasks and skills the interpreter should be able to perform in the course of fulfilling the duties of the profession. Standards describe what is considered best practice by the profession and ensure a consistent quality of performance. For healthcare interpreters, the standards define the acceptable ways by which they can meet the core obligations of their profession—the accurate and complete transmission of messages between a patient and provider who do not speak the same language in order to support the patient-provider therapeutic relationship.

This standard states that interpreters are to facilitate communication across cultural differences. It specifies that the interpreters are to strive to understand the cultures associated with the languages they interpret, including biomedical culture. It provides the example of the interpreter's responsibility of learning, for example, the traditional remedies some of their patients may use. It also states that the interpreter is to alert all parties to any significant cultural misunderstanding that arises. An example provided is when a provider asks a patient who is fasting for religious reasons to take an oral medication; an interpreter may call attention to the potential conflict (NCIHC, 2005, p. 7). It links these tasks to the related ethical principle listed in its code of ethics for interpreters to strive to develop cultural awareness of the cultures encountered in the performance of their interpreting duties. The NCIHC does not elaborate further than what has been described above, but the standard nonetheless gives clear guidelines and emphasizes the importance of striving to develop cultural awareness. The NCIHC standard does not address interpreters' activities within the framework of roles, so cultural roles are not described except for the one phrase where the standard states:

> When the patient's health, well-being or dignity is at risk, an interpreter may be justified in acting as an advocate (NCIHC, 2005, p. 10).

2.2.3 CHIA Standards (California, U.S.)

The California Healthcare Interpreters Association (CHIA, 2002) published the first and only standard for medical interpreters in the United States dedicated to a state region. This standard discusses the cultural realm of the interpreter's work and even provides specific tasks to address these issues. According to this standard, the fundamental purpose of healthcare interpreters is to facilitate communication between two parties who do not speak the same language and do not share the same culture. Various barriers in communication exist, including differences in cultural norms, and the standards describe roles and strategies available to interpreters to help the parties address these barriers.

The CHIA standard addresses interpreters' activities within the framework of roles. CHIA (2002) stipulated that interpreters have a fundamental role in helping both parties understand each other's explanations on health and illness. CHIA (2002) asserted that the *cultural clarifier* role goes beyond language clarification to include a range of actions that typically related to an interpreters' ultimate purpose of facilitating communication between parties not sharing a common culture. Interpreters are alert to the cultural terms and concepts that may lead to misunderstanding, triggering a shift to the cultural clarifier role (CHIA, 2002, p. 43).

In a similar manner to the other standards, CHIA (2002) gives specific examples of when interpreters may need to address cultural issues. The patient may perceive a provider's questioning strategy or remarks as culturally inappropriate. The same is true of the provider's perception of the patient's comments. This occurs more frequently when the patient and provider do not share a common understanding of illness and medical treatment. There is a section of the standard dedicated to the Ethical Principle 6: Cultural Responsiveness (CHIA, 2002, p. 31). It urges interpreters continually participate in cultural competency training and identify and monitor personal biases and assumptions that can influence wither positive or negative reactions in them, without allowing them to impact the interpreting. It also calls for interpreters to recognize and identify when personal values and cultural beliefs among all parties are in conflict, as well as identifying statements made by providers and patients indicating a lack of understanding health beliefs and practices. In these situations they are guided to use the applicable strategies suggested for the *cultural clarifier* role.

This role has it's own section in the standard document. The cultural-clarifier role goes beyond word clarification to include a range of actions that typically relate to an interpreter's ultimate purpose of facilitating communication between parties not sharing a common culture. Interpreters are alert to cultural words or concepts that might lead to a misunderstanding, triggering a shift to the cultural clarifier role (CHIA, 2002, p.43). It further explains the appropriate way to intervene:

> When there is evidence that either party, including the interpreter, may be confused by cultural differences, interpreters need to:
>
> a. Interrupt the communication process with a word, comment, or a gesture, as appropriate.
> b. Alert both parties to potential miscommunication or misunderstanding (Interpreters may say, for example "As an interpreter, I think that there may be potential danger for miscommunication/misunderstanding...").
> c. Suggests cultural concerns that could be impeding mutual understanding.
> d. Assist the patient in explaining the cultural concept to the provider, or assist the provider in explaining the biomedical concept. When requested, interpreters need to explain the cultural custom, health belief or practice of the patient to the provider, or educate the patient on the biomedical concept (CHIA, 2002, p.44).

Last, the CHIA Standard of Practice has a section on applying the ethical decision-making process, which may be helpful to interpreters when addressing cultural issues.

2.2.4 Canadian Standards (Canada)

The National Standard Guide for Community Interpreting Services (NSGCIS) of Canada (Healthcare Interpretation Network [HIN], 1996) is a standard that needs to meet the needs of interpreters working in many different settings and specializations, including healthcare. However, because of this, it needs to take a broader approach, limiting its guidelines to those that serve all settings and specializations. It takes a somewhat stricter and more nuanced approach to interpreting culture. According to the NSGCIS (HIN, 1996), community interpreting is defined as bidirectional interpreting that takes place in the course of communication among speakers of different languages. The context is the provision of public services such as healthcare or other community services, such as legal, educational, or social services, for example. Again, it is important to note that this standard needs to meet the needs of interpreters working in different fields, which includes interpreting in the legal field, where the environment, rules and regulations for conduct, objectives, and context, are quite different from the needs of the healthcare field.

HIN created the NSGCIS in 1996 in collaboration with Critical Link Canada (CLC), the Language Industry Association of Canada (AILIA), and the Association of Canadian Corporations in Translation and Interpretation (ACCTI). The creation of the Canadian National Standard was guided by joint efforts from multiple stakeholders across Canada, 24 members who represented governmental institutions, academia, interpreters, professional orders, and non-profit and private sector organizations composed the committee. In early 2010, AILIA announced a new certification program developed for Interpreting Service Providers (ISPs) under the NSGCIS. The NSGCIS is also used as the core document for ISP Certification in Europe through the Language Industry Certification System (LICS) Certification scheme.

NSGCIS includes the responsibilities of clients, medical interpreters, and ISPs. In section 8, entitled "Role and responsibilities of interpreters," point 6 specified "the interpreter must be able to understand and convey cultural nuances without assuming the role of advocate or cultural advocate" (HIN, 1996, p. 18). This is the only statement on the main document regarding the topic of interpreting culture. The text is clear in its direction, but ambiguous in its limitation. Some in the field may construe the task of understanding and conveying cultural nuances as one of the primary tasks of an intercultural mediator. If this is case, how is an individual to do this task without assuming this role of cultural advocate? What is a cultural advocate? This is not explained in the document and a clarification in a future edition on how the interpreter is to do this may benefit readers.

The clarification in Appendix A explains the reason for such limitation. In Annex A of the NSGCIS Standard (HIN, 1996), the publication explains the perspective of the Language Interpreter Training Program (LITP) Curriculum Development team on a move away from culture brokering, with arguments made by those professionals who believe community interpreters should not engage in this role of cultural advocate. It states that in Canada "historically interpreters were identified as 'cultural interpreters' with a role to bridge cultural misunderstandings between service providers and non/limited English speakers" (HIN, 1996, p. 18). Determining how and when an interpreter should intervene created conflicts for all parties for a variety of reasons. Although cultural differences can exist between individuals who do not share a common language, cultural differences can also exist between individuals who do share a common language. Given the complexity of factors that impact and influence an individual's culture, acting as an "intercultural mediator/bridge" goes beyond the scope of an interpreter's duty from the perspective of the LITP Curriculum Development Team. According to LITP, expecting an interpreter to perform that function contravenes the ethical principle and standard of practice to remain impartial, and furthermore begs the question of the demonstrated competence of the interpreter to perform that function. Therefore, it should be noted that the LITP Curriculum Development Team recommends that the role of the interpreter focus on the delivery of messages between individuals who do not share a common language rather than "cultural differences/nuance" of the speakers" (HIN, 1996, Annex A).

It is a recommendation; however, it is noteworthy to explore why it was made. According to those from the LITP Team, some of the reasons to recommend moving away from the cultural interpreter role were the following:

    a.   safety for limited English/French proficiency population (LEP/LFP) while accessing public services;

    b.   limited training: Training programs were limited on time and scope to include proper training on cultural interventions, historically, the average programs varied from 60-100 hours of instruction (in 2006, however, Ontario introduced a 180 hour training program);

    c.   equal access to public services, because if the interpreter provides advocacy service to the LEP/LFP, the question becomes who would provide this service to those immigrants who speak one of the official languages and are navigating the system without interpreters; and,

    d.   culture in relation to several factors, with language only one of them; sharing the language does not necessarily mean sharing the culture (HIN, 1996, p. 21).

It is noteworthy to mention that all mediation services in any industry are required to be neutral and impartial according to all the literature available on the profession of mediation (which would include intercultural mediation, a subset of general mediation). It is actually one of the most important ethical tenets of any type of mediation, according to a U.S. Mediation Association (National Association of Certified Mediators, 2015) in order to acquire trust from both parties being mediated. Therefore, the LITP statement that the mediation function contravenes the ethical standard of impartiality is confusing and merits clarification.

Since the group that recommended this limitation is the educator stakeholder group, perhaps the main reason for limiting the scope of work of the interpreter has more to do with the available education provided to interpreters on the topic. It also may be related to the fact that in the courtroom there is only room for cultural mediation when interpreting a dialogic conversation outside a legal proceeding. Within the courtroom proceedings, due to the nature of legal communication and procedures, cultural explanations in a courtroom could be seen possibly as mitigating or aggravating the behavior of the accused, victim or other party requiring interpretation. While intercultural explanations still have a place in the legal setting, it is mainly for clarification, and not per se mediation or brokering between two parties, as with healthcare. In legal settings, mediation is only possible and appropriate when interpreting between the accused and his lawyer, where the communication is collaborative. All other communications may not be collaborative and therefore cannot include mediation. It would take a higher level of interpreter education than currently provided in order to prepare interpreters for these nuances of protocol.

2.2.5   ASTM – F2089 Standard (International)

ASTM International Standard Practice for Language Interpreting (2015) (F2089) is the most recent international publication, a revision of an older F2089 standard, encompassing all specializations of interpreting. Like the previous standard reviewed, it is not limited to the healthcare specialization, but rather only discusses the protocols and tenets that apply to all interpreters. It includes very little on cultural issues, but the document does acknowledge that all interpreters, regardless of specialization, need to have certain skills related having the knowledge of culture-specific references and concepts, the ability to completely comprehend cultural subtext of the source language, and the ethical responsibility to recuse oneself should the interpreter lack adequately the cultural context. It lists these skills in the following context:

1.   *Cultural awareness*—Knowledge of culture-specific references and concepts that allow the interpreter to render the message faithfully.

2. *Comprehension*—Ability to fully comprehend meaning, subject matter, pragmatic intent, and cultural subtext of the source message.

3. *Competency*—The interpreter shall not knowingly accept any assignment beyond his/her interpreting ability or for which he/she lacks an adequate understanding of the subject matter or cultural context or both. In situations in which the interpreter cannot easily disqualify him/herself from an assignment, the interpreter shall inform the client of his/her limitations (ASTM International, 2015, p. 21).

While it addresses the need for cultural awareness and knowledge, it does not venture into the cultural activities interpreters may or not engage in outside the interpreted communicative event. It is noteworthy to point out that the previous version of this standard, published in 1996, did have a section on intercultural mediation in healthcare setting, and stated specifically that cultural awareness/sensitivity is the co-responsibility of the health-care provider and interpreter. "Special considerations, sometimes requiring consultation between interpreter and healthcare provider, should be given to situations involving sensitive medical information, conditions, or outcomes (for example, organ procurement, gender matching, HIV/AIDS, mental health, pharmacy, sex counseling, family planning, and end-of-life issues, among others)" (ASTM, 1996, p. 6).

The text brings up that interpreters provide cultural consultation to healthcare providers. According to Jalbert (1998), psychiatrists need these consultations, and in another study (Kimayer, Groleau, Guzder, Blake, & Jarvis, 2014), cultural consultations are considered as an important component of the work in the provision of culturally competent care. Considering that most healthcare systems are moving towards becoming more culturally competent in order to address the growing diversity of its patients, it is unfortunate that this very specific text was omitted in the most recent version of this international standard (ASTM, 2015). This newly revised standard does not address any role, task, intervention, or activity for interpreters to engage in when identifying cultural issues that affect intercultural communicative events they are involved in.

2.2.6 ISO–13611 Standard (International)

ISO is a worldwide federation of numerous national standardization organizations (ISO member bodies). In 2014, ISO published the first edition of an international standard guideline for community interpreting.

Similarly to the Canadian Standard and the ASTM Standard, it is not specific to healthcare interpreting, and needs to be seen in the light of being a more general standard that needs to limit itself to the protocols and tenets that apply to all community interpreters, without specifying specific guidelines for certain specializations such as healthcare. It is available via purchase at the ISO website at the cost of $123.00. This international guidelines document (ISO-13611, 2014) was developed in response to a worldwide need to accommodate linguistic, cultural, and ethnic diversity of people who interact via oral and signed communication.

These guidelines establish competencies for community interpreters and in the interpersonal skills section mentions the need to display intercultural competence and to use effective interjection skills when appropriate (ISO-13611, 2014, p. 8). It discusses the need for the role of the community interpreter to understand and convey cultural nuances (ISO-13611, 2014, p.11). When requested, or when possible, interpreters should interrupt to point out the existence of a cultural barrier, such as cultural custom, health belief, or practice (e.g. some ethnic groups can refuse surgery on the basis of religious beliefs) when such a cultural barrier can result in miscommunication or misunderstanding, being careful not to provide explanations, but to identify the misunderstanding clearly so that the end users can explore and clarify the misunderstanding with each other (ISO-13611, 2014, p. 12).

This guideline also limits the interpreter, stating the interpreter should be careful not to provide explanations, but to identify the misunderstanding clearly. When the interpreter identifies a cultural issue to the other two parties, or identifies the misunderstanding clearly, in effect the interpreter may need to explain why she believes the cultural issue is affecting communication. It seems that the intent of this standard is for the interpreter not to take over the issue but for the interpreter to start the conversation to allow the other two parties to discuss it.

2.2.7 NSW Guidelines (Australia)

A guideline is not the same as a standard in the sense that standards are measurable and can be used for certification purposes, while guidelines are recommendations and best practices. The differentiation between the two can be ambiguous and blurry. The New South Whales (NSW) *Guidelines for healthcare interpreters* (NSW, 2014, Australia) is influential enough to be mentioned, as it targets the medical interpreting specialization and is from another part of the world where healthcare interpreting profession is specialized to a greater extent than in other countries.

The NSW *Guidelines for Healthcare Interpreters* were published in 2014. The aim of the guidelines was to assist clients/patients from culturally and linguistically diverse backgrounds to access health services by providing professional and confidential interpreting. According to these guidelines, the role of the interpreter is to facilitate communication between two parties who do not speak the same language and may represent different cultural backgrounds. It is interesting to note that facilitating communication is not the same as rendering accurate interpretation. Thes guidelines showcase the role of the interpreter to be beyond interpreting messages, and instead to facilitate, or mediate communication. Since providers and patients who do not share the same language or culture, that means implicitly that interpreters are facilitating, or mediating intercultural communication. In transferring messages, interpreters make appropriate linguistic and cultural decisions in order to convey all aspects of the message and produce the same impact on the listener, as the original message would have. At times, in addition to interpreting messages, interpreters may need to intervene in their role of communication mediator to prevent misunderstandings. These guidelines state that, ultimately, the health providers and patients are both responsible for the resolution of the medical encounter. If one mediates the resolution of an encounter, does that not make one an intercultural mediator?

According to NSW (2014), the interpreter role includes the aspect of providing cultural information in an objective and professional manner, relevant to the clinical and social needs of the individual patient for whom they are interpreting at the time. These guidelines discuss timing and recommend briefing or debriefing with the healthcare professional before the assignment, where applicable, and that briefings should include cultural background information. Interpreters have a role in bridging the cultural as well as the linguistic gap between clients and can offer insights into cultural aspects relevant to the treatment of individual patients. However, it states that limitations apply and careful consideration is required in relation to when and how cultural information can be provided. Interpreters do not act as professional cultural brokers and take great care to avoid stereotyping. They generally provide cultural information at the healthcare provider's request or when the cultural gap is affecting communication during medical encounter.

Healthcare providers are encouraged to ask patients direct questions regarding any matters that they view as needing clarification, thus enabling patients to provide the information relevant to them as unique individuals. Cultural issues are sometimes discussed prior to or following an interpreting assignment, as initiated by the healthcare provider or by the interpreter.

Occasionally in the course of an assignment cultural issues arise that may affect the communication process or even the patient's diagnosis and/or treatment. Examples include superstitions and religious references in mental health. In such cases, the interpreter asks the patient's permission to explain cultural references and makes the health professional aware of the issue, and all parties are kept informed about what is being said. It is important for the interpreter and the healthcare provider to be mindful of variations in cultural practices within the same ethnic group due to factors such as educational background, religion, traumatic experience in the country of origin or during migration, different experiences of the healthcare system, and living conditions, etc. Interpreters accept that every client is an individual and are careful to avoid stereotyping, giving advice or volunteering unnecessary information. The guidelines even include specific guidelines or instructions about what professional scripts or phrases to use or not when addressing cultural issues:

> For example, the following phrase is a good way to introduce cultural information: "It is possible that some people who come from this country may have these beliefs..." Interpreter statements beginning with "in my culture..." are generally unhelpful. (NSW, 2014, p. 19)

The NSW guidelines include a section specific towards mental health:

> Assisting in assessment using specific tests such as the mini-mental examination can be challenging for the medical interpreter. These tests are often culture specific and the level of difficulty for the patient may be increased. It is helpful to discuss assessment tools with the clinician prior to the interview and alert him/her to potential areas of difficulty. These may include different calendars and seasons in different countries as well as the use of proverbs or spelling activities. The clinician and the interpreter can agree on the best strategy to deal with these issues. When interpreting for neuropsychological tests, in the briefing or post assessment, there may be issues related to the patients' difficulties relating to cultural bias on the test. (NSW, 2014, p. 11)

This last piece of advice discusses timing and demonstrates that not all cultural interventions are during an interpreted session, as they can occur before or after the encounter, in the briefing or debriefing. It also states, "In some specialized settings, such as mental health, speech pathology and neuropsychology, interpreters may be asked to provide feedback about the patient's speech and/or language. This is a legitimate requirement given the types of assessments in these settings" (NSW, 2014, p. 12). As stated before, cultural consultations are sometimes requested and required in order for the mental health provider to make a diagnosis or an accurate assessment of the situation, taking into consideration the cultural background of the patient. Medical interpreters provide cultural consultations upon request, but do not have specific guidance on what exactly they can speak on specifically within their scope of work other than answering their provider's questions to the best of their ability and recusing or asking the patient to elaborate on something that is not clear.

2.3 General Stance on All Standards

The documents reviewed in this chapter are the published norms, rules, and guidelines for the profession. Several of them were written specifically for the medical interpreting specialization with the healthcare realities, context, and needs in mind. These specialized standards (IMIA&EDC, NCIHC, CHIA, and NSW) carry more weight in this study as they incorporate the healthcare context without being limited or forced to encompass other settings of work that may have very different requirements (i.e. legal, educational, social services, etc.). Every single standard and guideline reviewed mentioned the responsibility of medical interpreters to address cultural nuances as part of their scope of work. However, these also prescribe professional constraints and limitations, and the need to use professional judgment when performing these activities as so not to have unintended consequences or work outside of the intended scope of work or against the goals and objectives of intercultural communication mediation.

Some of these documents include contradictory and confusing or ambiguous statements (NSGCIS Standard and NSW) that merit further clarification and study. Most concede that interpreters must identify cultural issues, but these two mention not acting as cultural advocate or professional cultural broker, respectively. Some trainers have been known to tell interpreter students not to add any professional information about culture, but only intervene to bring the matter to light and quickly return to the conduit role of interpreting to allow the actual cultural discussion to be primarily between the relevant parties. The reasoning behind this is that it empowers the primary parties (provider and patient) to discuss their cultural issues.

The difficulty lies in that it is almost impossible for an individual to discuss conflicting views when a participant is only cognizant of one view, or is not even aware of the conflict. There are those who state that in Canada one cannot engage in any way in intercultural mediation or act as a cultural mediator. However, this is not clear from reviewing their standards since it does request interpreters to convey cultural nuances. It is not clear if they mean within the interpretation or outside the interpretation, in the form of an intervention. In the explanatory Appendix A, the request is simply for interpreters to focus on the linguistic aspect of their work versus the cultural. This is a controversial issue due to the different weights that stakeholders may give to the linguistic and cultural issue, or strict interpretations of text. Which is more important? Which should the interpreter focus on? The study to be described in the next chapter did not ask such a question, as the core issue for our practice is not necessarily which is more important, but rather if it is or not part of the interpreters' scope of work.

These important standards of practice recognize that medical interpreters need to identify and convey cultural information, within professional constraints. The medical interpreter is also not an expert at cultures just by virtue of being part of two or more cultures, just as a bilingual individual is not qualified to be an interpreter (Phelan, 2010). As a healthcare professional who may not be sufficiently trained in cultural competency, or the patient's culture, the interpreter may actually act in opposition to the cultural norms and values of the patients or the providers served. However, one can argue that such an individual is not sufficiently trained to practice at all, according to the standards described for the profession, and unqualified professionals exist in all professions. Nonetheless, without sufficient training, the interpreter may not know specific language or strategies to address or discuss complex cultural issues with either party in a professional manner. The issue of interpreter education on addressing culture will be further investigated, and that data collected in this study will provide further insight to this issue.

2.4 Literature Review on Medical Interpreters' Cultural Work

Researchers have studied the issue of intercultural communication and the role(s) of the medical interpreter, from an ethnographic, cultural, social, medical, anthropological, sociolinguistic, and linguistic perspectives. For example, studies have been conducted by medical providers and published in medical journals focusing on the healthcare aspect of their work. This book focuses on the interpreters' perspectives about the cultural aspect of their work, and not necessarily observes what they actually do. It is a limitation of the study, but it also a strength. It provides readers with the interpreters' perspectives, via verbal reporting, on several factors: (a) why it is that they, as the ultimate practitioners, practice or not a certain way, (b) which activities they believe they should be engaging in, (c) under what guidelines and constraints, and (d) with what challenges and strategies they practice as intercultural mediators.

2.4.1   Trends in interpreting research.

Pöchhacker (1998) stated that research in the field of interpreting intensified since the late 1980s. The traditional scientific approach, focusing on the preoccupation with neuro-scientific or linguistic processes in simultaneous and consecutive interpreting (mostly in conference interpreting), has given way research related to the socio-psychological and sociocultural implications of other forms of interpreting such as dialogic interpreting (legal or medical interpreting). Dialogic interpreting involves interpreting between two individuals in an interpreter-mediated encounter within a very specific context of expectations and goals. Therefore, according to Pöchhacker (1998), conference-interpreting research has broadened to research of other specializations of interpreting.

These new specializations emerged in response to changes in the market requiring interpreting services in the provision of health and legal services, which in turn are linked to various issues of social and cultural policy, such as countries' efforts to provide culturally and linguistically appropriate services. In healthcare, for example, the goal of the provider is to provide appropriate treatment. For the patient, it is to restore optimal health or the absence of symptoms. The interpreter also has goals, such as facilitating communication, provide culturally and linguistically appropriate services, accurate interpretation, support the therapeutic rapport between the patient and the provider, and uphold the values and regulations of the healthcare system they find themselves working in.

Medical interpreting is one such specialization, which now counts with sufficient research to support new theories and paradigms of interpreting that take into account and better understand the context within which medical interpreters operate in. A focus on sociolinguistic questions and on considerations associated with the interpreter's presence and actions has led to different views in research, ranging from that of verbatim inter-linguistic reproducer, or neutral and invisible conduit, to that of an impartial yet visible active participant, as advocate, intercultural communication mediator, or communication facilitator or coordinator with self-agency. These are the two very different approaches to the field. This topic of this book explores how medical interpreters bridge the cultural gap in healthcare, so by definition the cultural aspects of the interpreter's work is supralinguistic. Interpreter-mediated communication is a complex activity that involves social interaction among all participants, and it is becoming increasingly important in today's globalized world to understand better the interpreted communicative event from a supralinguistic perspective.

2.4.2 Two theoretical models: Conduit or advocate?

Broadly speaking, there are two theoretical models for the profession of interpreting: At one extreme is the conduit model, with the interpreter seen as a mechanical device whose role is limited to converting and transferring messages or information between parties. This view focuses on the linguistic aspects of communication but not necessarily on communication itself. Communication does not occur unless the receiving party understands the message, so merely interpreting messages without checking for understanding is akin to providing someone with information that they may not have understood. Studies that focus only on the conduit or linguistic aspect of the interpreters' work will not be included in this research review, as they do not focus on the cultural issues interpreters face.

At the other end, the interpreter is seen as a mediator of intercultural communication between parties from different linguistic and cultural backgrounds, facilitating the interactions to achieve specific communication goals. Communication goals and interpreting goals are not one and the same. When the focus is on communication, in order to support accurate and complete communication, interpreters feel responsible for the parties to understand each other as if no linguistic or cultural barrier was present. This requires reformulating ideas and checking for understanding, and is somewhat different from the strict interpretation goal, which is to interpret everything that is being said accurately, without omissions, additions, distortions, or misinterpretation, not checking or being preoccupied for the participants' understanding. Most interpreters aim to strike a balance somewhere between the two extremes.

According to the latest research, the interpreter's role in dialogic communication is moving further along in the continuum towards greater visibility, from the conduit invisible model extreme into a moderate visible mediator or facilitator model (Angelelli, 2004; Dysart-Gale, 2005; Hsieh, 2006; Jacobs, 2002; Kaufert, 1999; Solomon, 1997; Tracy, 2002). This reflects a progression and the acknowledgement of the interpreter's need for agency, where the professional has decision-making responsibilities, and contributions to make towards the communicative event for optimal work and health outcomes (Hsieh, 2006). This exemplifies a newer paradigm for a better understanding of the interpreter's complex and important social and interactional role in the provision of culturally and linguistically appropriate healthcare services.

As stated in the previous chapter, there is ample research related to the direct link between culturally appropriate care and health outcomes and effects to patient care and compliance. The question remains to some if interpreters should provide services that are not only linguistically appropriate, but also culturally appropriate and competent. Another consideration is whether interpreters are simply linguists providing clients with linguistic services or ancillary healthcare workers, providing language and cultural mediation services as an integral component to the provision of culturally competent healthcare services. In other words, are interpreters providing a component of the healthcare service given to patients by the provider at hand, or are they simply providing a separate linguistic service that is unrelated to healthcare delivery quality? Does one service impact the other by virtue of this mediation?

2.4.3 Interpreter role typologies.

Relevant research about the cultural roles of interpreters will be described in this section. A seminal study (Kaufert & Koolage, 1986) focused on role conflicts among Cree and Salteaux language-speaking interpreters working in two urban hospitals, providing tertiary medical care services to native Canadians from remote northern communities. Over an 18-month period, participant observation and analysis of videotaped clinical consultations were utilized to develop an inventory of roles and situational contexts characterizing the work of native interpreters in urban hospitals. Roles identified for the interpreters observed included the role of *culture broker-informant* (when providing cultural information to the provider) and *culture broker-biomedical interpreter* (when providing biomedical information to the patient). This study showed that the practice of intercultural mediation was observed in healthcare as early as 1984 and included different types of cultural information to identify and convey to the parties involved (Kaufert & Koolage, 1984). These interpreters were bridging the cultural gap between patients and providers with very different cultures, not going against, but following the standards of practice for the profession previously reviewed.

Researchers have recognized that the assumption of invisibility is not what was observed in practice in the United States, and have proposed a model of interpreting based on visibility, along with others (Dysart-Gale, 2005; Hsieh, 2006; Jacobs, 2002; Kaufert, 1999; Putsch, 1985; Solomon, 1997). According to Angelelli (2004), interpreters bring their own "affect, age, ethnicity, gender, nationality, race, socioeconomic status, and solidarity" to the communicative event, and are therefore actively involved in co-constructing the interviews for which they interpret. Angelelli (2004) presented metaphors for interpreters as detectives, multi-purpose bridges, diamond connoisseurs, and miners. Some of the weaknesses of the invisibility paradigm in interpreting identified by Kaufert (1999) are that it does not account for issues such as social class, belief systems, or ethnicity. Solomon (1997) mentioned that ethical codes based on the invisibility paradigm to "intervene only when necessary," or "keep a low profile," promote neutral literalism, in place of the more desirable "nuanced interpretation." Dysart-Gale (2005) believed this approach does not allow interpreters to have a culturally appropriate interaction with the patient. Putsch (1985), Hsieh (2006), and Angelelli (2004) argue that invisibility does not accurately describe the medical interpreters' work.

Previous research in interpreting, which focused on the invisibility paradigm, served spoken language conference interpreters well, as they are often times hidden from the public in booths at the back of the auditorium of a conference interpreting mostly in one direction, and not between two individuals with a specific communicative goal in mind or problem to solve other than the accurate and faithful rendition of information being presented. Often spoken interpreters were not even seen at all by the audience and are truly invisible. The purpose of a presentation is to provide information or insight to an audience, but there is usually little or no interchange of ideas. However, sometimes there is a question-and-answer session at the end. However, the vast majority of conference interpreting research does not cover Q&A sessions or other interactive communicative events. Sign language interpreters, who are usually right at the side of the main speaker on stage, are much more visible physically than spoken language interpreters, who are usually in a booth at the back of the room. However, they are also interpreting in one direction, in a more static situation than an interactional communicative event.

Different cultures have a communication style associated with that culture. Low context cultures prefer direct low-context communication whereas high context cultures favor indirect and highly contextual communication (Hall, 1989). The paradigm of invisibility in interpreting follows a low-context communication style, where intention of meaning is best expressed through explicit verbal messages, such as in presentations where the communication is well thought out prior to delivery and mostly in one direction. High context communicators emphasize multi-layered contexts, and literal interpretation will not work well when interpreting high context communication. There seems to be a trend for the healthcare interpreting profession that is moving from the invisibility paradigm, mostly borrowed by other specialization (conference interpreting) to the visibility paradigm, more specific to the nature of dialogic interpreted communicative events in the healthcare environment.

Hsieh (2006) proposed a mediator model for medical interpreters, arguing that by recognizing interpreters as active participants, researchers will have the opportunity to move beyond a conduit model (linguistic conduit of interpretation). By seeing interpreters as mediators, Hsieh argued that researchers will have a more solid foundation to a new conceptualization of their performance and aim for neutrality and impartiality in that role. Unlike dispute mediators, she argued that medical interpreters do not presume the parties have conflicting goals. However, it is not uncommon for providers and patients to have different objectives due to cultural differences and treatment preferences (Hsieh, 2003). The challenge faced by interpreters is not to resolve conflict but rather to be vigilant and alert in identifying potential hidden differences in the provider-patient interaction, usually inferred and not explicitly communicated (Tracy, 2002). The mediator is therefore an active but neutral participant (Jacobs, 2002). He is active because the interpreter will identify and intervene when needed, and impartial and neutral when assisting the parties to resolve the issue. The IMIA Standards of Practice does mention 'managing conflict' as part of their scope of work. Managing is not the same as resolving, and as mediators or facilitators, interpreters would be careful not to overtake the negotiation or resolution process. However, mediation activities are still needed to address cultural dissonance in order for eventual cultural understanding and possible agreement to occur.

If interpreting involves mediation, what do professional mediators in other settings do? The ability to participate as a neutral party is crucial to a mediator or a mediation process in any setting (National Association of Certified Mediators, 2015). *The model standards of conduct for mediators* was prepared in 1994 by the American Arbitration Association, and the second tenet is the standard of impartiality. Some in the field have stated that interpreters cannot mediate because they need to be impartial (HIN,1996). However, these are not mutually exclusionary activities. Studies have confirmed that the act of participating and mediating a discussion does not make one partial; it is the opposite, as impartiality is key in objective and impartial mediation (Hung, 2002; Maiese, 2005).

It is important to note that the term *intercultural mediator* has been defined in various ways across countries, especially Europe (Theodosiou & Aspioti, 2015). The term is sometimes used to define medical interpreters in some countries, such as Italy or Belgium. Other countries define intercultural mediator a role that can be performed by many professionals in different settings who interface in intercultural communication. Lastly, the term sometimes defines a separate profession in itself for those who act as intercultural mediators in different settings, and these individuals may or may not also interpret. There are hospitals in Switzerland, for example who will have a medical anthropologist acting as an intercultural mediator between patients and the healthcare organization, mediating for parties who speak the same language, sometimes working with and with the assistance of interpreters, yet only focusing on the cultural issue that needs to be resolved, and not as an interpreter/mediator. This further confuses the definition of intercultural mediation. For the purposes of this research, cultural mediators in healthcare will refer to the interpreters who mediate and address cultural issues between two parties.

Perhaps due to these instances, some researchers (Phelan & Martin, 2010) see intercultural mediation and interpreting as separate professions. They propose that 'intercultural mediators' opinions should not be personal but be grounded in professional analysis" (Phelan & Martin, 2010, p. 12). Likewise, interpreters' cultural knowledge and opinions should also not be personal but be grounded in professional analysis. All opinions in a professional setting should come from a professional, and should not be personal. However, if an interpreter interjects with knowledge acquired through personal experience, versus training, it is still a professional opinion within the context of her work? Professionalism is important for both interpreters and mediators and both should withdraw from assignments if for any reason they cannot carry the assignment out appropriately. Interpreters' cultural opinions are not necessarily personal, even if their cultural experiences and knowledge come from tacit personal life experiences. Loenhoff (2011) claimed that most of the concepts of intercultural training rest thus upon this explicit knowledge. In contrast, this knowledge is not explicit but implicit knowledge, otherwise called "tacit knowledge," has crucial pragmatic relevance in the process of intercultural communication (Loenhoff, 2011, p. 57).

According to Phelan and Martin (2010), the role of intercultural mediator diverges from that of interpreter in that the mediator aims to empower the patient and help him/her make choices. They state that:

mediators have to provide cultural explanations, whereas interpreters usually allow the other participants to sort out a cultural problem by allowing them to ask more questions. Impartiality is important for both, but mediators have more flexibility in that they can meet with providers and patients alone. Mediators have to evaluate situations and propose a plan of action.

If the interpreter is intrinsically acting as an intercultural mediator, one may ask how can we better differentiate him or her from an intercultural mediator who is not actually an interpreter? These distinctions may seem nuanced but highlight two important role conflicts. As a mediating agent, the interpreter may have agency, and as such take initiatives independently of others, such as interjecting, introducing arguments, making comments, giving explanations, requesting clarifications, confirming understanding, and other tasks required of mediation. However, according to a number of the traditional researchers, the less an interpreter is noted the better (to keep a low profile). Sadikov (1981) compared interpretation efficiency with the degree of consciousness the parties have of the interpreter's presence. The premise is that the more natural the behavior of the main participants, due to not noticing the interpreter, the greater probability of communicative success.

Other researchers disagree with the naturalness principle and see an intrinsic contradiction. Uvarov (1981) maintained that the more professionally confident interpreters feel, the more they are noticed. As one can see, these two approaches, the invisible (Sadikov, 1981) and the visible (Uvarov, 1981) have coexisted for some time. This research showcases how the invisible approach may bind the interpreter to have less agency and only speak up as a professional when absolutely necessary, limiting himself to strict linguistic interpretation.

However, as stated before, the interpreter-mediated encounter in the healthcare setting is more transactional and personal then a public speech or presentation interpretation. Straniero (2007) noted that in dialogic communication (vs. a monologue presentation at a conference), interpreters not only have an interpreting role, but also a communicative role and a social role. Phelan and Martin's (2010) characterization of the work of medical interpreters and mediators are accurate. However, it seems to limit the agency of medical interpreters, and may not reflect their entire work; as it only acknowledges the interpreting role of interpreters. Are medical interpreters not providing professional opinions when intervening, as mediators do? Are they bridging the cultural gap between two parties in a neutral and impartial manner, as mediators do? Are they not assisting the parties in reformulating or even explaining cultural paradigms when requested? This study explored these questions. This study also investigated whether interpreters were engaged in some of the same activities as intercultural mediators or not.

2.4.4 Research on interpreting culture over the phone.

Oviatt and Cohen (1992) described some of the unique features of telephonic interpreting. They examined the discourse of telephone interpreting in real service-oriented encounters in Australia, while Wadensjö (1998) studied it in comparison with face-to-face interpreting. Nonverbal communication posed a challenge for interpreters working over the phone, as any information about non-verbal cues would have to be provided verbally, by one of the parties, to the interpreter. These are often not provided unless requested, since the parties are engaged in their own issue and are usually not aware the interpreter needs cues. For example, in long moments of silence, interpreters usually ask what is happening. Sometimes an interpreter will not understand the verbal message because the non-verbal cues are implicit to those in the room but not to the interpreter. The interpreter may need context in order to understand the message and interpret it accurately. In these studies, the interpreters expressed taking on a more passive role in identifying miscommunication or lack of understanding, as they could not see the parties they were interpreting for. Hsieh (2003) pointed out that the task of informing the involvement of cultural elements occurred less in interpreters working over the phone than those interpreters working on site with providers and patients. Likewise, the interpretation of nonverbal messages was active with on-site interpreting and not as possible for telephonic interpreting. Nevertheless, if there are cultural issues to address, telephone interpreters are still trained to actively inform physicians of such issues (Hsieh, 2001).

It would be worthwhile to look into how the limitations of telephone interpreting affect the quality of interpreting culture and how these challenges can be overcome. The findings of some studies, (Hale, 2012; Hale & Gibbons, 1999) suggest that the conduit model and/or invisibility paradigms (traditional ideology from unidirectional conference interpreting studies) are not being practiced among medical interpreters, even over the phone. According to these studies, interpreters are actively involved in the communicative process through specific communicative strategies, and the interpreters' choice of strategies is not solely dependent on their linguistic ability or interpreting competence (Forman, 2002). However, does the modality of remote interpreting (phone and/or video) affect the interpreter's ability to mediate culture? What about in video interpreting that allows for more visual cues? These are areas that require further research. It seems that researchers are now seeing the value of examining interpretation as a communicative activity, with a greater sociolinguistic and psycholinguistic lens. The dynamics and interactive nature of the practice of medical interpreting has significant implications for the practice within the healthcare field.

2.4.5 Interpreters as active participants.

In Bolden's (2000) analysis of a medical history taking sessions, for example, he observed interpreters only conveyed information related to the medical contingencies, leaving out information presented by the patient that was unrelated to that set of contingencies. This action may be interpreted as an omission, a grave error in the skills of linguistic interpreting; or worst, the interpreter may be seen as a gatekeeper of information. However, according to this study, this was intentional behavior where interpreters were acting as part of the medical team and making decisions that did in fact make the interpreter the gatekeeper of unrelated information, for the sake of the patient flow, time constraints and other medical objectives. In this case, the healthcare professional's pressures, provider expectations, ethics and obligations of the medical interpreter as a healthcare professional were at odds and seemed to trump the linguistic interpreting code of ethics of accuracy and transparency: to interpret everything without omissions. Some interpreters, therefore, act as agents of mediation, contributing to the stability or subversion of social structures through their capacity to redefine the context in which they mediate. This is a recent development in the evolution of the discipline (Pérez-Gonzáles, 2012).

Some research speaks to the fact that medical interpreting involves at least two immediate clients or consumers, the patient, and the provider. Some communicative events may involve more parties on the patient's side (as with pediatric care or when other family members are present) or on the provider's side (teaching hospitals where providers bring residents with them). This means interpreters are exposed to at least two sets of potentially different expectations, if not more, depending on the number of participants in the encounter, three being the minimum number for an interpreted communicative event. Davidson (2001), through 6 months of daily observation, witnessed and recorded the following overriding expectations or mandates given to interpreters: (a) to interpret all and only what was said, and (b) the goal of keeping the patient on track, or making good time, due to the pressures of time on the healthcare provider. This can cause intra-role conflict. For example, Japanese clients tended to rely more on the interpreter than the Australian provider, due to an inferiority complex that they are not competent in English (Davidson, 2001). Japanese individuals were more appreciative of the services than the providers, as they understood that it required a high level of skills, while the Australian providers tended to regard the interpreter as simply someone who speaks two languages. This caused interpreters to engage in countless adjustment activities with regard to their role in response to the different expectations of the parties involved.

This observation emphasizes the interactive and interpersonal aspects of an interpreter-mediated encounter, particularly in relation to communicative norms, demanding adjustment and flexibility as a strategy for meeting expectations, a parameter of successful interpreting (Takimoto, 2006). Considering that Japanese is a culturally laden language, and high context language, it is unrealistic to expect interpreters to convey the interpreted message in a literal manner without any alteration (Davidson, 2000; Hsieh, 2001).

In a study by Pöchhacker (1998) of perspectives of medical interpreter tasks, 62% of interpreters ($n=601$) reported *explaining culture* as one of their tasks, in addition to *alerting to miscommunication* at 96%. Spoken and Sign language interpreters within that group ($n=16$) reported their tasks separately (81% and 80%, respectively). It is interesting to note that spoken language interpreters had a lower level of agreement regarding *explaining culture* (61%) when compared to Sign language interpreters (81%). While the standards imply that most interjection are due to miscommunication, according to the study above, interpreters explain culture as well as alert to a possible miscommunication. This data challenges the notion that the interpreter is always the facilitator of information, whereas when one is explaining culture one is the deliverer or the information, constructing meaning, as a participant to the collective communicative space.

Researchers have also found that more experienced interpreters actively intervene in the dynamics and process of the provider-patient communication through their appraisals and interventions related to several factors, whereas more inexperienced interpreters are more likely to remain in the conduit role (Hatton & Webb, 1993) which is a safe role where the interpreter has no voice. Researchers have suggested that the results of their studies could be attributed to an institutional influence or constraints on the role of the interpreter (Elderkin-Thompson, Silver, & Waitzkin, 2001), as interpreters often lack institutional power. However, they may hold some power within the communicative exchange as a result of their bilingual and bicultural expertise, albeit to different degrees, as most professionals, depending on a myriad of variables. They may exercise this power by adopting various verbal and non-verbal strategies to negotiate, coordinate, facilitate, mediate, check for understanding, and other tasks that relate to re-establishing power relations balance or patient-centered culturally competent care and patient safety. In this framework, the interpreters are acting as interlocutors, empowerment or change agent figures, or mediators, within the neutral stance of the well-established mediator role (Mason & Ren, 2012).

Different healthcare institutions may be more culturally competent than others and they may promote an organizational culture of cultural competency, which promotes cultural sensitivity, competency, and interventions. Some may actually view healthcare interpreters as mediators and therefore allow the interpreters more room to intervene, when cultural issues arise, or outside interpreted encounters. Likewise, organizations with no understanding of how culture affects outcomes, may not give interpreters any space or agency to act or speak for themselves. This will be explored further.

This power of the interpreter has been addressed in a few studies. Traditionally, interpreters have been called parrots, mouthpieces, or conduits, and seen as a voice box, all these metaphors suggesting the invisibility and powerless of the interpreter (Angelelli 2004; Li, 2002; Roy, 1999; Wadensjö, 1998). This view had been reinforced by previous research, and codes of conducts that prescribed detachment, transparency, invisibility, passivity, and neutrality to mean that the ideal interpreter should not make people feel his/her presence. This view has persisted, to a lesser extent, in the field of medical interpreting. The IMIA was one of the first professional associations of the field that recognized early on when it first published in 1996 (IMIA & EDC, 2007) that medical interpreters were not black boxes and that they required professional judgment and intercultural sensitivity and agency. Mason & Ren (2012) described the interpreter as a power figure, exercising power as a result of the monopolization of the means of communication and having an unusually great impact on the structure of the entire situation. However, there seems to be a disconnect between what the standards of practice state and what interpreters are exposed to, especially in the short intensive occupational educational programs of only 40 hours of duration. According to the Canadian training group, with such little time to teach so much, it seems that the nuances of mediation may not be covered. This Canadian group teaches a curriculum of 120 hours that has been standardized in many colleges in Canada and is being raised to 200 hours. If it cannot be appropriately covered in a curriculum of 120 hours, then one can imagine that in a curriculum of only 40 or 60 hours, the ability to incorporate a more sophisticated and nuanced approach to teaching the higher-level skills of medical and healthcare interpreting are simply not attainable.

For instance, the interpreter should voluntarily introduce himself, establishing his identity and agency to a certain degree. Some will propose the meeting format, explain cultural differences, answer a question, make a suggestion, ask for clarification or for further explanation, facilitate, mediate or even conduct small talk with one or both parties. As gatekeepers, they may sometimes withhold information that they deem inappropriate (vulgar remarks, cultural taboos, things irrelevant to health of patient, etc.) even if they are trained not to do so in the purist form of interpreting language training. Davidson (2000) found that interpreters in his study in effect acted as gatekeepers who kept the interviews on track and the physician on schedule. In this way they are adopting more of a bilingual physician assistant role than a neutral non-participant interpreter. Sign language interpreters may sometimes consider themselves an ally of Deaf patients, identifying with their interests and exercising agency for them. In all these circumstances, the degree of the interpreters' intervention was governed by the interpreters' self-identification and their assessment of the participants' need or expectation for mediation. Rather, when interacting with interpreters, interlocutors should see interpreters as mediators (Wadensjö, 1998) and try to develop effective communication strategies that best suit the goals of the conversational task as a team (Hsieh, 2001).

A study by Mesa (2000) in Canada surveyed healthcare providers, and their expectations that interpreters should explain cultural values ranked low, and fewer respondents considered it important for the providers to receive cultural explanations from the interpreter. In contrast, most interpreters expressed their role as one to create a bridge between the two cultures. They attached great significance to explanations about culture (73%) in Canada, contrary to the implied limitation on their standard of practice.

In another study (Van de Mieroop, Bevilacqua, & Hove, 2012), interpreted interactions in a Belgian home for the elderly were observed. In spite of the theoretically clearly defined task of the interpreters to interpret only what was said by the other interlocutors, data taken from interpreted interactions show quite a different picture. The discursive norms to which an interpreter orients in reality are interactional and negotiated, rather than pre-discursively determined. The results demonstrated significant variations in the way breaches of interpreting norms were dealt with, both by the interpreter and by the provider, with the latter playing a particularly important role in shaping the norms that are observed in the course of the interaction. In this study, the provider was the party observed to have the most influence to shape the discursive norms utilized by the interpreters. Similarly, Rudvin (2007) argued that because medical interpreting as a profession is still very heterogeneous (Italy), the interpreters' role is often defined by how the institution's needs and how they are used. Providers, institutions, and even country status may have an influence on the interpreters' sense of agency and role.

A study of the working conditions of community interpreters in Sweden showed that these reflected how multiculturalism and multilingualism are viewed on a national scale in Sweden. Several factors were identified as undermining professionalism: bad working conditions, low pay, the feeling of being replaceable, and the feeling of the social status of interpreters being low. It seems that the respect and support of the provider, institution, or political situation of the country of practice may also influence the interpreters' sense of agency (Norström, Fioretos, & Gustafsson, 2012).

In one of the few studies that focused on the interpreter perspective (Messias, McDowell, & Estrada, 2009), researchers found that, according to the practitioners, the interpreting process needed to take on the social and cultural context into consideration, in order to enable intercultural communication. Their findings represented three core narratives:

(a) the challenging conduit role
(b) being in the middle and experiencing role dissonance and conflicting expectations, and
(c) being a bridge for social justice.

Interpreters expressed that the impersonal, impartial, invisible, and purely linguistically technical role with clear-cut boundaries was often impractical and sometimes impossible, due to the overarching communicative goals inherent and necessary to ensure the successful outcomes of the healthcare objectives at hand. One of the conflicting sets of expectations related to whether the goal is to provide accurate language interpretation (interpretation goal) and to ensure mutual understanding (communication goal).

Other researchers described interpreter roles and goals more closely aligned to that of healthcare professionals than linguistic professional (Jalbert's [1998] *bilingual professional* role) when participants stated that their main goal was to satisfy the needs of the patient, as ultimately, the health of the patient was the most important issue to them. It seems that in the face of competing expectations, according to this particular study, some interpreters have availed themselves of a more expansive role beyond the perceived prescribed role of an invisible, neutral communication conduit interpreter. In this study, bridging cultural differences and barriers was another way interpreters engaged in a larger role beyond the provision of language interpretation. Advocates of a more involved role for the interpreter usually cite power differentials between the provider and patient, and interpreter empowerment issues as the reasons to support their argument. They argue that there is a power difference between the two participants, provider and patient, and the interpreter therefore not only gives a linguistic voice to the speaker of the non-authority language (Angelelli, 2002) but also gives that individual agency. However, advocates of a less involved role claim that the empowerment of the interpreter may mean the disempowerment of the patient (Pöllabauer, 2004) and there is merit to this argument. It takes a very sophisticated set of skills to mediate and empower the parties involved, or a specific underpowered party. In the attempt to empower the patient, the ill trained interpreter may inadvertently take over the role of patient advocate, instead of allowing the parties to resolve their issues. However, some will argue that empowering an individual involves scalable intervention, and when the individual does not collaborate or take the opportunity, or is not able to due to their lack of personal agency, the interpreter may be justified to step in as an advocate, to ensure the dignity and well being of that patient, as stated in the NCIHC Standards of Practice (NCIHC, p.10).

Another study shows a shared social justice framework that provides another opportunity for nurses and healthcare workers (which included medical interpreters) to work together, where both can find considerable common ground in their roles of patient advocates, cultural brokers, and social justice workers to have successful and meaningful communications with patients (Messias, McDowell, & Estrada, 2009). From a healthcare provider and practitioners' points of view, experts quote collegiality as the rationale for a more involved interpreter role. Another study (Labun, 1999) analyzed nurses' experiences ($n = 27$) in working with interpreters to serve Vietnamese patients, and provided evidence of a shared brokering concept. This shared brokering concept provided a framework for providing complex, effective, and efficient care for these patients.

Another study (Larrison, Velez, Hernandez, Piedra, Goldberg, 2010) explored the ability of interpreters to integrate and alleviate the organizational climate at federally qualified community health clinics. It identified friction between interpreters and providers due to incongruent expectations. The organizational climate and the interpreters' commitment to the Latino community they served mitigated the impact of these tensions. Interpreter role identity and tasks are sometimes trapped between *prescription* (who they should be and what they should do) and *proscription* (who they should not be and what they should not do). The roles and work of the interpreter is constructed moment-by-moment through the social, relational, and intercultural context in which they perform. Their behavior, largely co-dependent on that of the participants, is shaped on a case-by-case basis as each communicative event is unique. This is why interpreting is regarded as a practice profession, and interpreters are regarded as practitioners. Other practice professions include police officers, lawyers, teachers, and healthcare providers. These professions have a high relational feature as problems are solved through encounters between clients and practitioners.

So it seems that in some research, interpreters are seen to hold more power, whereas in others the healthcare organization and healthcare provider hold the power. It will vary even within an organization as each department, provider, patient, and interpreter bring their own personal and professional approaches, skills, and agency in a particular moment and situation at stake. In other words, each communicative event is unique, so generalizations are difficult to sustain.

It seems by the literature review, that in patient-centered environments, the most effective collaboration between interpreters and providers involves a model of shared control over clinical communication in which both participants share the goal building a therapeutic relationship between provider and patient, including establishing communication and trust with the client (Bloom, Hanson, Frires, & South, 1966). Interpreters may be seen as language technicians (the invisible paradigm) and/or as intercultural communication practice professionals (the emerging paradigm), according to Witter-Merithew and Nicodemus (2012). Basically interpreters in the healthcare setting, are afforded or demand different degrees of autonomy and agency and within the context in which their work occurs. Interpreter power, professional autonomy, or agency is in reality relational as a result of the very social structures upon which it depends for its existence—legislative mandates, system-based policy, institutional support or constraints, and professional education, procedures, and practices. This is why it is important for research on this topic to influence and guide policymakers to take into account the medical interpreters' essential services when developing environments that support quality care for culturally diverse patients.

Appreciating relational autonomy requires an understanding of the patient-centered conditions fostering informed and transparent decision-making and those that restrict it. The provision of medical services has shifted in several countries from a provider-centered paradigm to a patient-centered paradigm. A shared social justice paradigm seems to fit better the new patient-centered paradigm, where all in the healthcare team, including the transporter or the dietician, will have the patient's unique needs in mind and will have the agency to adapt the services to meet those needs. Even in countries with a provider-centered paradigm, the interpreter may be seen more as a provider assistant, when such a professionalization exists, or in other countries, where it doesn't or is emerging, as a patient helper. Rarely however, is the interpreter initially seen as a neutral and impartial mediator, unless the interpreter takes ownership of their agency and presents a professional introduction that sets the stage and explains in a sophisticated manner the role of the professional medical interpreter in the healthcare setting.

Pistillo (2003) demonstrated how the interpreter's intercultural sensitiveness and competence can lead to better understanding between the two or more parties requiring interpretation. According to Pistillo (2003), the task of the interpreter as intercultural mediator, needs to be on the basis of his/her intercultural competence, to ensure culturally different attitudes and beliefs do not become the source of misunderstandings. The interpreter must recognize the communication strategy used by each interlocutor and, when such strategy appears unsuitable to produce the effect intended by the speaker, s/he may choose to accommodate it to the expectations of the recipient. This seems to find support in Kondo (1990), among others, who pointed out that the consummate communicator, whether he is a professional interpreter or not, is a person who can put himself in somebody else's shoes, so to speak, so that he would be able to adopt two or more world views and thus imagine how a certain message would be decoded or interpreted by the receiving party. Atwood and Gray (1985) had already proposed that the invisible model suggests the role of the interpreter to be less than the other persons communicating, and that interpreters bring their own culture and identity of being mediators between the Deaf culture and spoken culture.

Interpreters have argued that a successful intercultural medical encounter requires them to assume roles other than conduit (Dysart-Gale, 2005; Hatton & Webb, 1993). In a study (Hsieh, 2008) that examined self-perceived roles and their corresponding communicative goals and strategies, twenty-six professional interpreters were recruited. Interpreters expressed concern for other participant's goals, institutional goals, and their own communicative goals. The interpreters' desire to maintain neutrality influenced the communicative strategies they adopted when assuming other non-conduit roles.

Jalbert (1998) proposed a role typology, based primarily on the seminal work of the Winnipeg group (Kaufert, 1999; Kaufert & Koolage, 1984; Kaufert et al., 1996) to understand the varying roles of the interpreter.

1. When acting as the *translator*, the interpreter minimizes her presence as much as possible. In this role she simply facilitates the communication process, not interfering with what the speakers say. Often this role is called the conduit role in most research.
2. When performing the role of *cultural informant*, the interpreter helps the healthcare provider to better understand the patient. In this role, the interpreter uses her knowledge of cultural norms and values.
3. As a *culture broker* or *intercultural mediator*, the interpreter is a cultural informant but also a negotiator between two conflicting value systems or symbolic universes. In this role, the culture broker needs to facilitate, enlarge, provide explanations, or synthesize (not summarize) healthcare providers' and patients' utterances to help both parties arrive at a meaningful shared or accepted model (of care, of behavior, or belief, etc.).
4. Focusing on the role of *advocate*, in a value-conflict situation, the interpreter may choose to defend the patient to the institution or provider, or defend the provider or institution to the patient.
5. Finally, when working as a *bilingual professional*, the interpreter acts as a healthcare professional. She leads the interview in the patient's language, when filling out a form, for example, or assessing the patient's linguistic and cultural background, and then reports to the healthcare provider. She can do this because of prior training in healthcare or, in a more limited way, because the institution's norms for her assistance and her knowledge of institutional practices and routines (Kaufert, 1999; Kaufert & Koolage, 1984; Kaufert et al., 1996).

It is important to note that in the field of interpreting this bilingual (healthcare) professional role descriptor above may be confused with that of a clinical role, or that of an interpreter doing a healthcare provider's job, or a bilingual healthcare worker, such as a nurse. According to the study, this is not about the interpreter providing medical services, but about the interpreter relieving the colleague hospital staff person of sight translating text in a form that the interpreter can read to the patient directly in their language. Some educators in the field state that interpreters should require the healthcare professional to read it, whereas they simply provide oral interpretation, but providers will rebut stating that sight translation of a patient form is part of the interpreter's scope of work and doesn't require their presence. When interpreters are asked about this some state that they need to negotiate tasks with staff to truly be considered part of the team of healthcare professionals. With the added pressure of time and patients lined up for the provider and the patient, some interpreters have to make decisions about their practice that are practical and beneficial to the patient and their co-workers. If the patient had questions about the form, the interpreter would write them down and serve as the interpreter to clarify them with the appropriate healthcare professional. Some stated that they actually knew the answers to some practical and non-medical questions, since they had filled out the forms before with patients as healthcare workers. Interpreters in this study were seen as the professionals who will bridge the language and cultural divide, and as such were asked to conduct tasks beyond linguistic interpreting for the interested parties. This is still a very controversial issue in the profession, since interpreting usually requires three parties at a minimum, and the interpreter's work is rarely seen outside the context of a triadic communicative event.

In Jalbert's (1998) view, the intercultural mediation roles (cultural informant, cultural mediator, bilingual professional) appear in two primary scenarios: when there is the need of conveying missing cultural information, and when there are conflicting cultural values. According to the IMIA & EDC (2007) interpreters manage conflict between provider and patient, and assists the provider and patient in making conflicts or tensions explicit so that they can work them out between themselves (IMIA & EDC, 2007, p. 34). Therefore, they are not responsible for resolving such conflict. None the less, they may manage cultural conflict, and provide an essential contribution to its resolution by serving as facilitators and mediators, allowing the primary parties to come to an agreement or not.

2.4.6 Research on the difficulties of intercultural mediation.

The concept of neutrality or impartiality and a more interactive model of communication such as mediation do not have to be mutually exclusive (Zimányi, 2009). The act of aligning oneself primarily with one of the parties would contradict neutrality and impartiality. However, aligning with both parties who require interpretation allows the interpreter to remain neutral in assisting both parties as required. Mikkelson (2008) stated that it may be argued that medical interpreters should be held to a different standard than their counterparts in legal settings, given the collaborative nature of most healthcare interactions.

There are other concerns about interpreters mediating or interpreting culture. Medical interpreters do not necessarily have all the cultural knowledge to address all the cultural groups they encounter in their work. The amount of training they receive regarding addressing cultural issues may not be sufficient considering most training programs in existence are under 100 hours of duration. If they were not properly trained, they also may not have all the necessary skills and knowledge to mediate in a professional manner. Hale (2012) emphasized the need of adequate and more sophisticated pre-service training for the complex work of medical interpreters, so that they can better interact and manage the relational dynamics of working with healthcare providers and patients.

For example, Rice (2005) differentiated the resolution techniques of bilingual Mexicans, Cubans, and Colombians. Davidson (2001) further recognized these cultural differences when he explained that even interpreters from the same country as the patient may be culturally different. In his research interpreters were overwhelmingly urban, educated elites in their respective countries of origin (Mexico and Central American countries), whereas the patients for whom they interpreted for were overwhelmingly of rural backgrounds with little formal education (Davidson, 2001). Therefore, the studies above seem to suggest that care needs to be taken to ensure that the parties providing intercultural mediation are cognizant of these nuances to do so. This study will address the interpreters' perspective about their knowledge and training in the area of addressing cultural issues in the results section.

Most codes of ethics require interpreters to be impartial and neutral and to not interfere unless required, deferring the communication to the provider and patient. They are discouraged from developing relationships with patients and or making active judgments to facilitate provider patient communication (Hsieh, 2006). There is ample research in the field of interpreting about the interpreter's ethical responsibility to be neutral and impartial. However, the idea of neutrality should be challenged based on the settings in which the interpreter works (Bot, 2003). Some confuse neutrality and impartiality with negation of presence and lack of agency (invisibility conduit paradigm). Mediation does require neutrality and impartiality according to the National Association of Certified Mediators, which suggests that in mediation, neutrality and impartiality are not exclusive. However many in the field justify their warnings against the interpreter acting with agency outside of the interpreting conduit role as if one cannot be neutral or impartial in these other roles. If self-agency means the ability to make decisions and act on them verbally, should a professional medical interpreter be discouraged from making active professional judgments and decisions or have a voice in order to better facilitate the provider patient communication?

Intercultural mediation or facilitation requires soft skills that are deemed as sophisticated professional skills. These involve a high level of communication skills (such as active listening and the ability to speak in a culturally appropriate and clear manner), the ability to engage clients, build trust, honor transparency and validate opinions, create balance between the parties, as well as check for understanding. Sometimes, without proper training, the interpreter's effort to bridge cultural differences may lead to problematic practices. When editorializing the message to soften it using the justification of "cultural appropriateness," what may happen is that a different question and response may ensue. The interpreter's understanding or lack of understanding of the cultural issue may have an impact on his ability to effectively mediate culture. Interpreter misrepresentation of cultural situations may hinder the mutual understanding (Hsieh, 2006). Answers to these questions have considerable implications for interpreter education. The issue is not whether a mediation role is appropriate or not; as according to most of the research reviewed it is inherent in an intercultural exchange. However, can interpreters be effective in providing culturally competent services and avoid negative situations or outcomes under the present training conditions? The Canadian educator group that was a stakeholder in the development of the Canadian Standards of Practice for Community Interpreters, clearly expressed concern about the lack of training in this area.

Leanza (2005) recommended a new typology of roles for medical interpreters.

1) As *system agent*, the interpreter transmits the dominant discourse, norms and values to the patient. Cultural difference is denied in favor of the dominant biomedical culture.

2) As *community agent*, the interpreter plays the reverse role: the patient norms and values are presented and potentially equally valid. Cultural difference is acknowledged. This role can be played in various ways, more or less nuanced.

3) When acting as an *integration agent*, the interpreter finds resources to help patients to make sense, negotiate meanings, and find in-between ways of behaving. These roles take place outside consultations in everyday life.

4) As a *linguistic agent*, the interpreter attempts to maintain an impartial position. The process requires only linguistic

interventions (e.g., request for repetition, clarification of a term or utterance, transparency, paraphrasing, etc.).

This typology explains the medical interpreter's role in relationship to all the stakeholders involved (system agent > institution, community agent > provider, integration agent > community, and linguistic agent > patient/provider).

Gentile and Vasilakakos (1996) stated that when extra-linguistic problems arise in an encounter, the interpreter should always try to facilitate mutual understanding either by briefing the participants beforehand whenever possible or by interpreting in a more diplomatic way so as to soften the atmosphere and allow the communication to proceed. It seems the mere presence of someone who speaks the language of the patient made the patient much more comfortable in a health environment in which they cannot communicate. According to the researcher, children are more likely to heal if they and their parents feel comfortable when receiving treatment, and medical interpreters can provide a level of reassurance that puts pediatric patients more at ease.

Leanza's previous study (Leanza, 2003) reported that medical interpreters also identified themselves as *welcomers* or the institutional hosts of their patients. When the doctors in this study failed to make culturally appropriate greetings, the medical interpreters often stepped in to smooth things over. Leanza (2003) defined the intercultural mediator role not only as a cultural informant but also a negotiator between two conflicting value systems or symbolic universes. In this role, the intercultural mediator needs to enlarge, provide explanations or synthesize healthcare providers' and patients' utterances to help both parties arrive at a meaningful shared model (i.e., of care, of behavior etc.). According to the interviews with both the pediatric residents and the interpreters, more weight was given to the institutional discourse (biomedicine) than to that of the parents. According to the study, although interpreters were sometimes frustrated by not playing more of a mediator role, they found some satisfaction in playing the role of bilingual professional, which allowed them to experience a professional status quite different from that of their patients (Weber & Molina, 2003).

In a study about end-of-life care between patients and providers, results showed that there were role conflicts, including struggles concerning expectations to provide strict interpretation vs. being an intercultural mediator. Interpreters' recommendations for improving quality of care included providers having pre-sessions with the interpreter before the delivery of bad news (to negotiate a message that is culturally competent), and explicit discussions with interpreters about clarification of their role in healthcare in order to provide culturally and linguistically competent care (Norris et al., 2005).

Bot (2003) described the two approaches (impartiality and the partiality) in a unique way. She identified that in psychology, there is a one-person psychology (relationship of provider-patient is seen as manifestation of patient's psychology alone), a two-person psychology (without a relationship there can be no therapy), and a three-person psychology approaches (explicitly pays attention to the interpreted-encounter context in which the patient-therapist dyad functions). Bot described models of cooperation between the two professionals, by aligning the interpreting and therapeutic models. She stated that interpreters operating a conduit model work well with therapists who subscribe to a one or two-person psychology model, whereas interpreters with an interactive-model background can work well with therapists who prefer a three-person psychology approach. This model proposes the idea of the interpreter as an integral part of a three-person alliance, soliciting the interpreters' thoughts about cultural issues. These culturally sensitive providers are more likely to rely on interpreters as cultural consultants to help them understand the affect or cultural context of the patient's experiences, behaviors and metaphors.

Raval (2005), informed by Roy's work (1999), outlined the third role typology to be discussed, a series of roles specific in describing mental health interpreters. These include the following:

- *Interpreter*—interpretation done in a neutral and impartial manner,
- *Intercultural mediator*—explains and gives cultural and contextual understanding to either party,
- *Cultural consultant*—the interpreter acts as a cultural consultant to the provider,
- *Advocate for the patient*—the interpreter represents the patient's interests and speaks on his/her behalf,
- *Intermediary*—the interpreter mediates on behalf of both parties,
- *Conciliator*—the interpreter resolves conflicts that arises between the provider and patient,
- *Community advocate*—the interpreter represents the community concerns at the level of policy making,
- *Link-worker*—the interpreter supports providers in identifying unmet needs of the patient and helps the patient make informed choices concerning their healthcare, and
- *Bilingual worker*—the interpreter takes on a more involved therapeutic role in addition to providing interpretation.

to understand the contextual environment in which she works in order to be able to identify a contextual cultural problem, coming from the provider or the patient's part.

Stage 2 involves intervening conditions or culturally based factors that must be considered at all three stages: *analyzing the problem, devising appropriate strategies, and evaluating outcomes.* This also involves the intervention strategies of establishing trust and rapport, and maintaining connections between the parties. Specific elements of these culture-brokering strategies are the following: *advocating, mediating, networking, negotiating, innovating, intervening, and sensitizing.* According to Jeweski, anyone who is working as an intercultural mediator can utilize these specific skills to assist the parties in finding common ground. However, most in the field of medical interpreting would not agree that the interpreter should actually have the power to negotiate. However, the fact that the interpreter is the middle person and mediator of communication means the interpreter will in fact assist in the negotiation between the parties, taking an active part in the negotiated outcome by expressing the opinions of the parties involved to the best of his ability. This may include expressing their own opinions or formulations when checking for understanding, for example. This does not mean that the interpreter is in fact the negotiator who will decide the outcome, as the parties involved are the ones that need to express how they wish to negotiate a treatment or outcome. It simply means that at times the interpreter may need to be a participant in the negotiation, in his attempt to approximate the parties. As the formulator of messages, the interpreter will in fact be the key negotiation mediator, without being the negotiator himself.

There is an important distinction between participating in certain activities and being the head decision-maker of such activity. In the case of a negotiated agreement between the parties in an interpreted communicative event, the interpreter is indeed an active co-constructor of the very messages from both parties that have the intent to convey or even convince the other party of their point of view for a common-ground solution. As mentioned with identifying the problem, the actual skills of mediating need to be well addressed and studied by interpreters.

Most interpreters are unaware of the Jeweski model. It would be beneficial that it be included in their educational programs, as well as information about ethnocentrism and ethnorelativism, and other cultural concepts relevant to intercultural work. Currently the limited scope of information on this activity has not allowed interpreters to do much more than what is explained in the standards of practice of CHIA and IMIA. Educational textbooks need to be written specifically within the context of intercultural mediation by medical interpreters for them to have the tools to practice more confidently in this area. This book remains an introduction to the intercultural mediation activity as told by medical interpreters. At the time of this publication, interpreters are perceived to enter the field ill prepared, yet seem to gain extensive knowledge and experience in this area through their professional practice.

Stage 3 is *evaluating outcomes*, whether positive or negative. Success is achieved if connections are established between patients, the provider, and the healthcare system. Outcomes are unsuccessful if there is a gap in communication, continued miscommunication, or breakdown in service utilization. The question remains: To what extent should medical interpreters engage in intercultural mediation? In the medical interpreting field several terms have been used to describe the specific work of addressing cultural issues between two parties: culture interface, culture clarifier, culture broker, and intercultural mediator. This stage is very useful to medical interpreters as it is through evaluation that practitioners are able to better calibrate their knowledge and skills to better address cultural issues. Jezewski's (1990) theoretical model and framework for intercultural mediators is a tool that can be used to better understand the medical interpreters' work in interpreting culture. The CHIA Standard of Practice has a section on evaluating outcomes of all interpreter actions, and is useful for actions related to addressing cultural issues. This book is limiting itself to introducing readers to one theoretical model of intercultural mediation and one model of intervention, which can be applied to intercultural demands, or needs. The first is not limited to interpreters, but applies to all professions that participate in intercultural mediation, and the second is specific to interpreters, but not limited or targeted only for medical interpreters working in the healthcare setting. Both showcase the need of inclusion of more evidence-based content in interpreter education, to better equip interpreters to act in this arena successfully.

2.6 The Demand Control Schema (DC-S)

The Demand-Control Schema has been widely accepted by American Sign language interpreters, as it is a taught method of interpreted intervention in most Sign language interpreting programs of study in U.S. universities. It is slowly making its way into the world of spoken language interpreters. Dean and Pollard (2001) adapted the demand control concept from occupational research conducted by Robert Karasek (1979) and Törres Theorell (Karasek & Theorell, 1990). Karasek and Theorell (1990) theorized that occupational stress arises from the relationship between the difficulties (demands) presented by work responsibilities with respect to the interventions (controls or strategies) that professionals have to respond to in their daily work requirements. This framework of work stress challenged the traditional view that occupational stress is a function of a specific job category, such as an emergency medical technician (EMT) who works in an ambulance assisting patients in distress. Other occupations, including firefighters, pilots, or surgeons, were commonly viewed as high-stress jobs. However, Karasek (1979) demonstrated that such professions were not associated with high rates of stress-related illness when professionals had adequate resources (e.g., education, materials, experience, collegial support, and decision-making power) to perform their job requirements well. In contrast, when workers were least able to respond to high-demand job challenges (i.e., not enough training, materials, experience, collegial support, and decision-making power), stress-related illnesses were encountered.

Dean and Pollard (2001) used this occupational research theory framework to examine the nature of demands and controls in the interpreting profession. This model has evolved through the years and now is a well developed theoretical framework that meets the interpreting profession's needs as practitioners who have to make practice decisions beyond word choice.

Dean and Pollard defined four categories of job demands that act upon interpreters:

(a) *environmental demands*
(b) *interpersonal demands*
(c) *paralinguistic demands*
(d) *intrapersonal demands*

Environmental demands are challenges related to the assignment setting (e.g., the need to understand participant roles and specialized terminology specific to a given setting, space limitations, odors, extreme temperatures, or noise). Healthcare interpreters face many of such demands, as communicative events may take place in very tight situations, or where background noise may affect their ability to understand the messages they need to interpret. Safety conditions may play a role, as when an interpreter is interpreting for a highly volatile patient. The key factor in these demands is that interpreters need to identify and own the resolution of whatever environmental demands they face in order to provide optimal interpreting services. This type of demand does not involve cultural issues, although the issue of who is in the room with the patient or not may be identified as a cultural issue.

Interpersonal demands are challenges related to the interaction of the participants (e.g., the need to understand and interface between cultural differences, power differences, preconceptions, and encounter goals of the participants). By virtue of its definition, it seems that cultural differences and assumptions or preconceptions, and goals, all of which are affected by culture, are within interpersonal demands. Identifying these demands is also in the purview of interpreters. While these demands involve much more than intercultural issues, for the purposes of this book, it showcases that this DC-Schema is useful for addressing cultural issues, as part of a theoretical framework to address all issues that arise in an interpreted communicative event.

Paralinguistic demands involve challenges that relate to overt aspects of the expressive communication of Deaf and hearing consumers, what the interpreter sees and hears. Examples of paralinguistic demands are when a hearing individual has a heavy accent or is mumbling or when a Deaf individual is signing lazily, lying down, or has an object in his or her hands.

Finally, *intrapersonal demands* are challenges related to the internal physiological or psychological state of the interpreter (e.g., the need to tolerate hunger, fatigue, or distracting thoughts or strong emotions that emerge in a high-stakes situation). Strong emotions could have a cultural source, if the interpreter is not well trained in the skills of ethnorelativism, the ability to see different cultural norms and beliefs as valid. Interpreters need to be very attentive to intrapersonal demands that may have a cultural component.

According to the DC-Schema, intercultural issues is primarily an interpersonal demand (Table 2). However, it may be affected by intrapersonal demands.

Table 2
DC-Schema Demands

Demand	Description
Interpersonal demands	Challenges related to the interaction of the participants (need to understand and interface between cultural differences, power differences, preconceptions, and encounter goals of the participants.)
Paralinguistic demands	Challenges that relate to overt aspects of the expressive communication of Deaf and hearing consumers, what the interpreter sees and hears. (heavy accent, regionalism, etc.)
Intrapersonal demands	Challenges related to the internal physiological or psychological state of the interpreter (hunger, emotion, etc.)
Environmental demands	Challenges related to the setting (e.g., the need to understand participant roles and specialized terminology, noise, etc.)

What resources (controls) do medical interpreters, both spoken language and Sign language interpreters, have at their disposal and/or are utilizing to interpret culture? In the DC-Schema for interpreters, *controls* are skills, actions, or other resources that an interpreter may bring to bear in response to the needs and challenges (demands) presented by a given work assignment.

Controls for interpreters may include education, experience, actions, or interventions, assignment preparation or study, specific interpreting decisions, (e.g., specific word or sign choices, or explanatory comments to patients). The effectiveness and consequences of how one chooses to respond (or not respond) to a given challenge in interpreting culture is fundamental to the way the DC-Schema is applied during teaching, supervision, or self-analysis (reflective practice) of interpreting work (Table 3).

Table 3
DC-Schema Controls & Timing

Control	Description
Pre-assignment controls	Education *on patient culture(s), education on healthcare delivery and culture, knowledge of language proficiency and dialects, ability to assess cultural backgrounds,* assignment preparation, pre-session with the provider or patient, *intercultural experience, cultural humility and competency training, intercultural mediation training*
Assignment controls	Behavioral actions and decisions, made during the communicative event itself, *such as cultural interventions to clarify a possible cultural misunderstanding or lack of awareness*
Post-assignment controls	Follow-up behaviors *such as cultural education of either party after the communicative event,* post-session, debrief, consultations *or participation in cultural competency educational efforts outside interpreted communicative events*

Note: Italics added by author to connote controls specific to intercultural mediation.

The examples above are a partial list of the controls that can be applied to intercultural mediation. As seen above, the timing of such intervention controls is included in this model. When engaging in a DC work analysis, recognition of a given demand sparks consideration and critique of control options that may be employed in each of these three time periods. Therefore, the utilization of the DC-Schema on interpreting culture should be further explored. It is important to note that whereas the DC-Schema is widely accepted in Sign language interpreting professionals in the United States, it is a fairly new theoretical framework for intervention and most spoken language interpreters, and interpreters in countries outside the United States, are not very familiar with it. It has also not been specifically developed for the medical interpreting specialization. However, according to Dean (Dean & Pollard, 2001), one of the authors of the DC-Schema, it has had quite some attention from Australia, the United

Kingdom, and Europe. As an example, Dean and others regularly run online DC-Schema supervision groups from the United States for groups of interpreters in the United Kingdom and Australia. This is an important tool for all interpreters, and should be disseminated to the spoken language interpreters through higher quality training of longer duration. It is an intervention model that aids interpreters not only in interpreting culture, but also when the need to intervene due to other demand.

Thus far, readers have been exposed to three models for intercultural mediation, and one model for addressing all demands, which includes the interpersonal demand of intercultural differences:

(a) the IMIA & EDC (2007) model of intercultural mediation (IMIA & EDC, 2007 p.41),

(b) the CHIA cultural clarifier role (CHIA, 2002, p. 43)

(c) the Jeweski (1990), theoretical model of intercultural mediation and

(d) the D-C Schema (2001) to address all demands, including cultural differences.

Chapter Three

RESEARCH DESIGN AND METHODOLOGY

3.1 Objective

The study to be described in this book had as its main objective to study the professional medical interpreters' perspectives about their practice of bridging the cultural gap in healthcare between the providers and patients they serve. This book aims to redefine the professional role and scope of service based on the interpreters' own set of professional values and beliefs, using verbal reporting as the primary methodology. The aim is to shed light on the impact of the interpreter's provision of culturally competent care.

3.2 Need for the Study

There is a deficiency of studies related to the practitioner's perspective on interpreting culture. Most studies explore the cultural differences between providers and patients and how interpreters are observed to act to bridge those social and cultural gaps. The majority of these studies, as described in the previous chapter, utilize ethnographic observation techniques demonstrating and studying what interpreters actually do. Another popular methodology used in several of them was discourse analysis, where the transcription data of oral communicative events with interpreters is analyzed for linguistic, and other aspects of their practice. By analyzing the actual renditions of interpreters, researchers were able to analyze some of their actions. However, neither of these methodologies focus on what is happening in the interpreter's brain. When they are practicing, the aim was to explore what thought processes take place that inform the interpreter of what action to take next or not. This study attempted to bring to light the professional medical interpreters' views and perspectives as a powerful way to look at and understand their practice. How do *they* view their scope of work and/or limitations? What strategies do they use? Exploring their perceptions on the specific controls (strategies) at their disposal related to the demands (challenges) of interpreting culture in the healthcare setting is essential to better understand the reasoning behind their professional behaviors and actions.

3.3 Importance of the Study

This study assumes that the practitioner is the ultimate expert of his practice. Therefore, this study is important primarily because it honors the practitioner's perspective as the ultimate expert of his craft. This study will aid other stakeholders (providers, patients, educators, and policymakers) to develop more appropriate training, standards, guidelines, and institutional policies to support the medical interpreter's work in this area, as they are the ones in the trenches. Their cultural work is viewed in relation to the healthcare goals of providing culturally competent care. This study may have an impact on how interpreters are understood to support the various healthcare organizations' efforts to provide culturally appropriate care to culturally diverse patients.

3.4 Scope of the Study

This study was designed as an international study that focused on the specific experiences, impressions, and activities related to interpreting culture, including acting as an intercultural mediator when providing medical interpreting services to patients and providers who do not share the same language or culture. It does not focus in detail as to what specific cultural situations engender such cultural demands (challenges) or on the typology of such cultural issues. Therefore, only a few cultural case examples are given, mostly to illustrate the types of situations interpreters face when interpreting culture and their interventions and outcomes. The focus is on the interpreters work, which aims to look at interventions and outcomes, and not sources of cultural issues. Much has been written about the cultural dilemmas that are faced in the provision of healthcare.

Further study is needed on the perspectives of the cultural work of interpreters, from educators, providers, and patients. The scope of the study is limited to the medical interpreter's beliefs, values, and perception of the work of interpreting culture, in all its facets: its advantages, disadvantages, challenges, timing, strategies, stressors, and training. As such, data collection was limited to the understanding of the practitioners' perspective about this very specific component of their work. This study used the methodology of self-reported beliefs and practices, without verifying whether what they say is what they do. The value of studying what they think is that it may shed some light into the realities interpreters' face that may influence how they act or not depending on certain demands (challenges). This study and consequently this book, attempts to help readers see through the interpreter's eyes, leading to greater understanding of the complex multifaceted work of medical interpreters.

3.5 Expected Outcomes

The most relevant expected outcomes of this study are the following:

- to gain a better understanding of the practitioner's perspective of their cultural work
- to use the data to develop specific training curricula in this area
- to aid policymakers in establishing policies that support medical interpreters to provide culturally competent care
- to provide intercultural intervention models for medical interpreters,
- to increase the understanding of the medical interpreters' intercultural work.
- to document what medical interpreters have to say about their work of interpreting culture

3.6 Hypotheses

This study did not have a specific hypotheses as it is a primarily a qualitative study. Professional medical interpreters have their own perceptions about interpreting culture in their practice. They also have professional opinions about why, when, and how to act and when to intervene when addressing cultural issues. Lastly, they must understand the effects of their interventions or lack of interventions when interpreting culture. Understanding their perceptions about interpreting culture may inform cultural competency efforts and initiatives in healthcare. What greater role within the system does interpreting culture play in providing culturally competent care? This international study will help medical interpreters who read it to further define, understand, and standardize their practice about interpreting culture across regions and countries.

3.7 Research Questions

1. *When interpreting in healthcare, in what types of situations do medical interpreters find themselves addressing a cultural issue?*
2. *How often do medical interpreters have to intervene to address a cultural issue?*
3. *When do medical interpreters address cultural issues: before, during, or after an encounter?*
4. *What are the advantages of addressing cultural issues from the medical interpreter's perspective?*
5. *What are the disadvantages of addressing cultural issues from the medical interpreter's perspectives?*
6. *What are the challenges addressing cultural issues from the medical interpreter's perspective?*
7. *What are the strategies used when intervening to address cultural issues from the medical interpreter's perspective?*
8. *Did medical interpreters receive enough training to address cultural issues between providers and patients? If not, what areas need to be included in interpreter education?*
9. *How stressful is it for medical interpreters to interrupt a session to address a cultural issue, and why?*
10. *What else do medical interpreters have to say about addressing cultural issues?*

3.8 Research Design

This study selected verbal reporting as the primary qualitative methodology. The value of verbal reports is that they use a cognitive psychology viewpoint, where the data can be considered as accurate representations of the happenings of one's mind when completing a task (Ericsson & Simon, 1993). In introspective analysis, as opposed to protocol analysis, the goal is for subjects to express out loud the thoughts that occur to them naturally about their tasks. The qualitative data for the study was obtained in semi-structured interviews, one virtual focus group via online webinar, and an essay submitted by an interpreter on the subject.

Quantitative data was derived using a questionnaire delivered via an online survey. The survey included some open-ended questions allowing it to collect further qualitative data to inform the study further.

This research was designed with a mixed methodology design. The primary focus was to obtain the practitioner's perspective on the topic of interpreting culture. Therefore, qualitative data collection was the first and primary method of data collection. A focus group followed to collect additional qualitative data more efficiently. Finally, an online survey was developed using some of the coded language derived from the interviews and focus group for two reasons. First, it allowed the researcher to reach a greater number of participants in a broader area, and second, it enabled the researcher to see if the data collected quantitatively corroborated with the initial qualitative results. The quantitative data also allows for objective comparisons. A comparison analysis of the quantitative data was done using various variables, such as general education, specialized training, experience, country, etc. Last, there was a desire to embrace a large variation of cultural interactions and perspectives, and for that reason it was important for the study to have an international scope. The study ended up involving practitioners who practiced in 25 countries.

3.9 Qualification of Participants

The target population for this study was professional medical interpreters worldwide. Some research defines the interpreter as the individual who interprets, not distinguishing between the bilingual family member or bilingual healthcare provider who is called in to interpret informally, and the medical interpreter who trained and tested to be deemed competent to interpret in the healthcare setting. Since this is a study focused on the practitioner's perspective, it was important that only practicing professional medical interpreters be interviewed. Therefore, interpreter researchers, managers, or educators, who were not interpreters, were disqualified from participating, as they would not be giving the perspective of practitioners. There was no minimal experience qualifier, so that the researcher was able to compare responses between interpreters with varying degrees of training or experience. Consent to participation was required, so if an individual refused consent, he or she was disqualified. Therefore, there were only two disqualifiers: (a) if the individual was not a trained practicing professional medical interpreter or (b) if the potential participant did not consent to the study. Because the study was an international study, target populations included medical interpreters practicing in different countries. The selection process was based on a random sample. With randomization, a representative sample from the medical interpreter population provides an improved ability to generalize to that population. There were no specific training qualifications due to the varied and limited training available to medical interpreters.

3.10 Ethical Considerations

All research must respect and be transparent with the participants, and as such an informed consent was developed and approved by the primary professor of this research, Dr. Nakamura, and later by the Institutional Review Board (IRB) of Osaka University. All interview and focus group participants filled out the same form for the interviews as well as for the focus group. The survey had an abbreviated form of the consent form, as approved by the primary professor, and instead of a signature, the participant simply had to answer yes to the question of consenting to participate. Any participant who answered no was sent to a disqualifying webpage thanking them for their interest and explaining that consent to participate was a requirement for participation. The informed consent form (Appendix B) included the following important elements:

1. The right to participate was voluntary and the right to withdraw at any time;
2. The purpose of the study, so that participants understood the nature of the research and its impact on their work;
3. The procedures of the study, so that participants could reasonably know what to expect in the interview, focus group, or survey;
4. The right to ask questions and obtain a copy of the results;
5. Their right to have their privacy respected, as this was an anonymous study, where excerpts of what was said would be shared, but not the names of participants;
6. The benefits of the study and possible future applications;
7. Any foreseen discomfort or negative outcomes, for which none were identified or shared; and
8. Requirement of a signature from the participant and the researcher for the interviews and focus group, or in the case of the survey instrument, the positive answer of consenting to the study electronically obtained.

In addition to obtaining consent from all participants, the researcher also took care to send the transcription to all participants or medical interpreters in order to verify the data that were collected and to ensure that all data shared had the approval of the participants. The term *participant* was utilized vs. *subject* or *respondent*. The study also uses guidelines by the American Psychological Association (6th ed.), which requires unbiased language that is sensitive to labels or stereotypes, and to acknowledge participation in the study. The interpreter is referred to as a medical interpreter and also as healthcare interpreter, as both terms are used to describe the profession. They are also referred to as he or she interchangeably. The researcher was mindful and ethical not handpick participants, or to suppress, falsify, or select findings to meet the researcher's needs. This statement serves as a proactive stance in writing by the researcher not to engage in such practices.

3.11 Research Instrumentation

The instrumentation developed and utilized to collect data for this study involved three different instruments: (a) the interview instructions and questions, (b) a focus group presentation, and (c) the online survey. Each will be described in greater detail this chapter.

3.11.1 The interview instrument.

The interview was the primary data collection tool for this survey, and comprised the interviewer's instructions, nine demographic questions, and the eight research questions, providing the participant with the ability to add any statements they wished to about the topic at the end of the interview. The questions in the interview were very close to the research questions of the study. The interview document was mostly an internal tool for the researcher, to perform all interviews in a consistent manner with the participants. The interview instrument was not shared with the participants.

3.11.2 The focus group PowerPoint presentation.

A focus group PowerPoint presentation titled *Interpreting culture: Exploring the professional medical interpreters' perspective*s was developed to aid participants of the online live focus group who are visual and need to see the questions as they discuss them. As a token of appreciation for their participation, the PowerPoint presentation also included information about the most common culture bound syndromes and a cultural competency self-assessment as two incentives to participate. The researcher also applied for the event to provide continuing education credits for certified medical interpreters to document their learning experiences. It was delivered utilizing software called www.GoToMeeting.com, which allows for the delivery of live online webinars. This webinar had the technical capability for 20 participants and the on the actual scheduled date of the focus group, 16 participants were present. Steps were taken in order to give each participant equal opportunity to provide their opinions about the research questions.

3.11.3 The online survey instrument.

The online survey was developed using software called SurveyMonkey and titled *Interpreting culture: Exploring the professional medical interpreters' perspective*. The questions were reviewed and approved by the primary professor of the study. This online tool allowed for the easy dissemination of the survey via an online web link to reach a larger random sampling of participants. It also provided the researcher with the ability to code some of the responses received in interviews to see if the quantitative data corroborates with the qualitative data. The online survey instrument comprised of 35 questions. Its first section included an introduction explaining who the researcher was and the topic and purpose of the study. This was followed by nine definitions with the intent of standardizing participants' usage of some of the relevant terms in the field, and to avoid miscommunication.

A consent form came next with the two qualifying questions: the consent question, and the question about being a practicing medical interpreter or not. The second section, the demographics section, followed by 12 questions. The third section had the purpose of asking questions about the medical interpreter's cultural background, level of acculturation, training, and perception of cultural knowledge and skills. This section was comprised of eight questions. The fourth and last section, titled *Addressing cultural issues in your work*, had 13 questions, which included the research questions, with a format allowed participants to respond by agreeing to multiple sub-item responses regarding their agreement. Last, a thank you page thanked participants for their participation. The survey included another thank you page for disqualifying candidates. The online survey asked a few additional questions that could not be addressed in the interviews or focus group. These included questions exploring other facets of interpreting culture, such as level of acculturation, training, cultural knowledge and skills, importance of addressing cultural issues, and level of competency needed. The majority of the questions were close-ended, multiple choice, some with a question about frequency of incidence which included a Likert scale from "never" to "always," for example. Most questions that were open ended and provided ready-made answers, all allowed for the participant to provide a different response. The last question also provided each participant with the ability to share any idea, comment, or opinion that he or she may have on the subject matter.

3.12 Data Collection Methods

Data collection was longitudinal, collected over a period in time between March 2013 and August 2015. The researcher utilized the main e-mail list server and social media sites in the professional field of medical interpreting to disseminate the need for participants. The researcher also asked professional colleagues in different countries to disseminate the main promotional research message to other medical interpreter contacts they knew, and this mix of dissemination provided for a healthy random sample pool for the study. Several organizations assisted in promoting the survey primarily (Appendix C).

3.12.1 Data collection of interviews.

The researcher performed 18 semi-structured interviews in a period of 24 months. They were executed in three modalities: by phone, by Skype (communication software with video), and in person. All participants were given the consent form to sign either in person or electronically. Hard copy and electronic consent forms were signed and given or emailed back to the researcher. Scheduling interviews was challenging due to differences in time zones and the availability of the participants and the researcher. However, all scheduled interviews were performed and while some interviews were rescheduled, there were no cancellations or medical interpreters who refused to sign the consent form. The interviews were recorded and then transcribed by the researcher. The transcription was then emailed to the participant for the participant to verify the accuracy of the text and if there was any correction requested, the correction was made so that all data utilized was approved by the data source.

Most interviews were performed in English, and some were done in Spanish or Portuguese, as these were the only other common languages between the participant and the researcher. In the cases where the participant did not share a language with the researcher, which also occurred, these interviews were executed with the assistance of a professional medical interpreter. Interpreting for these interviews occurred in Japanese and Hebrew and were rendered by professional interpreters. The researcher acknowledges Michal Schuster, in Israel, and Kazumi Takesako, in Japan, for their role of interpreters in the study. Without them, the researcher would not have been able to collect this data in these countries from interpreters who did not speak English. For those interviews that were done with an interpreter, the language of the interpreter, English, is the language that was transcribed. The recording of the interview contained the original utterances by participants in their language, and the interpretation in English. The transcripts generated the English renditions of the participants' contribution.

The modality was determined based on location, availability, and preference of the participant. There was no observable change in the length, quality of interaction, or the quality of data obtained. Whereas face-to-face or video interviews provided the benefit of the researcher's ability to see the body language of the participant, most of the affect was provided by non-verbal cues that are not necessarily visible (tone, hesitations, repetitions, etc.). The probing of the questions was done mostly for clarification when the participant did not have much information or opinions to offer, with care not to guide the participant in any direction. Occasionally, when a participant stated something that was unexpected or rarely discussed with the researcher, such as bringing a new perspective on the subject matter, the researcher would ask the participant to elaborate further. Otherwise the interviews were straightforward and specific to the ideas and questions that were being researched.

The length of the interviews varied: the shortest at 15 minutes and the longest at 1.5 hours long. The average length of interviews was 38 minutes. The length of the interview was mostly affected by two factors: how much information the participant had to give for each of the questions, and secondly, whether or not a medical interpreter was present, as the utterances need to be stated twice in each language, which takes longer.

Before each interview started, the researcher would read a script that included three definitions. Since there are so many roles and terms utilized in the field, the researcher wanted to make sure that during the interviews, all participants had the same understanding of the main terms and concepts to be discussed in the interview. It read as such:

Script from interview:

Before we start I want to define three terms so that we all under the same understanding regarding the main concepts behind this research study.

Culture clarifier: **(also known as interface, mediator, and/or broker)**	When the medical interpreter acts as a bridge between two cultures.
Cultural issue:	A value, belief or practice in health practices or in general that may affect intercultural communication.
Cultural intervention:	When a medical interpreter intervenes in order to address a cultural issue (prior, during, or after a clinical encounter).

3.12.2 Data collection of focus group.

The focus group was a one-time meeting that took place on June 17, 2015. It was entitled *Interpreting culture: Exploring the professional medical interpreters' perspectives.* The promotion of the event was done similarly to the interviews and survey. The researcher utilized the main list serves and social media sites in the field of medical interpreting to disseminate the need for participants. However, the interest or availability in such a meeting was not as significant as expected and the researcher had to cancel two previously scheduled focus groups due to lack of participants. This may have been due to the fact that contrary to the interviews, the times and days of the events were pre-set and not done at the convenience of the participant, as with the interviews, essay, or survey.

An organization called Culture Advantage, LC, based in Newton, Kansas, was instrumental in assisting the researcher for this survey, as this organization allowed the researcher to use their software platform, GotoMeeting, in order to perform the focus group webinar, which was a live online meeting with the ability to showcase presenter slides, counting on a chat box that allows participants to write their comments and questions on the online white board, when the facilitator or any participant is speaking. This allowed for two data sources: the recording of the entire webinar, and the chat box data which includes all the notes and information participants chose to write in the whiteboard. The focus group took place on June 17, 2015, from 6:00 p.m.–7:30 p.m. EST. Results were shared in the results section of the thesis paper.

3.12.3 Data collection of online survey.

The online survey entitled *Interpreting culture: Exploring the professional medical interpreters' perspectives.* The online survey was developed utilizing the coded responses given by the first two data sources in order to test level of agreement and concordance of those statements by a larger participant base. It was designed as a self-administered questionnaire to be administered online, remaining open for 90 days and to be done at the time of the participant's choosing by simply clicking on a link. The participant could even leave it half done and come back to finish it later.

Performing a pilot survey was an essential part of testing this instrument. Consequently, a pilot survey instrument was sent via survey link to 10 experienced medical interpreters who volunteered to review the survey for content and also for technical glitches. Several small issues were identified and modified or corrected by the researcher before the survey was finalized and sent to the participants. There was only one comment that was not changed and that was related to why this study was not asking questions about the provider or patient's opinions about interpreting culture. The researcher explained that this study was focused on the medical interpreter's perspective, and that any questions about the opinions of other stakeholders would have to be asked of them directly, and not through interpreters. Since most of the questions in the survey are for medical interpreters, it was not possible or advisable to double this survey for the purpose of asking the same question of another stakeholder group. The responses from the pilot survey were then discarded, in order to edit the survey, as the final survey was a modified version of the pilot survey.

The rate of return cannot be verified with the methodology used, as the researcher did not have the names or emails of possible participants to track who responded. The survey software provided a link to the survey, and this link was distributed through electronic means (e-mail, social media sites, and list servers) by the researcher and other collaborators who shared these links. The benefit of obtaining a true random sampling of the field and also of securing more participants for the study were greater and of more importance than the benefit of getting a response rate, which would have limited the researcher to send the survey instrument out to a specific list of individuals. The survey software allowed the researcher to check periodically online to see responses in progress and also to see who was responding. The software also provided the means to group open-ended responses in an electronic fashion, aiding the researcher in coding the responses. The interview instrument is available to readers of this thesis (Appendix D).

Chapter Four

RESULTS

Interpreter-mediated intercultural communication in healthcare is a complex activity that involves social interaction among participants of different cultural backgrounds, values, beliefs, or traditions and customs. It is becoming increasingly important in for all stakeholders to hear the practitioner about what facilitates or impedes their work. This may be the most important section of the book, as it brings to light the voice of the professional healthcare interpreter on this subject matter. While one may agree or disagree with the opinions of participants, the results were conclusive in many areas where there was a clear majority. Read this section carefully and mark specific areas that particularly interest you.

This chapter lists the data collected from the doctoral study. The first part showcases the general profile of the participants by showing the demographical information of the four data sets combined. The second part showcases the interpreters' perspectives on how medical interpreters bridge the cultural gap, in their own words, from a practitioner's perspective via case studies obtained through one on one interviews. This chapter follows with an extensive section showcasing the results grouped by research question and theme.

As stated before, this study collected data from different sources, qualitative and quantitative. The four data sources provided the research a richer set of data that can be triangulated. The first data source was qualitative, involving collecting data from 18 interviews of professional medical interpreters about the topic of study. The second data source was qualitative, obtained through a focus group with 16 participants discussing the same questions that the interviews addressed. The third set of data was quantitative, with 423 respondents providing mostly quantitative responses to some of the topics and situations uncovered by the qualitative data. Some qualitative data was obtained from the survey, as several questions allowed the participant to comment, if the answers did not fit their response need. The fourth and last source of data was collected from one medical interpreter who requested to provide an essay on the subject rather than to participate in an interview.

4.1 Demographic Data

4.1.1 Number of participants.

There were 18 interview participants and 16 focus group participants. One participant requested to provide an essay instead of an interview, and it was accepted as a fourth data source. The 18 interview participants provided the study with primary qualitative data. The 16-participant focus group allowed for more participants to provide qualitative data in a group environment in a quicker manner, and in order to focus on the research questions, demographic data was not asked. The essay provided one more participant the opportunity to participate, and while unconventional, was another unique manner to give interpreters a voice.

The online survey obtained of a total of 437 participants, however not all qualified. Of all those who participated, only two responded that they did not consent to participating, so the survey took them to the end of the survey and thanked them for their time and consideration. There was an error in the online survey that allowed some to skip the consent question and 10 participants did not answer the consent question. These 12 surveys (two who did not consent, and the 10 who skipped the consent question) were disqualified. This lowered the number of participants to 423 qualified survey participants. Therefore, the study generated a total of 458 participants when all data sources are combined (Table 4). The qualitative and quantitative data will be presented by theme.

Table 4
Matrix of Data Sources

Data Source	$N = 458$
Interviews (qualitative)	(18)
Focus Group (qualitative)	(16)
Online Survey (quantitative and qualitative)	(423)
Written Essay (qualitative)	(1)
TOTAL:	(458)

4.1.2 Age of participants.

Age-wise the top three categories of age groups were as follows: 37.01% were 45–54 years old, followed by 21.19% who were 35–44 years old, and 18.64% were 55–64 years old. When grouping the top two categories the majority of medical interpreters, or 58.2%, are between 35 and 54 years old (Table 5).

Table 5
Age Distribution of Majority of Participants (N = 458)

Data Source:	Interviews	Focus Group*	Online Survey	Essay
18 – 24	0% (0)	NA	3.60% (13)	
25 – 34	16.6% (3)	NA	14.40% (52)	
35 – 44	27.7% (5)	NA	20.78% (75)	
45 – 54	27.7% (5)	NA	37.40% (135)	
55 – 64	22.2% (4)	NA	18.84% (68)	100% (1)
65 – 74	5.5% (1)	NA	4.71% (17)	
75 or older	(0)	NA	0.28% (1)	
Skipped	(0)	NA	14% (62)	(0)
Total (458)	(18)	(16)	(423)	(1)

*Note. Focus group timing did not allow for demographic questions to be asked.

When comparing the data from the 18 interviewees and the 423 online survey participants, one can see that the two highest categories remain as 35-44 years of age and 45-54 years of age. This confirms what is seen in the field as well as in salary surveys, since most medical interpreters have entered the interpreting career as a second or third career, and not straight out of college. This is because there are very few academic programs specific to interpreting, and even fewer for the specialization of medical interpreting. The majority age of participants is between 35 and 54 in most salary surveys and other surveys utilizing medical interpreters as participants. These include the five annual IMIA salary surveys since 2008 (IMIA, 2008), as well as that of an interpreting marketplace study (Common Sense Advisory, 2010). It is noteworthy to mention that in the field there has been much discussion about whether the minimum age of entering the field should be 21 years of age, and not 18 years of age, due to the fact that medical interpreters engage in some very difficult life situations that require a level of psychological maturity not seen in most individuals who are under 21 years of age. However, most training programs and certification programs have kept the minimum age for study at 18 years of age for inclusion. Note that a very small number of most participants (2.94%, $n=13$) were between 18-24 years old, of a total of 442 participants. The total number of participants asked about their age is 442 participants, as this excluded focus group participants, who were not asked the age question. This issue of the minimum age to enter the profession merits further study, as putting individuals between 18 and 21 years of age in difficult ethical and emotional situations may put these individuals in a very inadequate and uncomfortable position.

4.1.3 Gender of participants.

There were 80.56% female participants, whereas 19.43% were male. This is congruent with most of the surveys that have been done in the field about medical interpreting, such as IMIA (2008), and Common Sense Advisory (2010). It is also congruent with studies and common knowledge that women tend to enter the language careers at a greater pace than men. Are women more in tune with cultural issues than men? The study compared whether or not there were significant differences of opinion on the issue of addressing culture due to their gender or not, but this comparison did not generate any significant differences. The data were examined by data source and the online survey data had a higher incidence of women, but also had a much higher number of participants, as seen on the Tables 6 and 7, below.

Table 6

Gender of All Participants by Data Source (N = 458)

	Male	Female	N
Interviews (qualitative)	33.33% (6)	66.66% (12)	(18)
Focus Group (qualitative)	31.25% (5)	68.75% (11)	(16)
Online Survey (quantitative mostly)	18.43% (78)	81.56 % (345)	(423)
Written Essay (qualitative)	0% (0)	100% (1)	(1)
Distribution from all data sources	19.43% (89)	80.56 %(369)	(458)

4.1.4 Cultural and linguistic diversity of survey participants.

There were certain questions that were only asked to the survey participants, since the qualitative data focused on the research questions. The survey data allowed for additional questions that could later be utilized for a comparative analysis. Therefore, the following section will only show survey data. Of all the participants who did the online survey ($n = 423$), they were born in 68 different countries, with the largest group being born in the United States (35.69%), followed by the rest being from all the other countries. Survey participants interpret in 76 working languages in 25 countries. A working language is a language for which an interpreter has a high enough proficiency in that language to interpret accurately. Medical interpreters may speak four languages but only be qualified to work in two, so they were asked to list only their working languages, not all the languages they speak at varying fluencies. Of the 76 languages, the top 10 languages of participants are listed in the Table 7, listing the percentage and the number of participants for each working language in descending order. Certain languages dominate the market in certain countries (i.e., Spanish comprises 75% of the demand in the United States) (IMIA, 2008). The other 66 languages therefore were comprised of less than nine participants each.

Table 7

Top 10 Working Languages of All Participants

1	Spanish	55.65% (197)
2	English	51.99% (184)
3	ASL	10.45% (37)
4	Arabic	5.37% (19)
5	Portuguese	5.37% (19)
6	Russian	4.80% (17)
7	Japanese	3.39% (12)
8	French	3.39% (12)
9	Italian	2.82% (10)
10	Hindi	2.26% (9)

Note. Percentages will not add up as some participants listed multiple working languages. ASL stands for American Sign Language.

Participants stated that they work in 25 countries (Appendix E). The top five countries were the United States (68.08%), Canada (6.93%), Japan (1,94%), United Kingdom (1.66%), and Australia (1.39%). It is impressive to note that even though the United States dominates the data, there was noticeable diversity of where the data came from, with data arriving from an additional 20 countries. This may be due to several reasons. Medical interpreting is not a developed professional specialization in many parts of the world, it seems it is in development in many countries. The fact that the survey was in English limited the number of participants who live in non-English speaking countries that could participate. The United States undoubtedly has the largest market for medical interpreting services. It is the country with the most medical interpreters worldwide, and is also one of the largest in population, making it difficult to have a more equal spread when doing an international survey. The researcher also lives in the United States, at the time of publication of this study, and this certainly affects the origin of results, even though the survey was sent to international venues. More international surveys will need to be translated into several languages order to obtain responses from a larger spread of participants. The data allowed for comparisons between participants working in the United States (68.08%) and the rest of the world (31.92%), with no significant differences found. The study also compared the Canadian responses with all the others and found that Canadians are slightly more conservative than others when addressing cultural issues.

The interviews only had a distribution of 50% U.S. and 50% non-U.S. participants. Half or 50% of participants (nine) who did the interviews were done in the United States and the other interviews were performed with non-U.S. participants living in the following countries: Japan (5), Israel (3), and New Zealand (1).

When asked if they were born in the country where they practice interpreting, 43.28% stated that they did and 56.72% did not. The data confirms that the majority of medical interpreters are not born in the country they practice, however with a narrow margin. The data showed that almost half of the medical interpreters who participated in the study were born where they work and not in the countries where their patients come from. Interpreters may speak the patient's language, look like the patient, and have a similar cultural background, making the interpreter appear closer culturally to the patient than the interpreter is to the provider. If a significant number of the medical interpreters are born in the dominant culture (43.28%), then this may affect the data in terms of how closely they actually align with the patients or providers, depending on their own cultural background. This can have implications also on whether or not they feel competent in addressing cultural issues. However, comparisons between those who have lived in the country over 20 years (68.96%) with those who have lived in the country less than five years (4.78%) did not generate significant differences in their opinions about addressing culture in their work.

4.1.5 General education of all participants

In terms of education, 73.61% of all participants had a general education of a bachelor's degree or higher, which is significant (Table 8). General education data show that 38.12% graduated from college, 7.33% had some graduate school, 24.05% completed a post-graduate master's degree, and 4.11% had completed a doctoral degree. This is also congruent with IMIA salary survey data (IMIA, 2008), which showcases that in every salary survey of 2008, 2009, 2010, 2011, 2012, and 2015, the majority of medical interpreters had a bachelor's degree.

Table 8
General Education of All Participants (N = 458)

Answer Choices	%
Did not graduate from high school	0.58%
Graduated from high school	3.45%
Some college	21.91%
Graduated from college	38.33%
Some graduate studies	7.78%
Completed a Masters Degree	23.92%
Completed a Doctoral Degree	4.03%
TOTAL	100.00%

4.1.6 Interpreter education of survey participants

As far as specific training and education, responses were more varied. Absent laws or regulations regarding medical interpreting education hours, interpreters are being educated in a variety of ways (independent study, workshops, intensive courses in private companies, in-house training courses in hospitals, and colleges/universities). Private for profit and non profit organizations tend to favor short intensive educational programs lasting from 40 hours to 200 hours. The majority have a duration of 40 hours. There are very few bachelor programs focusing on medical interpreting worldwide, as it is a specialization of the field of interpreting, but there are more generalist programs in translation and interpretation, or in Sign language interpreting, in most countries. The first Masters in Healthcare Interpreting program was launched in 2015 in the US, but it is limited to English and Sign language interpreting. The vast majority of interpreting programs specializing in medical interpreting in colleges involve non-credit certificate programs, according to the IMIA Educational Registry (http://www.imiaweb.org/education/trainingnotices.asp).

4.1.6.1 Estimated hours of medical interpreting education.

The most common duration for programs is believed to be of 40 hours, at least in the United States (Table 9). The data generated the largest response in the 41-60-hour range. Perhaps this is because several 40-hour programs are expanding into 54 or 60-hour programs in order to better accommodate the materials that cannot be taught in 40 hours. Both the NCIHC (NCIHC, 2011) and the IMIA (CMIE, 2014) have written positions stating that 40 hours is simply not enough. However, in the absence of legal mandates to require more hours, private companies will continue to teach in this manner. According to the data, as expected, the highest range was 41-60 hours (16.95%), followed by 61-100 hours (15.82%), and 101-200 hours (15.54%), and these top three categories add up to 48.31% of participants. So almost half (48.31%) of medical interpreters have 41-200 hours. When comparing the highest four categories with the lowest four categories, one can see that 49.16% have over 60 hours of specialized training to enter the field, 50.84% have less than 60 hours of training. Roughly a third had attained university level interpreter education (28.16%) and 71.84% were educated in occupational educational programs run by non-profit or for-profit companies. Whether or not occupational education affects the professional status of medical interpreters needs to be studied further.

Table 9

Hours of Interpreter Education for Survey participants (n=244)

Answer Choices	%
Under 8 hours	10.73%
8-20 hours	10.17%
21-40 hours	12.99%
41-60 hours	16.95%
61-100 hours	15.82%
101-200 hours	15.52%
201-400	6.50%
Over 400 hours	11.30%
TOTAL	100.00%

Two organizations have put forth guidelines for medical interpreting education. In the United States, NCICH has put forth a document that is called the *National standards for healthcare interpreter training programs* (NCIHC, 2011). Internationally, the IMIA developed accreditation standards for medical interpreter education (Commission for Medical Interpreter Education [CMIE], 2014), run by the CMIE, which sets forth measurable guidelines for training organizations to meet via onsite auditing services in order to become CMIE accredited, a voluntary accreditation. At the current moment, both NCIHC and CMIE acknowledge that 40 hours is not enough due to the complexity of the work involved. However, they themselves accept this as the minimal requirements since the demand for the work is so high, and there are not enough university training programs in the country. CMIE now requires 60 hours of education as of January 1, 2016, and 80 hours of education in 2018 for training organizations to receive CMIE accreditation. This is an initiative to help training programs to make the decision to increase the number of hours of their programs. It is important to mention that in 2015 Canada launched an accreditation program for community interpreters that required 180 hours of training (http://www.occi.ca/). These are attempts in the field to improve the educational opportunities for medical interpreters. Without the development of more university level programs, and the requirement of such university level education, medical interpreters may remain to be seen as an occupation and not as a bona fide profession. This study did not ask about continuous education experiences, only about basic education to practice the profession.

According to a study conducted and led by Flores (Flores et al., 2003), common medical interpreter errors include the following: (a) omission—when the interpreter leaves out an important piece of information, (b) false fluency—when the interpreter uses words or phrases that don't exist in a specific language, (c) substitution—when a word or phrase is replaced with another word or phrase of a different meaning, (d) editorializing—when the interpreter's opinion is added to the interpretation, and (e) addition—when the interpreter adds a word or phrase that is not in the original or source message.

Flores' subsequent study showed that medical interpreters with at least 100 hours of training made fewer errors overall, and made fewer errors of consequence. "These findings suggest that requiring at least 100 hours of training for interpreters may have a major impact on reducing interpreter errors and their consequences in healthcare, while improving quality and patient safety" (Flores, Abreu, Barone, Bachur, & Lin, 2012). This study compares survey data between participants with under and over 100 hours of specialized training to see if there are noticeable differences between the groups in their perspectives about addressing cultural issues.

4.1.6.2 Educational paths into interpreting.

Note that some participants responded not only with their specific number of hours of training, but also how they were educated to work as medical interpreters. With the options given, there was an *Other* option, which generated a few qualitative responses. These data show that they believe their educational backgrounds in other areas, such as general interpreting, nursing, medicine, etc. are relevant to their medical interpreting education.

Below are examples of what was deemed to be medical interpreter-specific training:

1. General Spanish interpreter training.
2. I have a bachelor's degree in communication and have been a practicing interpreter for over 10 years.
3. I don't have any interpretation training but am a legal interpreter and I have 9 years of experience working in a hospital where I interpreted.
4. Associate degree in nursing.
5. I have an MS (master's) degree in nursing.
6. Two years of medical school in Argentina Agnese. Haury training for federal court interpreting (got a 77).
7. I did interpreting coursework as part of my master's degree.
8. I have a degree in Hispanic studies and Spanish literature and have attended workshops and conferences on medical interpreting and more.
9. I have a bachelor degree in translation, Arabic/English, from the University of Mosul in Iraq.

These examples above demonstrate how interpreters enter the field with various educational backgrounds and not all with specific medical interpretation background. Some come from a medical or healthcare background, and others come from a linguistics or communications background; still others come from other types of interpreting, such as generalist interpreting or legal interpreting. This may affect the medical interpreter's view and identity as a professional and some may see interpreters as linguistic professionals, others, such as nurses or other healthcare providers, may see medical interpreters as healthcare affiliate professionals. Due to the lack of standardization of medical interpreter education, or availability of training, many have entered it without a program or coursework in medical interpreting per se. The United States, Australia, Canada, United Kingdom, and a few other countries require medical interpreter education or testing prior to practice in most hospitals, but did not before. Some countries do not have specialized programs to require specialized training to hire someone to work as a medical interpreter. National certifications for spoken language interpreters in the US require only 40 hours of specialized training.

4.1.7 Professional experience of survey participants.

With respect to professional experience, the majority of the participants are experienced (Table 10). There were 65.43% of participants who had 6 or more years of experience. The largest group was comprised of 31.09% who stated they had 6-10 years of experience, followed by 25.64% who stated that they have 11-20 years of experience.

Table 10
Estimated Years of Experience of All Participants (N = 453)

Answer Choices	%
Under 2 years	11.43%
2-5 years	23.14%
6-10 years	29.43%
11-20 years	24.57%
Over 20 years	11.43%
TOTAL	100.00%

This study compared the opinions of those with over 20 years of experience (11.43%) to those with up to 2 years of experience (also 11.43%), as well as those with under and over 10 years of experience, to see if there were significant difference in the following: (a) confidence of addressing cultural issues, (b) the stress levels of addressing cultural issues, or (c) the frequency of addressing cultural issues. It is interesting to note that while there were no significant differences between interpreters with over 100 hours vs. under 100 hours, there was a much higher level of confidence, less stress, and an increased frequency of addressing cultural issues with the group with over 20 years of experience, versus the group with under 2 years experience.

4.1.8 Certification status of survey participants.

The employers, to ascertain if the individual had the skills to interpret accurately, have historically done the testing of medical interpreters. However, healthcare administrators are not experts at interpreting testing, developing in house exams that could be as short as a list of medical terms to translate. Therefore interpreter testing has varied in quality as much as interpreter education has. Certification, on the other hand, is a third party testing system performed by testing professionals, or Psychometricians, that certifies competence through a rigorous testing process. Most professions have some sort of certification to ensure competency. Since the 1970s, Sign language interpreters in the United States have had a generalist interpreter exam, as in several other countries. In Australia NAATI certifies a community interpreter in a large number of languages. In the UK there is a public service interpreter certification system in place as well. However, only the United States has a certification system specifically designed for medical interpreters. Since 2009, the United States has counted on two national certification systems for spoken language medical interpreters, and even medical interpreters abroad have been taking the exams when one of their languages is English. Interviewees were asked if they were certified. The interviewee ratio was 60% certified, 40% not, and the survey data show that 47.46% were certified for medical interpreting practice and 52.54% were not. This was significantly higher rate than expected due to the fact that national certification for medical interpreters has only been available since 2009, available in seven language combinations with English. Therefore, this does not reflect the general international population. It is possible that certified medical interpreters are more engaged in the field and therefore were more likely to participate in this study. Certified interpreters are also on certified interpreter registries, which received an invitation to participate. Of those who were not certified as medical interpreters, 37.01% had other interpreter certifications, such as generalist or other specialized certifications, such as the state department, conference or legal/court interpreter certification. The research compared the responses of certified vs. non-certified medical interpreters and found there were no significant differences of opinion regarding the cultural work of participants.

4.1.9 Number of years in the country of service.

Survey participants were asked how long they have lived in the country where they interpret. The number of years living abroad is not an exact measure or indication of acculturation, due to different rates of acculturation. However, it is safe to assume that those with over 20 years of living in a country and who are bilingual individuals may feel more comfortable in the dominant culture than those with a shorter exposure to the country of practice. The data indicate that 68.96% answered that they have been in the country for over 20 years. These data may reflect that a majority of interpreters are considerably assimilated enough to understand the dominant culture (Table 11) well. These data were surprising as in the United States most medical interpreters are immigrants with less than 20 years in the United States. However, this study included medical interpreters working in other countries, which has shifted the data to reflect all 25 countries covered in the study.

Table 11
Number of Years Living in the Country of Work

Answer Choices	%
Under 5 years	4.78%
5-10 years	6.87%
11-20 years	19.40%
Over 20 years	68.95%
TOTAL	100.00%

Note. n=335.

4.1.10 Perceived knowledge of patient and medical culture.

Survey participants were asked how knowledgeable they were about the patient(s) cultural group(s) they interpreted for (Table 12), 85.67% responded *Extremely knowledgeable* (39.10%) or *Very knowledgeable* (46.57%). 11.64% or participants stated they were *Moderately knowledgeable,* and only 2.69% stated they were *Slightly knowledgeable* or *Not at all knowledgeable,* when these were combined.

Table 12
Perceived Knowledge of Patient(s) Cultural Group(s)

Answer Choices	%
Extremely knowledgeable	39.10%
Very knowledgeable	46.57%
Moderately knowledgeable	11.64%
Slightly knowledgeable	2.39%
Not at all knowledgeable	0.30%
TOTAL	100.00%

Note. n=335.

Data show 85.67% of survey participants have a high level of confidence in their knowledge of their patient(s) cultural group(s) (*Extremely knowledgeable* or *Very knowledgeable* combined). In order to bring some clarity to this issue, participants were also asked about the training they received about patient cultures they interpret for. A small majority, 55.22%, responded that they did *not* receive any specific training on their patient(s) cultural group(s). This means that only 44.78% received any training about their patient's culture. The level of confidence is revealing, based on several facts:

(a) a large number of medical interpreters were not born in the countries of their patients,

(b) the majority has been living in the dominant culture for over 20 years, and

(c) only 44.78% of participants received training in this area.

The qualitative data, to be shared later, indicate that some of the confidence and knowledge comes from the interpreters' personal life experiences and not necessarily from formal training. It is argued that cultural knowledge is mostly obtained through tacit learning, and is not easily taught in a classroom. However, there are basic concepts about different cultural groups and their health practices that are important for all medical interpreters to know. Living in a country may not give one this information unless one is in contact with such practices. Many medical interpreters will not know about traditional medicine or alternative practices in the patients' country unless they learned them while growing up from their families, or in an educational setting or had experiences with their traditional health practices, and not only Western medical services. Some medical interpreters who are born and raised in the same country as their patients would not be aware or knowledgeable of such alternative practices unless they actually practiced alternative medicine themselves. There are medical interpreters who work with multiple cultures, and therefore need to know about more than their own cultural background. Last, even individuals who are quite familiar with their culture, may not know of specific health practices or culture-bound syndromes that affect their target patient populations.

Survey participants were also asked how knowledgeable they were about medical culture and if they had received training on medical culture (Table 13). Regarding how knowledgeable they feel about medical culture, 29.25% answered they were *Extremely knowledgeable*, and 48.66% stated that they were *Very knowledgeable*, with a combined confidence response of 77.91%. Only 1.79% stated they were *Slightly knowledgeable* or *Not at all knowledgeable*. The other category was *Moderately knowledgeable* with 20.30 %. Therefore, data show a confidence level in biomedicine culture of 77.91%.

Table 13
Perceived Knowledge of Medical Culture

Answer Choices	%
Extremely knowledgeable	29.25%
Very knowledgeable	48.66%
Moderately knowledgeable	20.30%
Slightly knowledgeable	1.79%
Not at all knowledgeable	0.00%
TOTAL	100.00%

Note. n=335.

Whereas the level of confidence is not as high in their knowledge of medical culture, when compared to their knowledge of patient culture(s) at 85.67%; however, 77.91% is still a significantly high level of confidence, especially for those who were not educated in a training program that viewed this as a healthcare career or included medical culture knowledge in its curriculum. Most healthcare providers learn about biomedicine culture through multiple years of education (e.g., clinicians, nurses, and specialists) and these issues include, but are not limited, to:
   (a) the culture of efficiency,
   (b) scientific inquiry
   (c) evidence-based data
   (d) patient safety
   (e) healthcare system
   (f) specialization cultures
   (g) protocols, teamwork among healthcare providers
   (h) disease and treatment identification methodology
   (i) therapeutic rapport
   (j) clinical trials
   (k) provision of culturally and linguistically competent care
   (l) medical errors, etc.

Regarding the training about medical culture, a small majority of medical interpreters (56.76%) stated they had received training on biomedicine culture. The level of confidence may seem high, considering that a large number of interpreters (43.24%) have not received any training on the subject whatsoever (Table 14).

Table 14
Training Received on Medical Culture

Answer Choices	%
Yes	44.78%
No	55.22%
TOTAL	100.00%

Note. n=335.

There is the possibility that some medical interpreters have obtained that medical culture knowledge from a previous medical profession or education, as stated earlier, since some interpreters did arrive at interpreting after practicing a medical profession in their country. For some participants, it seems their medical background may have enhanced their knowledge of medical culture. Others may have learned it through their interpreting experience and continuing education. The data, however, imply that there are training programs that are not teaching basic medical cultural concepts that are important for the medical interpreter to function and understand the context of their work environment. Some of these programs may be unfamiliar, as many interpreter instructors are not actually practicing medical interpreters. This is important for interpreters to enhance their own professional knowledge of the medical culture, to better navigate it and have the ability to identify cultural issues that come from the medical culture, not just the patient's culture. The results may also indicate that medical interpreters may be over evaluating their knowledge of both their patients' culture(s) and/or medical culture.

4.1.11 Perceived competency in addressing cultural issues.

Data show, as with knowledge, that medical interpreters have a high level of confidence in their competence related to addressing cultural issues (Table 15) as they stated they were *Extremely competent (23.97%)*

and *Very competent* (53.72%) creating a combined confidence level of 77.69% Only 2.48% stated that they were *Slightly competent* (2.07%) or *Not at all competent* (0.41%). The category of *Moderately competent* received 19.83% of the responses.

Table 15
Perceived Competence in Addressing Cultural Issues

Answer Choices	%
Extremely competent	23.97%
Very competent	53.72%
Moderately competent	19.83%
Slightly competent	2.07%
Not at all competent	0.41%
TOTAL	100.00%

Note. n=242

The figure of 77.69% of those who stated they were *Extremely* or *Very competent* can be considered a high level of competency, and perhaps the fact that 65.43% of medical interpreters have 6 years of experience or more has had an effect in their perceived competency in addressing cultural issues. The researcher later compared the competency paradigm of those with the most experience (over 20 years) that is at 11.43% with the two lowest areas of experience (under 2 years) that comprises of also 11.43% of participants. As expected, those medical interpreters with over 20 years reported a much higher level of self-declared competence than those with under 2 years of experience.

4.1.12 Perceived importance of addressing cultural issues.

When asked about the importance of addressing cultural issues, 90.08% stated it was *Extremely* or *Very important*, 45.87% and 44.21% respectively (Table 16). There seems to be no question among participants that this is an important issue and that the task of addressing cultural issues is important.

Table 16
Importance of Addressing Cultural Issues

Answer Choices	%
Extremely important	45.87%
Very important	44.21%
Somewhat important	9.50%
Not very important	0.00%
Not at all important	0.41%
TOTAL	100.00%

Note. n=242.

If it is as important as the data indicate, that means that this subject matter needs to be appropriately covered in educational programs and testing, or certification/accreditation. It also means that it is important for healthcare organizations and healthcare providers to understand how important addressing cultural issues is for medical interpreters. These organizations need to provide an environment to their medical interpreters that allows for cultural intervention, when needed, in order to provide culturally and linguistically appropriate care. Educating all those who work in the healthcare system on the fact that medical interpreters need to be able to provide cultural information and support when needed or deemed appropriate may be very helpful to interpreters, and ultimately to the patients they serve.

How cultural competency affects patient outcomes, patient satisfaction, and patient compliance is still very little understood by healthcare providers in some countries with a low number of diverse patients with little interest or no policy in cultural diversity. Several countries, however, have developed initiatives and strategies to make their healthcare system friendlier and more culturally competent in their countries or regions, according the latest research report on intercultural mediation for immigrants in Europe (Theodosiou & Aspioti, 2015). The individual who submitted an essay in lieu of participating in the other data collection formats (interviews, focus group, online survey), made a significant comment about the importance of addressing cultural issues:

> *The cultural differences are as important as the linguistic differences in communication. Practically, we are unable to know all of the cultures in the world. However, we can exercise*

> *humility to continue learning new things from each other*
> *and working as a team to provide the best possible healthcare*
> *for our patients." (Essay participant, United States)*

This statement suggests that some interpreters feel that the cultural differences are as important as the linguistic differences. If this is true, the interpreters' responsibility and activities in interpreting culture needs to receive significantly more attention when discussing their work or the provision of culturally and linguistically competent care. The essay participant seems to be aligned with the goals and objectives of the medical team, which is to provide the best healthcare for patients. In this participant's view, addressing cultural issues is required to provide the best care for patients. Finally, this participant seems to see the profession to be beyond the scope of linguistic interpreting, and within the larger scope of providing intercultural communication services and healthcare services, as in her own words she states she works as part of a team (healthcare team) to provide the best possible healthcare for her patients. More research is needed on the issue of how the medical interpreter professional identity affects their beliefs and behavior in the workplace, ethically and otherwise.

4.2 Qualitative and Quantitative Results Presented by Theme

The next set of data address the practitioners' perspectives in the key research questions regarding all aspects of the work of addressing cultural issues as medical interpreters. Different aspects of interpreting culture were addressed in the qualitative data obtained via interviews, the focus group, and an essay.

These data will be presented thematically as follows:

(a) cases where interpreters address cultural issues,
(b) frequency of addressing cultural issues,
(c) healthcare areas that encounter greater cultural issues,
(d) advantages of addressing cultural issues,
(e) disadvantages of addressing cultural issues,
(f) challenges of addressing cultural issues,
(g) strategies of addressing cultural issues,
(h) timing of addressing cultural issues,
(i) stress of the activity of addressing cultural issues, and
(j) training on addressing cultural issues.

For each theme, the qualitative data from the interviews will be presented first, followed by focus group data and essay, when applicable. To conclude, the survey data will be presented to explore and understand the level of commonality of these issues between the qualitative and quantitative data sets.

4.2.1 Intercultural Case Studies

Interviewees were asked to provide an example of a situation that they encountered that required their cultural intervention. Survey and focus group participants were not asked to give examples of cultural interventions. In all cases shared, the names of the parties involved, specifically patient information, were not shared, due to health confidentiality laws in several countries. The focus of the study was not to analyze the cultural issues in these cases in detail, as far as the essence or categories of the cultural problems encountered. Participants provided realistic examples of what the medical interpreters mean when they refer to cultural intervention. These self reported case studies give us another angle to better explore and focus on the interpreter's ideation of their work in this area of interpreting culture. The cases give us a window into how the participants believed their action in a particular real work scenario, constituted addressing a cultural issue. The purpose of describing examples of their work was to better understand which situations interpreters believe require them to address cultural issues. It was not to study the cultural issue itself, so they were only asked to provide a short summary as an example. Therefore, these are not in depth case studies, but vignettes that showcase examples of interpreters addressing cultural issues. These reported real cases provide readers with "snapshot pictures" of the participants' cultural work. Each case provides interesting facets of this cultural work that perhaps are not verbalized by the participants' other qualitative data. These cases shed light into the real outcomes and perceived benefits or problems with addressing culture in the healthcare setting.

The 32 cases shared by the 18 interviewees were analyzed to see if the interpreter was playing roles of *cultural informant* (Jalbert, 1998) when providing cultural information to the provider, *bilingual professional* when providing medical practice or norms information to the patient, Leanza's (2005) role of *integration agent* (the interpreter finds resources to help patients to make sense, negotiate meanings, and find in-between ways of behaving), *community agent* (the patient norms and values are presented and potentially equally valid), or, last, *linguistic agent* (the interpreter attempts to maintain an impartial position). When the intervention took place was also noted for each case. Table 17 provides an overview of the cases, and then a discussion of a few of them and what new ideas they bring to the table regarding interpreting culture in healthcare.

Table 17
Summary of Real Life Medical Cultural Cases

Case Study	Type of Cultural Issue	Role of Interpreter	Time	Cultural Issue	Intervention in the Interpreters own words	Health related outcome
1	Alternative medicine	Cultural informant & Bilingual professional & Integration agent & Linguistic agent	D	Provider was unaware of patient cultural healing practice.	*I informed the nurse of commonality of this practice and informed the patient about how practice not common in U.S.*	Nurse is informed of cultural practice. Better nurse-patient rapport and herb use to be discussed with doctor. Provider is informed of common health practice.
2	Communication style and/or register	Cultural informant & Community agent	D	Provider was unaware of patient's cultural background.	*I asked the provider to explain a medical term to the patient each time the provider uses high register language* (note: in the specific case reported, the patient did not ask for an explanation, the interpreter intervened and asked for the patient).	Provider more aware of importance of adapting to cultural background of patient. Patient understood concepts better.
3	Prescriptions from another country	Cultural informant & Integration agent	D	Provider was shocked that patient was taking several different antibiotics and unaware of ease of obtaining medication in some countries.	*I informed the provider of how in some countries some prescriptions are easy to get and I asked the provider to explain to the patient how it works in the U.S.*	Patient learned not to use medications without the knowledge and consent of his provider. Provider informed.

#	Topic	Role		Description	Action	Outcome
4	Treating fever	Cultural informant	D	Provider was unaware of common treatment of sweating out fever by covering child vs. keeping child cold.	*I informed the provider of the different treatment in the patient's country and beliefs related to heat/cold.* Objective: to prevent patient lack of compliance.	Patient understood reason for different treatment and agreed to comply. Provider informed.
5	Treating burns	Bilingual professional & Cultural informant & Linguistic agent & Community agent	D	Provider was unaware of common treatment of putting ointments on burns vs. keeping burn uncovered and dry.	*I let both parties know that this treatment is the opposite of what they do in his country.* Objective: to prevent patient lack of compliance.	Patient understood reason for different treatment and agreed to comply. Provider informed.
6	Religious	Cultural informant	A	Provider unaware of belief in ghosts as a culturally accepted belief. Patient and mother believed there were ghosts in their home. Provider was about to refer patient to inpatient mental health setting.	*I informed the provider this was a common belief that could be solved with the recommendation of a priest blessing in the home.*	Patient was not hospitalized and mom was happy with the suggestion. Provider informed. Healthcare costs saved.

7	Diversity of cultures in Korea – over twenty dialects and treating elderly	Cultural Rephrasing and Reformulating	D	Patient expectations not congruent with communication in country. Doctor asks questions in a particular way to an elderly patient from a small island in Korea the same way he would any other patient.	*I needed to interpret in a different way to match the messages they expect or they will not trust the provider.*	Increased trust from patient, but with the risk of possible distortion of message. Culturally competent delivery of interpretation may require distortion of original message from a linguistic point of view to elicit same response as if stated in target language.
8	Female modesty	Cultural informant & Community agent	D	Patient expectations not congruent with care in country. Patient goes to ED on an ambulance at night but refused to be seen by male ob-gyn doctor until a female doctor arrived that morning.	*Sometimes it is in our culture to hide these things, and the patient would be hesitant to speak up, there is insecurity within them, but she refused treatment. Doctors were furious and I had to explain the cultural issue at hand.*	Patient now knows that hospital cannot guarantee a female doctor and that she needs to call first. Providers informed.
9	Timeliness	Bilingual professional & Integration agent	B	Patient expectations not congruent with Western medical care. Patients arrive late and the staff sees it as a lack of respect.	*I have to explain to patients that in Japan all patients need to arrive on time or they will not be seen.*	Proactive action to improve patient compliance with timeliness.

10	Perceived health problem	Bilingual professional & Community agent	A	Patient expectations not congruent with care in country. Grandfather wants baby grandson to get medication for throat. Doctor says there is nothing wrong and grandfather is upset stating to interpreter that he will go elsewhere to get alternative care.	*I came back to the provider with this information and the doctor decided to see the patient again and give the baby placebo drops.*	Grandfather was happy and continues to come for care. Provider informed.
11	Blood removal	Bilingual professional & Community agent	D & A	Patient expectations not congruent with care in country. Patient wants blood drawn to improve health, a common idea in Ethiopia. Doctor wanted blood tests every 6 months. The patient stated: *if you do not draw blood I will get myself hospitalized so that they will take blood from me.*	*I asked for a team meeting to discuss this common request, which was frustrating to the providers. I suggested they accommodate or these patients will continue to get hospitalized just for this reason. Three clinics did a pilot where they now draw just 0.1cc of blood from the patient regularly. Now other clinics are doing it to keep the patients happy and avoid unnecessary hospitalizations*	It saves money, hospitalizations, and all patients are happier feeling that the clinics and providers understand and accept their practices better now. Providers informed.

12	Patient request for occupational health consult	Cultural Informant and Community agent	NA	Patient expectations not congruent with care in country. Patient can't work and comes to clinic to ask to see an occupational physician.	*I explained to the patient that they have to go to the welfare office and not occupational health, if they are not working. In Israel you can only go to occupational health if you are working.*	Patient now knows where to go and does not show up for an appointment where he will not be able to be seen and waste resources.
13	Patient question on work accident and request for time off	Bilingual professional & Integration agent & Cultural reformulation within interpretation	D	Patient expectations not congruent with care in country. The patient did not know that their boss had to sign a paper for them to get a day off from the national insurance.	*The doctor explained, but I added "This is the way it goes in Israel."*	Patient knows that in Israel the supervisor needs to sign a letter.
14	Language used for unknown diagnosis	Cultural informant & Community agent	D	Provider not aware of common description for multiple ailments. Patient said she had gastritis and provider took her word for it.	*I explained that in Salvador many people think a lot of problems are related to gastritis, so I explained this and asked the provider to probe further.*	Improved and accurate communication–avoidance of miscommunication. Provider informed.

15	Different healthcare systems	Bilingual professional & integration agent	A	Patient expectations not congruent with care in country. Patient confused with U.S. health system	*I have to explain to the patient how it works here in the U.S. vs. Japan.*	Increased patient knowledge to navigate U.S. healthcare system (compliance)
16	Cultural news about giving bad news	Cultural informant & Integration agent	A	Patient expectations not congruent with care in country. U.S. doctors tell patients bad news straight and it does create a shock to the patient, as they are not used to receiving information this way.	*I explained to the patient that U.S. doctors cannot hide diagnosis, as they are not in a position to do this by law.*	Improved patient-provider rapport. Patient trust in doctor enhanced. Patient informed of law.
17	Fasting during Ramadan	Cultural informant & Community agent	B	Patient expectations not congruent with care. Provider not aware of when is Ramadan. When female patients fast during Ramadan it can affect their health.	*I informed the obstetrician prior to the session starting.*	Improved context for provider to treat patient. Improved patient safety. Provider informed.

18	Custom of applying honey in baby's upper lip right after birth	Cultural informant & Community agent	D	Patient expectations not congruent with Western medical care. Provider not aware of this practice. At first midwife refused because in Japan babies are not allowed to have honey for first year.	*After my explanation of this ritual, they allowed the patient to do so.*	Hospital makes cultural accommodation to make the patient feel more comfortable. Providers informed.
19	Different healthcare systems	Bilingual professional & Integration agent	A	Patient expectations not congruent with care in country. Most do not know that in Japan prescriptions expire in 4 days.	*I explained to the patient after the session. That way, patient will fill the prescription within 4 days and will not have to come back for a new prescription.*	Improved utilization of healthcare system. Patient informed.
20	Ziaar food	Cultural informant & Community agent	D	Doctors don't know about our foods, how many calories or other scientific properties.	*I explain that it is a sugarless grain, eaten with lentils and in special occasions with mint and we slaughter a cow or sheep.*	Provider gains understanding of type of food and is better able to treat patient.

21	Zäar ritual	Bilingual professional & Community agent	D	Providers not aware of Zäar. In Israel, providers consider it as a mental health illness when the patient starts talking about spirits. Ethiopians consider it differently, like a prophecy or message coming to heal one.	*I explain that this is a cultural custom and different way of looking at healing where all participate as a group to heal an individual.*	Provider does not hospitalize individual. Provider informed.
22	Female modesty	Bilingual professional & Community agent	D	Provider not aware of this Muslim custom. Female patient refusing to be treated by male doctor	*I explained to provider that this is a very important part of their culture, that men do not see their body parts.*	Hospital makes cultural accommodation to make the patient feel more comfortable. Provider informed.
23	Cultural norm	Bilingual professional & Community agent	D	Patient expectations not congruent with care. Older ladies from Punjab wear a veil on their heads and when they go into surgery they want the veil in their head. In Western culture they need to wear a cap.	*I asked the providers if she could wear the veil under the cap and usually they agree.*	Hospital makes cultural accommodation to make the patient feel more comfortable. Provider informed.

Table 17 continued

#	Category	Agent role	Code	Description	Quote	Outcome
24	Cultural diversity of English speakers	NA	D	Provider not aware of diversity of patients who speak English. Assumption by doctors that all English speaking patients share the same culture	*I have to explain where the patient is from and tell them that I am not familiar with the patient's culture if they are not from the U.S./Canada.*	Increased provider understanding of the fact that English is not the patient's first language or culture.
25	Traditional practices	Linguistic agent	D	Provider not aware of traditional practice. Woman was making young girl sit on hot bricks because she was urinating in bed.	*I knew what was going on but I let the doctor figure it out.*	Provider learned from patient about cultural practice and prescribed medical treatment.
26	Healthcare system utilization	Cultural informant & Integration agent	NA	During pre-session I found out that the patient had breast pain and was there to see an OB/GYN.	*I explained to patient that this is not the type of doctor that treats breast problems.*	Patient was redirected to appropriate appointment. Patient informed.
27	Female modesty	NA	D	Provider not aware. Female patients do not want a male doctor or sometimes even a male interpreter.	*I interpret over the phone; they will accept this better than an in person interpreter.*	Hospital makes cultural accommodation to make the patient feel more comfortable.

#					
28	Cultural background Assessment	Pre-session: Interpreter cultural and linguistic assessment.	NA	Not an interaction between provider and patient but between interpreter and patient prior to clinical session starting.	*I use my linguistic and cultural assessment skills to ensure that I am the right person for that assignment*	Cultural or linguistic issues can be addressed with the provider prior to the session starting. Interpreter can withdraw if necessary.
29	Communication style and/or register	Co-constructor of message	D	Provider not aware of difference in communication style. ASL is a high context language, where English is not.	*I may rephrase my interpretation in order to get a more concise answer.*	More efficient communication between parties due to time constraints.
30	Communication styles and/or registers	NA	A	Patient gets confused when interpreter speaks in the first person.	*I switched to third person just for the patient but remained in first person for the provider.*	Improved communication between parties.
31	Body language	NA	NA	Provider believes that the Mayan young patient is not honest because she is not looking at the provider's eyes	*I didn't intervene but I wish I had.* Note: Sometimes interpreters wish to intervene but can't for several reasons, to be addressed in the theme of challenges.	Trust and therapeutic rapport between patient and provider is compromised.

| 32 | Educational level | Cultural informant & Cultural consultant | D | *I explained that from my point of view the results were not clear, as even if the patient was 100% sound, the patient would not have the knowledge to answer the questionnaire. The provider then asked more questions specifically to ascertain the patient's level of education to test this possibility.* | Provider believes patient did not pass psychiatric evaluation possibly due to educational level but is not able to ascertain this due to not listening to the patient in English, knowing that interpretation may skew the educational level. | Mental health misdiagnosis averted. Provider informed of how some psychiatric evaluations are culture-bound do the country of service. |

Note. Time: B=Before; D=During; A=After the clinical encounter; NA= Not applicable

4.2.1.1 Interpreter roles and activities.

These cases showcase the variety of roles and activities that medical interpreters engage in when interpreting culture, as well as the roles and activities that are beyond linguistic interpreting. In three of the cases, they described how they needed to rephrase or reformulate the content to make it culturally appropriate, without any intervention or transparency. This will be further discussed later.

In most of the roles used for analysis (i.e., bilingual professional, cultural informant, integration agent, and community agent), the interpreter informs either the patient or the provider/institution. It is interesting to note that the information provided to either patient or provider may be useful to them not only in that instance, but also in future encounters. In one role (linguistic agent), the interpreter informs both parties as they are working within the constraints of the interpreting ethic of transparency.

It is interesting to note that even when engaged in interpreting culture, interpreters can and should always be engaged as a linguistic agent. Transparency means that every time that an interpreter informs one of the parties, the interpreter is supposed to interpret/inform the other party of what was just explained so that all parties know what is being communicated, including all side conversations. So even though the message, or information was intended to one of the parties, the interpreter must relay the conversation, via interpretation, to the other party(ies) for transparency. This increases the party's trust in the interpreter and allays fears of either party to be unaware of the content of side conversations. This does not seem to be the case in practice, based on these interpreter verbal reports, at least in the 28 cases that involved triadic encounters. Some interpreters seemed to prefer one role over another. When one interviewee was asked whether or not he ever explained anything about Israeli culture to the patient, the answer of one of the interviewees was, "I don't. Usually the need is the other way around. The provider doesn't understand our culture, that's why my two examples are about that." This needs to be further explored, and the reasons may well be practical (time constraints) and/or related to the medical interpreters' focus on the medical goals or provider expectations of the appointment and not necessarily the linguistic goals.

4.2.1.2 Situations prompting intervention.

Of the 32 cases in the study, 15 of them were due to the provider not being aware of a cultural belief, value, or practice, and in 14 of the cases the patient's expectations of treatment were not congruent with the country they were being cared in, due to their lack of knowledge of how the healthcare system works. However, as seen by the data, other reasons and situations also prompted cultural intervention. The other cases did not fit either of these needs.

Regardless of the specific cultural situation, these data suggest that the primary trigger for medical interpreter cultural intervention is not miscommunication, but the lack of cultural information or context, from providers about patient cultural practices, or from patients about the medical system, respectively. This showcases the need for provider education on different cultural paradigms, and for patient information about the healthcare system they are utilizing. Patients also need better information of how to integrate into the local system of care. Providing this education to patients and providers would greatly improve the situation and may preclude or diminish the need or frequency of medical interpreter cultural intervention. Many hospitals around the world are attempting to do this provider education, but limited resources, as well as other equally important priorities make it difficult to do. Some may also not see the relevance of cultural education in medicine, not understanding the direct link between cultural competency and patient healthcare outcomes. Some countries are incorporating this type of education into medical schools. All interviewees mentioned the lack of information about other cultural paradigms as key to the need for their cultural work. This topic will be discussed in further detail when the themes of challenges and difficulties are addressed.

4.2.1.3 Cultural rephrasing.

In three of the cases, 7, 29, and 30, the medical interpreter rephrased and/or reformulated the source language with a specific intent of making it more palatable to the culture of the patient. In all three examples, the cultural accommodation was made for the benefit of the patient. This rephrasing goes beyond finding the linguistic equivalent, and goes into the realm of finding a cultural equivalent so that the patient, or receiver of the information, receives it as if someone of his/her culture had said it in his/her language. There is a distinction to be made between cultural rephrasing (a linguistic activity) and cultural reformulating. Reformulating the communication to include cultural norms of communication may include adding and deleting information in the source language, when interpreting into the target language in order to be more culturally appropriate or to provide a cultural norm. In case 7, the medical interpreter explained that the elderly from Korea do not trust anyone. This is a generalization that he has found to be congruent with his experiences. The interpreter stated the following:

> *If you don't understand the situation of the elderly and what they are going through, then you can't understand them. We have to understand what cultural value they have, who they are and where they are coming from. When you have experience, with a few words in the pre-session, I know where in the country they are coming from. I know these differences. I have to rephrase the question to the thinking of the elderly lady's thought of accepting the question. I interpret, but in a different way. I need to interpret in a different way to match the messages they expect, or they will not trust the provider.*

In case 29 the medical interpreter was using this rephrasing strategy to bridge differences in communication, specifically the difference between indirect and direct communication. This may be more due to time constraints and provider expectations than cultural differences, but the source of the problem (cultural communication styles) are cultural.

In case 30 the medical interpreter used first person with the provider, however choosing to utilize third person with the patient for the sake of better understanding and to ensure meaningful communication was truly taking place. In the interpreter's words:

> *Traditionally interpreters interpret in the first person, with the same voice and aspect, but in a mental health setting we have the leeway to step out of the first person when there is an indication that there is something impeding understanding, with body language, for example. It can be confusing to hear someone speak in the first person for another person, as if being their voice, and usually that is not an issue in physical medical appointments, but it is in mental health. This is not something that the professionals would be able to assess, as they are not familiar with Deaf culture, so I am the one who makes the decision and the provider is not even aware of it. I switched to third person just for the patient but remained in first person for the provider.*

The IMIA Standards of Practice (IMIA & EDC, 2007) address this cultural issue and guides medical interpreters to use professional judgment when deciding to switch into third person, and it is usually only done due to a party who is confused as to who is speaking for who, or it could also be due to the fact that in a few cultures speaking in the third person is in fact the norm as a show of respect, so in other words the third person would be the form to address another, and as such would be interpreted as such. The main reason for switching to the third person is to enable meaningful communication and understanding of all parties.

4.1.2.4 Cultural informant goals and strategies.

The *cultural informant* is a role that is closely aligned with the goals of making the care more culturally appropriate for the patient, in an attempt to help the healthcare provider learn a more ethno-relative worldview. The first case involved a mother who had given birth and the nurse was asking about the mother's breastfeeding with the medical interpreter. The mother mentioned that she was already giving the baby chamomile tea, a common practice in their culture. The nurse stated she should ask her doctor about that. The interpreter noticed that mom was astonished that the nurse seemed to have an issue with it. The medical interpreter decided to interject, stating that this was a common practice and known herb for colicky babies in the patient's country. This may not be considered a needed intervention, as there was no miscommunication per se.

Others may argue or interpret this as a cultural miscommunication. The participant was asked why she intervened, and she stated she wanted to make sure the nurse did not make faces when the next patient told her that, and that she wanted to make sure that the nurse knew of this very common practice, and she wanted the nurse and the mom to have a good relationship, as they would see each other again, and as a bad attitude can create lack of trust from the patient. In her words "when the patient does not trust the nurse or doctor, everything goes downhill." What seemed to prompt her to intervene was double faceted. On one hand, she wanted the provider to know that this was not something bad that mom is doing, that it was cultural, so she was acting as a cultural informant and as a community agent. This was determined by the medical interpreter to be a needed intervention based on the body language of the nurse as she reacted to that news with concern.

Second, as an interpreter, one of her goals is to ensure not only that the communication is smooth, but also that she supports the provider-patient rapport that seemed strained, and was not specifically related to culture. The interpreter stated that the nurse did not know of that cultural tradition;

it was obvious by her reaction, and she was not interested in asking or learning why the mother did this, again a perception from the interpreter of the nurse's reaction. Linguistically the nurse understood well what the patient said, via the medical interpreter. However, she did not know or ask why the mother was giving chamomile tea to a newborn, even though she addressed concern. In the absence of her asking for clarification, the interpreter jumped in and provided it.

This example alone shows that some medical interpreters feel comfortable intervening not only where there is a cultural issue affecting the communication, but simply to provide cultural information for the present situation and for future benefit and to improve rapport on the spot. Whether or not this was a serious enough situation to intervene is debatable; however, it is the medical interpreter's decision on how to act based on her assessment of the situation at that moment. The amount of intervention may also vary depending on the objectives of the interpreter.

In the IMIA & EDC Standards of Practice B-2 (cultural interface), item B states the following as a task: prompts the provider and patient to search for clarity (IMIA & EDC, 2007, p. 41). In this case when asked, the medical interpreter stated that she did not prompt the nurse to ask the patient why she gave chamomile tea, but she justified this because she believed the nurse was clearly not interested, based on her body language. When asked why she didn't prompt the mother to explain that this was done in her country in her own words, empowering patient autonomy and agency, she stated that she did not think the mother would want to defend her tradition if asked. It seems the medical interpreter had thought of it and a reason not to prompt either party, based on her professional knowledge and experience. She therefore made a conscious choice to intervene and explain to the nurse, then explain to the patient (transparency) that she explained to the nurse that this is a common practice in their country, but it isn't in the United States. Making this comment helped the mother understand that the nurse did not have anything personal against her, but that she simply didn't know; she lacked that information. As already established, the medical interpreter perceived a level of discomfort in the patient due to cultural issues and decided to address it immediately. In the IMIA Standards of Practice (IMIA & EDC, 2007), it also stated as a task to address the patient's comfort needs, and in this case, the interpreter felt she was doing just that through her intercultural intervention. It seems that patient comfort may be tied to culture at times.

It seems that several of the objectives of medical interpreters that prompt cultural intervention may not be the fear or identification of a cultural misunderstanding, but due to other goals and objectives.

Addressing patient comfort level, support the provider-patient relationship, or ensuring trust between the parties seem to be prominent in the medical interpreters' minds when deciding to intervene. It is by addressing these nuances, which have nothing to do with the actual linguistic interpretation, that they are able to meet those objectives. In this case, there was an additional objective that is not commonly in any standards of practice, but that has been observed in the research presented in the literature review. This includes the task of informing providers of cultural issues that may help them in the future, even without their request to do so.

To summarize, the goals and reasons behind cultural intervention are varied, and this needs to be further evaluated and explored. The common professional protocol to only intervene when a miscommunication is imminent is not what is being practiced, according to the data obtained in this study.

4.1.2.5 Pre-session between the medical interpreter and the patient.

Case 2 is interesting for two reasons. Some may consider requesting rephrasing to lower the linguistic register to be a common linguistic issue, which it is. This goes contrary to most codes of ethics that require the interpreter to maintain the linguistic register of the speakers. However, according to the medical interpreter, it is also a cultural issue. The interpreter made an assessment of the patient's cultural background, which included level of education, and knew that the patient would not understand the provider's rendition. Therefore, he requested that the provider rephrase the explanation into simpler terms, as is usually done, in lieu of lowering the register. If the provider lowers the register then the interpreter can provide an interpretation with greater fidelity.

When the researcher asked if he requested permission from the patient or verified understanding first, the interpreter ascertained that he knew and there was no point in asking, and that is why interpreters do a pre-session, to understand where the patient is coming from and their level of education. It seems the medical interpreter is acting with the intent of ensuring optimal communication and preventing miscommunication that may affect the treatment. He did not say this, but time may also be a factor. This example illustrates that sometimes, when a pre-session is conducted, the medical interpreter may know more about the patient's cultural background than the provider may know, which seems to make the interpreter more aware of the context of the communication needs of the parties involved even before. Providers rarely do a cultural assessment of patients prior to starting the session.

4.2.1.6 Timing of cultural interventions.

Medical interpreters may intervene at many different times. They may occur with the patient or provider. In a pre-session with the patient, the interpreter uses a small conversation to assess the patient's linguistic style and cultural background (i.e., origin, education, and any clues as to other cultural factors). It may occur in a pre-session with the provider, where the interpreter may say something about the patient or if it is with the provider the provider will share information that may be relevant to the medical interpreter before the session. A pre-session is not the same as an introduction, and those sometimes are confused. During an encounter, the interpreter may provide an introduction, where the interpreter notifies both parties of the interpreter's role to bridge the cultural and linguistic gap, that he may intervene if there are any communication issues, and other protocols of interpreting. If during the introduction the medical interpreter explains he may need to interrupt and intervene, in order to explore or clarify something that was stated or due to a behavior observed, both parties will be better equipped to know what to expect. Interpreter introductions set the state and allow the interpreter to set the rules for his or her facilitation. Without this introduction, it will be very difficult for the interpreter to manage the flow of communication and provide optimal interpretation.

Often responses indicated that timing depends on the context and needs of each unique situation. Others explained that it was important to include in the introduction that an interruption may occur if a cultural or linguistic issue needs to be addressed. This seems to be a pre-emptive strategy, which then helps the parties not be surprised when the medical interpreter brings something up. If addressing cultural issues does not happen all the time, or in every encounter, perhaps some practitioners do not find it necessary to state that warning about possibly addressing cultural issues in the pre-session. Three participants stated that addressing issues after was ideal, as it avoids interrupting the encounter, but that issues that arise during the session often need to be addressed when they arise. Sometimes, it may be ideal for the intervention to be addressed in the post session. However, it is not always possible for remote medical interpreters, as providers will hang up unless the interpreter interjects asking for the provider not to hang up. One participant explained:

> I only interpret incoming calls. So anything that is to be addressed will be within that call. Any clarification has to be made with permission from the client, and as brief as possible.

With telephonic and video interpreting, the end users will disconnect the medical interpreter when the encounter ends. The interpreter can ask the provider if he or she can stay on the call after the patient leaves. However, the same question is usually not asked to the patient, unless the interpreter is the one who initiated the two or three-way call (not common), due to concern for the provider's time constraints. Regardless, since there may be no time at the end of the appointment, it may be that remote interpreters will feel more urgency to address the cultural issue when it occurs during the encounter. Future studies comparing interventions and modalities may provide relevant information about how the interpretation modality affects the medical interpreter's ability and frequency of intervention for whatever reason. This interpreter reminds us how time is always an issue, forcing interpreters to be able to deliver clear and meaningful messages in the shortest amount of time possible. One participant explained how the type of intervention might dictate when to intervene:

> *Timing depends on the nature of the encounter. For example, when going into palliative care encounters, it is helpful to brief the provider on any known issues so there is adequate preparation. In these instances, the interpreter would likely be aware of what cultural issues could arise. In the emergency medicine encounter, an intervention during the encounter can allow the provider to proceed with all necessary information at hand. When addressing U.S. healthcare culture with patients, I generally perform that intervention after the encounter and after informing the provider of the intervention.*

In this statement, she was describing three different types of intervention, and a different timing for each one. In the first case, she describes a situation that is likely to require cultural intervention due to the subject matter, in her example, palliative care. In these foreseeable cultural situations, she prefers to intervene with the provider before the encounter. In an emergency medicine encounter, where it cannot be foreseen, she may address it during the encounter. For additional explanations about U.S. healthcare to the patient, clearly a helpful but not required set of information, she prefers to address it after the encounter, as this would be akin to working as a patient advocate and cultural interface at the same time, helping the patient utilize the healthcare services in a more appropriate manner. One medical interpreter felt strongly about what not to say:

> *Some people think that saying something about culture*
> *in the introduction goes way beyond the bounds of what*
> *an interpreter should say, because an interpreter shouldn't*
> *assume that all doctors are like that.*

This is an illuminating comment, where the medical interpreter is connecting the need to address a cultural issue with the ability of the doctor to be able to know what to do with all culturally diverse patients. No matter how culturally competent a provider is, he or she may not have a specific information about a specific culture that could be helpful for that specific encounter. However, some providers work often with diverse patients, and can become very skilled in this area. Interpreters may know the provider beforehand and may adapt their introduction to the provider met at each encounter.

Discussing the need to possibly address a cultural issue may not be due to any assumptions the medical interpreter may have, but may be needed simply to inform the provider about the scope of work of the interpreter, which may be unknown to the provider. The provider may know that information, but the interpreter cannot assume one way or the other, and therefore as a professional may need to ask vs. assume. Many medical interpreters start their introductions asking the provider if he or she has worked with interpreters, and foregoes their introduction on how to work with an interpreter when the provider answers in the affirmative. In that case, the interpreter may be assuming that the provider knows the scope of work of a medical interpreter just by virtue of having worked with her. Unfortunately, even those who have worked with interpreters before, may not have worked with professional medical interpreters, and may still not know their scope of work, or worst, may assume and/or have strong beliefs that interpreters exist simply there to 'repeat' or 'translate' word for word.

When analyzing the survey question about when it is best to intervene, 59.92% answered that the intervention should be during the encounter. 12.81% stated before the encounter, and 7.02% stated after the encounter. Another 22.2% answered the *Other* option, and most reiterated that it was dependent on the situation at hand, and when it was necessary to do so, vs. responding with a general preference. The data suggests that most medical interpreters probably intervene during the medical encounter. Depending on the issue at hand, the issue itself may require clarification and resolution when the topic of discussion is taking place.

4.2.1.7 Cultural diversity of patients within a language group.

Several interviewees mentioned that patients are more diverse than the country they are from. One of the focus groups participants stated the following:

> *Just because the interpreter speaks Spanish doesn't mean that they are Hispanic. There are so many Spanish-speaking cultures. You can't know all of the cultures that speak Spanish; you have to get back to the culture of the individual patient.*

In this statement she is making it clear that it is difficult for medical interpreters to know the cultures of their patient, and that speaking a language does not mean that you understand that culture, as one language may represent many cultures. The term *Hispanic*, for example, only exists in the United States, where all who speak Spanish are bunched up into one category and most believe Hispanic culture is the same, since there are similarities. Another interviewee described how generalizations hurt cultural competency efforts and how unrealistic it is for medical interpreters to know all the cultures they work with:

> *Providers learn about the variety of cultures. All Indians are not the same. India is huge and people come from all parts of India. It would be difficult to learn about all the different regions. What is ok with an European may not be ok with Indians.*

Another interviewee elaborated on the subtle differences of even neighboring cultural groups by bringing in her own experiences:

> *If the interpreter is not correctly informed about a particular practice or tradition in a culture, for example: I am from Central America, and if I assume that all Central Americans behave the same way as I do in Costa Rica, that could easily give the wrong explanation for the particular behavior, tradition, or whatever. Someone may know what they are doing, but it may create a huge obstacle in the communication.*

Another interviewee stated the difficulty of having providers assume that you understand the patient's culture when as a medical interpreter you may not be as familiar as they would think:

> One of the issues that I am encountering a lot is the assumption on the part of the hospital and the patient that I understand everything about that particular patient's culture. I do not deal only with native English speakers. Here in Japan we have people who come to teach English but they are not coming from an English-speaking dominant country. Maybe they got married to a Japanese person, and they don't even communicate well in Japanese, and English may be their second or third language. So as a result, sometimes the patient expects me to know their cultural understanding of hospitals and cultural situations that are common in their countries, but that is not my experience, as I come from America. The providers don't realize, for example, that a patient is European, like from countries I am not familiar with, like Germany or another country. They lump them all up as a foreigner 'gaikokujin', a person outside the community. This is the label given to anyone who is not completely Japanese, including myself, since I was born in America, though of Japanese parents, I am not considered a Japanese national by many here.

Any interpreter whose working language(s) encompass more than one culture may experience this scenario. Medical interpreters, for example, interpret in English, French, Spanish, Russian, or Arabic, or even Hindi, as these may be a second or third language to some patients. Interviewees reported that these languages are spoken in many different countries and therefore it is not realistic to assume they have the same culture, although most are combined into one culture, with the assumption that one language equals one culture.

Likewise, individuals even from the same country, such as the previous example about India being a large nation, showcase that many other factors affect cultural beliefs and practices. Regional differences can be larger than assumed. There are also many other factors that contribute to culture. Age, region, religion, economic status and educational background can be strong influencers and molders of cultural beliefs and practices. Several interviewees spoke about the importance of understanding that patient culture is unique to the specific patient in question. Almost all interviewees, and four of the 16 focus group participants, mentioned that culture was unique to each individual and that stereotyping cultural groups was counterproductive to culturally appropriate descriptions or explanations of any cultural issue.

4.2.1.8 Healthcare outcomes to cultural interventions.

When looking at the cases provided by the interviewees, some addressed issues of comfort and helpful information to enhance or promote the provider-patient relationship, which are goals of the medical interpreter as per their standards of practice. Other cases described specifically addressed situations where the interventions actually affected the health compliance, understanding, or a possible outcome for the patient. More research is needed that explores how an interpreter's cultural intervention may actually affect the course of treatment a patient ends up taking. In the study cases reviewed, there were several cases that point to the medical interpreter's direct impact in healthcare improvement. One of the focus group participants spoke about this in more detail:

> *When you facilitate communication, you help the provider make a better treatment plan for their patients; it's huge! It's like a light bulb lights up and they say, "Now I get it." It's the same with the patient, as they become familiar with the healthcare system it helps them navigate it.*

Another participant stated the following:

> *I am an English Russian interpreter. There are benefits for both [parties], the patient's well-being and health in particular. Many of my Russian patients are of the Orthodox religion and some treatments are suitable for them while others are not. If a cultural issue is properly addressed, then the patient will agree with the treatment even if the treatment is against his or her religious belief, due to the help of the interpreter.*

When asked about how the medical interpreter was able to do this, she explained that knowing when to intervene was important and that the cultural aspect has to be acknowledged, as it is very important to the patient. By putting it out in the open, the provider is now privy to important considerations for the patient's decision-making process. This gives the provider the full context of the situation, allowing him or her different ways to explain to the patient why it is important for them to consider the treatment as the best option. One participant gave an additional example of how a cultural intervention may assist the delivery of healthcare:

> *First, Western medicine is exposed to our traditions and then they can understand the patients better and give them what they want. There is an expression: my heart aches... it does not mean what they say. They will end up referred to a cardiologist to do an EKG but this is an expression; they are not speaking about the heart as an organ. When the patients say this I inform the doctor that it may be a symptom of distress. Maybe you can ask him to define more clearly and show where it hurts. It is an expression. [Interpreter cannot ascertain meaning from that utterance]. This is to show the doctor that the phrase has many cultural aspects.*

It seems that the medical interpreter here is explaining how easily a provider may misunderstand a message, and if so, that the patient could be referred to the wrong care, wasting time and money, and most importantly, not addressing the patient's ailment. As professional guidelines dictate, the interpreter did not assume it was a case of mental illness, but alerted the provider for the need for clarification. Again, here the medical interpreter's main focus was in accuracy of communication and the health of the patient.

The cases presented by the interviewees include several where there was a clear relationship between the cultural intervention and the healthcare outcome, even if minor. In case 3, the patient agreed not to use prescriptions from other countries without the knowledge and consent of the provider. In case 4 the patient agreed to a treatment that is contrary to his cultural practices because of a cultural discussion about different treatments. In this case the patient's treatment method was not looked down on, but acknowledged as a possible treatment. In case 6 the medical interpreter's intervention not only prevented a hospitalization, which would have been costly, but the interpreter proposed a culturally appropriate solution to the problem at hand. Case 9 is perhaps not unusual, as many interpreters stress to their patients the need to arrive on time in their country of practice, avoiding delays and the possible need to reschedule a visit. In case 11, the interpreter not only provided a culturally appropriate solution (drawing small amounts of blood to keep Ethiopian patients happy in Israel), but also avoided hospitalizations that had occurred before due to the lack of understanding of the Ethiopian cultural practices related to blood removal as a form of healing. Providers had no idea that the patients would get themselves hospitalized just to have blood removed. Several other examples showcase the medical interpreter navigating the patient to the appropriate location or office, improving their use of the healthcare system. In one particular case, case 14, where the interpreter explained that in El Salvador patients use the term "gastritis" to mean several ailments, the interpreter basically intervened to allow the provider to inquire more and not take that term for its value as it had ambiguous meaning in El Salvador. In this case, the interpreter is using his or her cultural knowledge to assist the provider in making a correct diagnosis.

What if the medical interpreter did not know this fact about El Salvador? In that case, the interpreter would not have caught this cultural nuance. However, because one interpreter didn't know one cultural piece of information, it does not mean that another interpreter, who does have this information, should hide it or avoid speaking up because there is no miscommunication. Often miscommunication is not overt, and the interpreter is the only person in the room that knows that one party may not understand accurately what the other party is saying. Is this miscommunication or lack of information? In any event, lack of knowledge prevents optimal safe communication. Perhaps medical interpreters are going beyond engaging in safe accurate communication that is void of communication problems, but it seems many are also engaging in ensuring that both parties have full context in order for the communication to be accurately understood as if it were spoken in the receiver's language and culture.

4.2.2 Frequency of addressing cultural issues.

It was important to attempt to assess how often this knowledge and skills are required of a medical interpreter, considering that 'every single human encounter is cross cultural' (SenGupta, 1996). This question was asked of all data sets. Interviewees all struggled with this question for a good reason. Most said occasionally or that it depended on the situation at hand. One participant showed that the level of cultural competency of an institution or its providers may affect the level of need for a medical interpreter to intervene. She stated, *"Hospital providers and hospital staff had become accustomed to take care of Muslims, so recently the need for explanations has diminished."* Another also spoke of how providers are getting more knowledgeable about their diverse patient populations:

Most understand that the Korean older generation are different but they understand the choices people make, so eventually things are getting better, thinking of the future, we will be all together, no translation or interpreting will be necessary. Everyone is learning from each other so the differences are diminishing.

A different interviewee emphasized the need for clear guidelines on when to get involved: *"There have to be clearly defined lines when we should get involved, whenever there is a danger or complete miscommunication, or misinterpretation."*

There is plenty written on professional standards about this topic, as listed in the literature review. However, it seems that some medical interpreters are still unsure about the professional protocols and standards regarding interpreting culture, based on the comment above. Another interviewee listed that certain medical environments required a greater frequency of addressing cultural issues. She listed the following: *"We interpret in many medical fields; in mental health there are a lot of cultural issues, practically in every conversation with psychiatry, whereas family physician work, it is not so often."*

One interviewee mentioned the level of cultural awareness and competency of the medical interpreter will impact the frequency of their interventions. This participant had a master's degree in intercultural communication and this may have an effect on her outlook:

For me, every situation has a cultural component. The healthcare provider, the patient, and myself these are three different cultural frameworks. It really is pretty constant that something is slighted; maybe it is after the encounter or during it, or even previous to an encounter. I see culture in everything: For example, how many wines are there? For some it is three; for others they will see the intricate differences. The more you perceive these differences, then you can't not see them. Sometimes people ask the interpreter to redirect the patient. I don't like doing that, as it is better to allow the patient to say what they want to say, it is their voice, this is their healthcare and they have the right to communicate the way they prefer. I let them speak and try to construct, can we put it in this order? And that clarifies it for someone who is not familiar with circular communication.

It seems the number of interventions a medical interpreter makes also depends on the cultural group(s) he or she is interpreting for. For example, one of the interviewees explained that for one cultural group the interventions were significantly lower than for the other:

> *For Russian patients I intervene less often, but for my Uzbek patients, more often, because they are Muslims. Usually when it is a female speaking to a male provider, the patient has stress answering the questions. There has to be some balance, to serve my primary role, so I do not put my opinion up front, but I explain to the patient "this is America; they are neutral." I don't think I have expressed any advice to the patients.*

Focus group participants focused on the types of medical environments that required more cultural intervention, stating it depended on the setting, but that these were the settings that required greater cultural intervention:

(a) mental health,
(b) family planning,
(c) reproductive health,
(d) women's clinics,
(e) palliative care and end-of-life situations, and
(f) organ donation.

Survey participants who gave ranges and seemed to relay a higher level of occurrence than the interviewees. When asked how often they intervened, the largest group (45.67%) stated *Somewhat often*. Participants stated that it was *Extremely often* or *Very often*, (36.54%) and only 17.79% stated that it was *Not very often* or *Not often at all*. The interview data stated that it didn't come up very often. However, the survey data showcased a higher frequency, as only 17.79% stated that they intervene not very often or not often at all.

In the survey, a long list of medical specialties was included, which included the categories given in the qualitative results of the interviews, to see which ones scored highest by the survey participants (Table 18). There were eight categories that obtained more than 30% of participants stating that cultural issues were *Extremely often*.

Table 18

Highest Frequency of Cultural Issues in Specific Healthcare Areas

Specific healthcare area	Extremely often
Mental Health	43.81%
Labor and Delivery	36.77%
Family Medicine	35.12%
Maternity	34.30%
Emergency Medicine	33.47%
Pediatrics	32.23%
Gynecology	31.81%
Palliative Care	30.17%

Note. n=433

There is another way to look at the data. When combining the responses that matched *Extremely often*, *Very often*, or *Somewhat often* there were 10 categories with over 50% agreement. These include the following (Table 19):

Table 19

Frequency of Cultural Issues in Ten Specific Healthcare Areas?

Specific healthcare area	Extremely Often + Very Often + Somewhat Often
Mental health	65.71%
Maternity	64.05%
Labor and delivery	64.04%
Family medicine	62.35%
Emergency medicine	61.98%
Gynecology	61.56%
Pediatrics	56.61%
Immunology	54.14%
Infectious diseases	51.66%
Neonatal care	51.24%

Some of the comments rightly pointed to needed areas that were not listed, such as cardiology, nutrition, physical therapy, rehabilitation, tropical diseases, oncology, surgery, blood transfusions, and diabetes. The list was not an extensive list and the *Other* option was given precisely so that participants could give other healthcare areas that may require cultural intervention.

Both analyses show some validation of what the interviewees and focus group members stated when they listed healthcare areas. It seems mental health is the area where cultural issues will occur the most, in general, and agreed by all medical interpreters. Then, all the areas related to childbirth (maternity, labor & delivery) and children (neonatal, pediatrics) had higher scores. This may be due to the fact that there are many cultural practices that relate to birth and child rearing. There were two areas in which interviewees stated it did not occur as frequently, but survey participants disagreed and listed them as one of the top eight and top 10 categories of a total of 22 categories presented in the survey. It appears that in family medicine and emergency medicine there is a large variety of situations that can occur, so perhaps this is why they were able to obtain higher scores than expected, based on the qualitative data. It seems that the qualitative data was more reticent, with all stating that it was *Not often* or *Mostly occasional*. None of the interviewees or focus group participants stated *Often* or *Very often*, or even *Somewhat often*. When asked this question, interviewees quickly dismissed it, stating that they couldn't answer it as it depended on the situation. When probed, some listed the types of departments, and the others responded it occurred occasionally, or depended on the language, and that they intervened based on goals of the communicative event.

In contrast, it seems that more survey participants agreed with the categories of *Extremely, Very,* or *Somewhat often.* The options were clearly listed in the quantitative data, and that may have had an effect on the frequency discrepancy between qualitative and quantitative data. Deeper analysis of the data demonstrates that there are several factors that influence the frequency of cultural intervention. There is research on specific health areas that encounter cultural difficulties, but no study has been published to date that does a thorough comparison of frequency of cultural issues and medical specialty. Table 20 shows some of the factors that were found to affect the frequency of cultural intervention based on the data collected.

Table 20

Factors Affecting the Frequency of Intercultural Intervention

Specific healthcare specialty	Certain specialties encounter more cultural differences than others.
Cultural competence of the interpreter	Lower the level of cultural competence of the participants engendered lower levels of intervention.
Cultural competence of the organization and/or providers where the interpreter is working.	The higher the knowledge and skills of the providers and the institution, the less medical interpreters need to inform or intervene.
Cultural group the interpreter is interpreting for.	Some interpreters interpret for different cultural groups and one group may have greater variance with the country of practice than the other(s).
Level of education, religion, race, economic status of the patient	These patient cultural factors will affect the level of intervention needed.
The knowledge and skills the interpreter has of a particular patient culture	The less the interpreter knows about a patient's culture, the less likely he will intervene.
The interpreter's approach (conservative approach vs. liberal approach)	Some interpreters believe they are to intervene only when there is miscommunication, whereas others intervene for multiple reasons. According to the study, very few ($n=2$) believe they should never intervene (0.44%).

4.2.3 Advantages of addressing cultural issues.

One of the research questions was related to identifying the advantages of addressing cultural issues. Interviewees had many comments on this topic. One of the interviewees described it as increasing clarity and peace of mind:

> *There are more advantages than disadvantages. I only intervene if I see there is a gap in understanding. If I get the sense that it is due to culture then I pause and intervene to both parties and explain what the cultural issue means, to both parties so both parties are on the same page (transparency and impartiality). It dissipates frustrations or fear especially in the case of the client (patient), like when they are expecting the diagnosis. It increases clarity and peace of mind.*

Clearly there may be a certain level of frustration and fear in the provision of healthcare, according to the participant, mostly by the patient. Increasing clarity and peace of mind are intangible benefits, and dissipating fear and frustration as well. Whenever an individual does not speak a language, and goes for care, it is safe to assume that being in a place where you can't easily communicate is stressful. When that communication is related to your health even more so. Most people who have not experienced this cannot imagine the level of stress and discomfort this can cause a patient. There are current studies taking place to hear the perspectives of patients in this regard. Fortier is working on one such study in progress, at the time of the publication of this study, under the auspices of Diversity Rx and Osaka University, to hear the opinions and experience non-Japanese speaking patients have in Japan when seeking care (Fortier, 2014). An interviewee identified an advantage for the patient:

> *The advantage for the patient is that he is at ease, and can get comfortable. They feel included, it's very important for them to feel included and respected. They feel that their culture is being taken into account, it is important.*

It seems that in addition to providing clarity and peace of mind or ease (lack of stress) to patients, it seems to this medical interpreter that their presence helps the patient feel included and respected. This can go a long way in improving patient trust levels that can ease collaboration in treatment plans. There are studies that have showcased how trust in the provider increases patient compliance. Understanding how to incorporate patient preferences is an important move towards patient-centered system. In the patient-centered care model of shared decision-making between providers and patients is based on a partnership of equals. Patients, who do not adhere to physician instructions, or recommended follow-up treatment plans, are difficult to manage, and often present significant risk management concerns for the physician (Bontempo, 2012). Despite their best efforts to educate patients, some providers are faced with behaviors that indicate patients are putting themselves and the provider at risk by not adhering to the prescribed treatment. Compliance increases if patients are given clear and understandable information about their condition and progress in a sincere and responsive way. How patients feel about the message and the messenger may be a factor in their compliance.

The interviewees had a myriad of thoughts about the advantages of addressing cultural issues, focusing on both providers and patients:

1. *Providers learn about the variety of cultures.*
2. *One of the immediate advantages is clarification to one or both parties, who are then better informed. Awareness for medical staff of things that they will probably deal with if they continue to serve LEP (Limited English Proficient) communities of that particular ethnicity. It could help a safety issue or even prevent a legal issue due to a misinterpretation of a behavior that is being construed when it is common in that culture, such as coining, or, in Somali communities, the burning of the hands, etc.*
3. *The provider can understand more and it can open his mind, his horizons, to understand the patient where they are coming from, from a cultural aspect. There are no disadvantages; I can't think of one. Discussion the cultural issue helps the provider and the patient. First, Western medicine is exposed to our traditions and then they can understand the patients better and give them what they want.*

Several interviewees discussed the effect of clarification and better-informed providers and staff as they continue to serve culturally diverse patients. In a way it seems that medical interpreters, through their small interventions, may have a significant role in educating providers on the spot, where the learning moment is most relevant. When engaging in informing providers or patients about certain cultural issues, it seems interpreters are acting as cultural educators, or according to Jalbert (1998), these would be the roles of cultural informant, intercultural mediator, or healthcare professional.

Traditionally educators (mostly in the United States) have relied on the framework of four roles (conduit, clarifier, cultural interface, advocate), developed by the Cross Cultural Healthcare Program in 1999. It has been referred to as the incremental intervention model for medical interpreters, and is only used by this specialization. This framework is limited to four roles, and may not address all the roles or functions medical interpreters undertake. The term cultural educator may be more appropriate than cultural informant, as the interpreter is not only informing the parties, but also in doing so educating providers to provide a more culturally competent service in the future. Providers have access to cultural training at different levels, but the specific circumstance and relevance is best applied when the issue takes place. As the participant described earlier, cultural intervention can also prevent negative medical or legal impact to a specific case in point.

The responses indicate the relevancy and benefits of allowing medical interpreters the space to enter this cultural dimension in order to provide better care. The cultural educator and cultural mediator roles seem to be relevant to improving the cultural competency of all stakeholders involved in the patient's care, including the organization that provides the service. An interpreter may not know all the facts and nuances of a particular culture. These situations may improve as medical interpreters are better trained in this area. The educator can only teach what they know, and, thus, will have varying levels of knowledge about different cultures, just as any educator will have different levels of knowledge of what they are teaching.

Some participants have argued that it can cause more confusion, or that an educator may teach wrong information. This is true of any teaching role when done inappropriately, and it is up to the medical interpreter instructors to do better job educating interpreters how to act as a cultural mediator, with all the intricacies and nuances involved. Due to the scarcity of quality training, there are instructors in the field who, unfortunately, are not bilingual, and some have not even practiced as a medical interpreter, and this translates into an inadequate level of training, to be discussed in more detail later in this chapter. Another statement from an interviewee discussed her role as a medical interpreter:

> *The providers feel that they get more than linguistic help.*
> *For the role of bridging, the staff knows me well, after*
> *15 years; even some patients know me well. We are staff*

*interpreters and are allowed to advocate, we are part of the
healthcare team much more than a voice. We are part of the
healthcare team. Helping with even a smile, making the
patients appreciate those things. It's an ambassadorship,
so the patients know that you are there to make their
experience better. When there is this trust, then they will tell
you. For example, the patient may tell me "I didn't mention
but I used this herb." They feel more comfortable stating
this to us rather than someone else. I never pretend that I
have any answers, but I want the patients to communicate
in the manner that they feel comfortable. Well, certainly
they have a better understanding of how the healthcare
system works in the U.S. so they can adjust themselves to
receive good care in the U.S.*

Above, the interviewee is explaining that one's role in the institution
may make a difference in accepting the interpreter as more than a voice,
or a mouthpiece. In the case of staff interpreters, they are more seen as
healthcare professionals (not clinical) but nonetheless as team members
to the healthcare team. This means that all parties have accepted the
interpreter as an integral piece of the puzzle of intercultural healthcare.
This would not be the case with a contracted interpreter who shows up
in a hospital for the first time and meets with strangers as *the interpreter*.

Her use of the word *advocate* is vague and refers to it as actions that
involve more than being a voice. However, we can extrapolate from her
positioning as being part of the healthcare team that she is not speaking
of representing the patient against the healthcare team, as she is part of
one. The term *advocacy* is used loosely in English, with many connotations,
as it can mean simply promoting an idea, as in advocating for clear
communication, to representing an individual's interests and speaking on
his or her behalf, such as advocating for a patient against a case of overt
discrimination.

The focus group agreed that patient safety and improved effective
communication were the primary advantages. There was a strong focus
on the medical goals of the profession, which may sound surprising to
readers who do not see the medical interpreter as a medical professional.
Some of the statements referred to the importance of the medical goals of
the encounter, and the patient's safety. Patient safety, a concept that was
borrowed from the airline industry, and that has been used in the United
States in the last 10 years, mostly describes the importance of a do-no-harm

environment where the main goal is to prevent negative health outcomes or accidents. One of the focus group participants explained it well:

> *The first thing I think of is patient safety. If we can intervene and help the patient and provider stay on track, great. The focus needs to be on the medical reason why we're all there. Cultural competence, and emotional, or other issues are secondary. This is the standard use: The patient safety model. It trumps everything else.*

Clearly accurate communication will assist in ensuring patient safety is safeguarded, and this may be the most important benefit from the perspective of the patient's health. This also showcases that when medical interpreters are treated as integral members of the healthcare team, they may have the same goals in mind. The linguistic goals seem to be secondary to some as other tasks and goals, such as improving the provider-patient relationship, or ensuring complete understanding of all parties. Other responses included the following:

1. *It (addressing cultural issues) dissipates frustrations or fear, especially in the case of the client (patient), like when they are expecting the diagnosis. It increases clarity and peace of mind.*
2. *Hospital staff members, including healthcare providers, dieticians, etc., can take care of foreign patients calmly, not upset.*
3. *A connection is made that wouldn't be made without it. Patients are able to communicate and know that they are being understood.*
4. *The providers feel that they got more with that help. To give better treatment, to give more peace of mind to the patient. The doctor can understand his/her patient better.*

The first participant comment is speaking to the fact that receiving care without speaking the language can be quite stressful, from the patient's perspective, and the simple presence of a medical interpreter can greatly improve the patient's experience. Further research is needed to ascertain the perspectives of patients on the effects and benefits of working and communicating with professional medical interpreters. The second focus group participant also showcases that working with a patient who does not speak the local language of service can be stressful and that interpreters dissipate this frustration by making it possible not only for them to communicate with their patients, but also to be able to do their work in a safe and effective manner. The third speaks of the provider-patient rapport.

The last speaks of the effect of her interventions on providing a better treatment, and also the importance of understanding in communication. Other participants stated the following:

1. *One of the immediate advantages is clarification to one or both parties, who are then better informed. Awareness for medical staff for things that they will probably deal with if they continue to serve these communities of a particular ethnicity. It could help a safety issue or even prevent a legal issue, due to a misinterpretation of a behavior that is being construed when it is common in that culture, such as coining, or, in Somali communities, the burning of the hands.*
2. *Everyone is learning from each other, so the differences are diminishing.*
3. *The provider can understand more and it can open his mind, his horizons, to understand the patient, where they are coming from, from a cultural aspect.*
4. *Providers learn about the variety of cultures.*

The participants above speak of the educational component of their work in addressing cultural issues, as these experiences and knowledge learned through a cultural intervention or information may be helpful for future appointments. There seems to be a resistance in the field in Canada (HIN, 1996) to allow medical interpreters to act as cultural educators, although the standard does state that the interpreter needs to understand and be able to convey cultural nuances. The fact that providers do not have time puts pressure on the medical interpreter NOT to interrupt the session, even though from a professional perspective, the interpreter needs to convey cultural nuances and ensure understanding. This will be discussed later when the focus is on provider attitudes.

Focus group participants also discussed how addressing cultural issues is a way to address patient comfort, which is a task for medical interpreters in the IMIA Standards of Practice (IMIA & EDC, 2007). A participant stated the following:

> *We don't do it only for patient safety reasons, but also because the patient is not comfortable. Then the staff will understand it is due to the patient's culture, and not something else.*

Three other participants spoke of the provider-patient rapport and the relation between facilitating this relationship and addressing cultural issues:

1. *It is important that we support the patient-provider relationship, to facilitate that relationship. Anything the medical interpreter does not understand or identifies as a cultural barrier we must ask for a clarification and ask the patient to explain, we can't make the assumption that the patient can't.*
2. *Sometimes the relationship between the provider and the patient can be difficult. In the case where the patient cannot trust the provider, for example.*
3. *We help create bonds (between provider and patient). If they do not discuss it [the cultural issue], it will affect the communication (negatively).*

The fact that the provider and patient are from different cultures and cannot communicate provides for a wider separation than a culturally and linguistically congruent patient would have. This means that improving the provider-patient relationship may require a cultural agency component, as that may be precisely what separates the two parties. One participant commented on how he believes that telephonic interpreting affects the encounter:

There is really no relationship over the phone but in person the provider gets it that they need to partner up with the interpreter and that brings satisfaction to our work.

It appears that the participant above prefers the greater visibility that medical interpreters have when working in person with providers and patients. There are many advantages and disadvantages to in person and remote interpreting to describe here. However, visibility and agency is usually more prominent in person than over the phone.

The online survey participants were given eight examples of possible advantages, including improving the rapport with each party, better understanding, opportunity to adapt the healthcare service to the patient's cultural preferences, the opportunity for the patient to adapt to the healthcare system, and learning something new about each culture (Table 21).

Table 21

Advantages of Addressing Cultural Issues (Survey participants only)

Answer Choices	%
The rapport between the interpreter and the provider improves.	37.30%
The rapport between the interpreter and the patient improves.	31.97%
The rapport between the provider and the patient improves.	70.90%
There is a better understanding of the reasons behind the participant(s) ideas and opinions.	66.53%
There is an opportunity for the provider to adapt the services to the patient's cultural preferences.	64.46%
There is an opportunity for the patient to adapt better to the healthcare system serving him/her.	57.44%
The delivery of services is more culturally competent when we are able to address these issues.	68.80%
The parties I interpret for learn something new about teach other's culture.	42.56%
Other	6.61%

According to the survey participants, the top advantage of addressing cultural issues was the improvement of the rapport between the provider and the patient, with 70.90% level of agreement. This supports the qualitative data, where interviewees and focus group participants discussed the importance of improving the rapport of the provider and the patient. This research now showcases the relation between improving provider patient rapport and addressing cultural issues. It is important to note that the improvement of the rapport between the medical interpreter and the provider (37.30%), and likewise of the interpreter and the patient (31.97%), were secondary in importance to the interpreter when compared to the therapeutic rapport between the provider and the patient, as encouraged in all the standards of practices for medical interpreters.

The second ranked advantage with 68.80% was regarding the increased understanding of each party as to the reasons for their ideas.

Without understanding there can be no communication, so it seems that the participants are very aware of the importance of increasing understanding in order to improve the communication of two parties. When we view the medical interpreter just as an invisible conduit, or a mouthpiece, it does not take into account two important goals and tasks that medical interpreters have been speaking about in the study. First, the interpreter, in a triadic encounter, feels a responsibility to ensure accurate and complete communication (for patient safety reasons) through a variety of subtasks in addition to that of consecutive or simultaneous interpretation, or reformulation of messages into another language. Second, the interpreter is constantly working to improve the provider patient therapeutic rapport and that is an important task in a triadic encounter, where, without the interpreter's constant subtle interventions, would be a triadic rapport.

The third sub item with the highest level of agreement (68.44%) was the benefit of the delivery of services being more culturally competent when the medical interpreter is able to address these cultural issues. It seems that participants are keenly aware of their overall responsibility of providing culturally and linguistically appropriate or competent services to those they work with. How they act and behave in this regard has an impact on their cultural competency as well as that of the organization's cultural competency in delivering healthcare. In hindsight, the sub item could have specified if it was referring to the delivery of healthcare services or interpreting services, as these are separate and can be delivered in a culturally competent or in a culturally incompetent manner. This signals the importance to the healthcare organization to create a corporate environment that allows and encourages all parties, including medical interpreters, to engage in making their interpreting services cultural competent and enhance the ability of the provider and organization to provide not only linguistically competent services, but also culturally competent services.

There were two sub items that discussed the possibility of a positive side effect or advantage of the provider can know how to adapt to the patients' cultural needs (64.75%), or that the patient can know how to adapt to the healthcare system (57.79%). It seems that by this response, participants believe that even though adaptations need to happen on both sides, healthcare providers (including the institution) have the highest burden to adapt in order to truly provide culturally and linguistically competent services to their patients. Both of these adaptations can make it easier for the patient to comply with the treatment and medications prescribed. Upon review of the written comments to this question about advantages, participants stated the following about the advantages addressing cultural issues:

1. *The communication is clear between the client and the Non-English speaker.*
2. *Better care and better results.*
3. *It is done when there is an issue that will affect treatment and outcome.*
4. *The interpreter must always intervene to provide better health outcomes/overview to the provider.*
5. *Communication needs to be clear so that medical services can be provided appropriately. Rapport is secondary; I am more interested in things that will affect a person's safety or health.*
6. *With our interventions, the patient and hospital staff can engage in the most appropriate treatment, based on a better understanding of the patient and the patient has a better understanding of why things are the way they are and is more likely to be compliant. Everybody rubs along better.*
7. *Delivery of services is just more satisfactory to the patient and the provider, and is successful.*
8. *Patient care and health outcomes improve.*
9. *Saving money and saving patients.*
10. *The patients can evaluate the doctor based on how they were treated, rather than on their skills as a healthcare provider. The more comfortable they feel, the more they will follow up and do what they need.*
11. *To avoid behavior or language that could be offensive to either party.*

The survey comments are similar to the interview and focus group responses where medical interpreters stress the need to address cultural issues for several reasons that are inter-related. These responses showcase the high level skills required to accomplish the communicative work of medical interpreters, with linguistic interpreting of messages being but one of many tasks, albeit the most visible one. It is true that interpreters provide linguistic services, which involves interpreting consecutively and simultaneously, as well as providing sight translation when required. However, they are also engaged simultaneously in many other tasks and activities before, during, and after a triadic encounter that go beyond their linguistic domain or scope of work. The linguistic component may be but one of three components of their scope of work. This issue will be further discussed in chapter six.

4.2.4 Disadvantages of addressing cultural issues.

Interview participants had difficulties addressing the disadvantages, as if they had not thought of this issue before. Several of them mentioned time as a disadvantage:

1. *The amount of time the provider has to stay with a patient. They are always in a rush. I keep interpreting and remain on point by conveying the message, and it doesn't allow the interpreter much room for intervening.*
2. *It depends on which doctors you work with; some doctors don't want it; it has to go fast.*
3. *It will take more time for understanding each other, so that the consultation time becomes longer, which is sometimes difficult for other patients who are waiting for a long time. And for the doctor, it takes more time to see one patient. However, those are small matters, as I believe both sides usually appreciate the intervention.*

Time is certainly a disadvantage, as consecutive interpreting requires all utterances to be stated, and then interpreted, so it should double the time of the encounter. Since most encounters are anywhere from 10 minutes to an hour or even more, doubling the time would not be possible from a practical perspective. Unfortunately, most healthcare organizations do not book more time for providers to meet with patients who require interpreting services than for patients that do not. This means that the provider must accomplish the same discussion with all patients, regardless of their need for a medical interpreter, which in a normal condition would double the time. One can extrapolate that this provides a definite difficulty for the provider time wise. In order for the provider not to run behind, he or she has several options. One must either cut some of the conversation that would be had otherwise in order to make up for time. This explains why providers who provide verbal and non-verbal communication state that time is of the essence.

Medical interpreters are keenly aware of this, and, therefore, attempt to provide an easy and fast flow of communication. Intervening at any moment, even for a linguistic clarification, can delay the time of the appointment and make it difficult for the provider to finish on time. This adds stress in the intercultural encounter. This may have an effect in the ability for providers as well as medical interpreters to provide culturally competent care. Ideally, healthcare organizations that aim for cultural competency would consider providing extra time for the appointments of patients that require medical interpreting. The only way and possible trend for the future is for remote technology to enable simultaneous interpreting so that the time will not be an issue. In that case, only interventions and clarifications would require more time, but the appointment would follow through naturally as if there were no linguistic barrier or delay.

Another disadvantage speaks to the fact that any intervention will inevitably interrupt the flow of the discussion:

1. *Sometimes the service provider carries on and pausing to make a clarification becomes difficult as the party speaking may lose their train of thought so timing is important, and depending on the situation intervening is necessary. I note where we stopped so we can resume from there.*

2. *I think if you as an interpreter are not able to control it and do it in a professional way, it could definitely hinder the flow and the professional development of an interpretation. What I mean is that it can become like a show where the interpreter becomes the star, and he/she will continuously interject and really destroy the flow, which should be the patient-provider interaction.*

3. *Like I said the interpreter may be green and have the tendency to stop the session and say "doctor my experience with the patient from Guatemala..." I think the interpreters are too quick to want to help, out of a good heart, I'm not saying it's bad, but it is not our role as interpreters. Communication may not be clear and then obviously yes, you do have to get clarification. A lot of times we are too quick to stop and interrupt the dialogue. The interpreter loses the focus as a facilitator of communication.*

The first medical interpreter who made this statement has a strategy for this, but invariably a speaker may still have difficulty returning to the point before the interpreter intervention. Maintaining a natural flow of communication is one of the goals and tasks of the interpreter, which means that any intervention will risk the interruption of the flow of communication. This showcases how certain tasks may be in opposition of others, making the work of the medical interpreter more complex than that of just interpreting. What if the communication becomes even more confusing? These participants speak to the fact that sometimes a cultural intervention can have the opposite of the desired effect:

If the interpreter is not correctly informed about a particular practice or tradition in a culture, for example, I am from Central America, and if I assume that all Central Americans behave the same way as I do in Costa Rica, that could easily give the wrong explanation for the particular behavior, tradition or whatever. Someone may think they know what they are doing but it may create a huge obstacle in the communication.

Inappropriate interventions may upset the party that feels an assumption was made of them, or have another negative consequence, such as eroding the trust the parties have on the medical interpreter. An interpreter should know not to generalize and stereotype, but as all professionals, there will be some that are more or less competent in this area. If an interpreter clarifies the issue with the patient or provider, asking them to confirm and explain the issue before deciding to provide any intervention, this should not happen.

A focus group participant explained how the patient is the one who needs to explain their cultural issue: "The patient needs to be the one to explain." Four other focus group participants brought up the fact that there are times when the patient is not able to speak up:

1. *Here's a situation. The patient didn't know his date of birth and the nurse got very upset and I had to explain that this was common for this person's culture, so then she understood.*

2. *For some cultures, it is not possible to speak up about all that is culturally relevant. It is impossible as it is something that is not supposed to be spoken but to be understood. We also have to act as to not lose the trust of the patient or provider on the interpreter. The interpreter should not interject personal bias, but the rules for the provider are different. The provider can allow himself or herself their cultural issues.*

3. *I empathize before sharing, I check with the patient, to correct or to make sure that they are comfortable, I don't want to explain but sometimes they want me to so I clarify with the patient if it is ok to go ahead. I will tell the provider that the patient is afraid to share. It is their (providers) responsibility to make it a safe space to disclose cultural information.*

4. *The patient is embarrassed about admitting to using or preferring a traditional home remedy and may not want the interpreter to tell the provider.*

Cultural beliefs and values are often difficult to explain. As the first participant explains, it is not something commonly discussed or compared. One cannot explain one culture in relation to another if one does not know the other. Those who understand the two beliefs or values to be compared can only make comparative explanations. For example, in the example given above, where the patient didn't know his date of birth, that is not something that the patient would know to explain that in his part of the world some people do not know their dates of birth, because that same patient may not even know that this phenomenon is uncommon in another country. Often values are believed to be absolute (believed by all) unless challenged. That patient may not even know why the nurse is upset. This is a situation where the interpreter may interject not due to an overt miscommunication, but due to other goals: improve provider-patient rapport, correct the nurse's misinterpretation of the patient's response due to lack of knowledge about that culture, educate the nurse about this issue so that when she or he encounters other patients who respond the same way, the nurse will know why. The medical interpreter was observing not only the patient's non-verbal communication, but also the nurse's non-verbal communication, and made the decision to intervene without the permission or clarification of the patient. When the interpreter was asked during the focus group why she did not ask the patient first if she could explain that in the patient's culture sometimes patients did not know their date of birth, the interpreter answered that she did not want to embarrass the patient and that the patient may not understand why she is stating this.

It seems that interpreters have their reasons for requesting permission or not and that this is a decision the interpreter needs to make in every unique scenario based on their professional judgment and factors present. The last comment about this clearly suggests that sometimes the patient does not feel comfortable or empowered to explain the cultural issue. Some interpreters are very skilled at empowering the patient, when necessary. However, the interpreter cannot force the patient to speak. Also, if the patient requests the interpreter to explain a cultural concept, the interpreter is obliged to do so.

There is another disadvantage stated by a participant that can occur when interpreters address cultural issues: *"Hospital staff members may depend on interpreters too much. We may have to take care of patients everything sometimes. It's a big burden for the U.S."*

When asked about this statement, the interpreter explained that sometimes the provider will simply work with the patient by communicating with the interpreter, avoiding eye contact and communication with the patient, as in communicating in the first person. The interpreter stated that the provider would ask her the questions that he should be asking the patient. This comment, within a real work experience, does not seem to be related specifically to addressing cultural issues, but to the tendency of some providers to believe that they may not need to learn how to work with the patient, so long as they have an interpreter present who will be the one who knows how to work with the patient. Interpreters need greater agency and presentation skills in order to set the triadic encounter in a manner that explains to the provider that it is important that he or she speak to the patient directly and have a therapeutic rapport with the patient and that the interpreter is there to help the provider achieve that, but that the goal is not to encourage the main rapport to be with the interpreter and patient but that it be the therapeutic rapport of the provider and the patient.

Online survey participants were given six disadvantages to rate, based on the qualitative responses of interviewees. Survey responses follow below (Table 22):

Table 22
Disadvantages of Addressing Cultural Issues (Survey participants only)

Answer Choices	%
Sometimes it does delay the time of the encounter.	55.37%
Sometimes it causes more confusion than clarity, as the parties really cannot conceptualize or accept the ideas being put forth about the other culture.	41.74%
I can end up being reprimanded for getting too involved with the patient and healthcare provider interaction.	19.01%
The provider may not want me to address cultural issues, and if I do, the provider may get upset with me.	23.55%
Other	19.83%

As can be seen by the online responses, similarly to the interviewees, online survey participants listed the delay of time (55.37%) as the primary disadvantage of addressing cultural issues. Time is a very real obstacle to quality services and should be further evaluated in the attempt to provide equitable care to diverse patients. This has not been discussed in any interpreter study and merits further research. If patients who do not speak the local language are given less time to address their issues (due to the consecutive interpretation time taking at least half of the time of the speaker's utterances), how are they to receive equitable care, and how is the provider able to assess the patient's condition in half the time? These are important questions that should be addressed in further research.

The second disadvantage, with a 41.74% agreement, is that this is a complex issue and if the parties cannot conceptualize or accept the ideas being put forth about the other culture, the communication can be challenging and require high level diplomatic skills from the perspective of the interpreter. Confusion can ensue and clarity is not always attainable. This is a risk that medical interpreters need to weigh in every time they are considering addressing a cultural issue with an intervention during the appointment.

The third disadvantage, with a 23.55% agreement, relates to the provider not wanting the medical interpreter to address cultural issues and if done the provider may get upset with the interpreter. This shows a very strong deterrent for addressing cultural issues. If the medical interpreter does not feel that the provider will appreciate the cultural information, the tendency will be not to intervene. Some interpreters are being trained to intervene only with the provider's authorization, even if the provider is unaware of the importance or relevance of addressing cultural issues in providing culturally and linguistically competent healthcare services. This will be further discussed in the section where cultural training is discussed. The comments section of this question online presented a few interesting responses worth sharing:

1. *Every time you intervene as an interpreter you enter into a conversation that is not yours and you can impact the way the patient and provider relate to each other, you can become the center of attention and you can derail the flow of the encounter and interfere with what the actual speakers are trying to say to each other* (flow of communication and invisibility of interpreter).

2. *I don't see any disadvantages if the interpreter takes the approach of having the provider and the patient work through the cultural issue and the interpreter supports that process* (invisibility of interpreter).

3. *I risk frustrating either patient or provider if I reveal that I need clarification on a possibly culture based confusion* (flow of communication).

4. *Delaying the time is a consequence, but that can happen with any other clarification the patient could need* (delay).

5. *It takes more time in a crowded hospital when many patients are waiting* (delay).

6. *I don't think any disadvantage overrides the importance of cultural sensitivity.*

7. *None. Because they mostly involve medication, it would be dangerous not to intervene* (patient safety first).

8. *It may cause confusion if interpreter does not know how to address cultural issues effectively. Many times providers believe that interpreters are the culture experts, when in reality it is the patient who is expert in his/her own culture (confusion).*

9. *It may upset and confuse the patient even further* (confusion).

The first two comments speak of how an intervention puts the interpreter at the forefront of the discussion and how this is uncomfortable for an interpreter who has the simultaneous goal of remaining in the background and supporting the provider-patient relationship. The other statements above reiterate some of the options and also relay the primary dangers of an intervention causing a delay, breaking the flow, and causing confusion. It is important to state here that 23 participants responded in the *other* section, stating that they did not see any disadvantage in addressing cultural issues, as this was not listed as a sub-item. This may signal that there is a portion of medical interpreters who believe that there may be no disadvantages to addressing cultural issues, just challenges, which will be discussed in the next section of this chapter. The essay participant did not mention any disadvantages.

Upon reviewing all four data sets, there seems to be a consensus that there are fewer disadvantages than advantages in addressing cultural issues. The main disadvantages were clearly the time delay, the interruption of the flow of communication, and the possibility of the intervention itself causing confusion to either party. These seem to be the clear disadvantages of negative consequences to addressing cultural issues. The time issue is not one under the interpreters' control. However, there are other demands, according to the D-C schema, which can be controlled by the interpreter with skills and strategies that are specific to each case. As stated before, this schema may be very useful for medical interpreters of spoken languages who are not familiar with it, to rely on when making decisions about cultural matters in their work. Training all interpreters in the D-C schema will greatly equip them to handle these challenging situations in the most professional and tactful manner possible. The next section will discuss the results related to the challenges of addressing cultural issues.

4.2.5 Challenges of addressing cultural issues

The participants of this study were asked what the challenges were that they faced when addressing cultural issues. The responses showcase the variety of difficulties and challenges that medical interpreters face when attempting to do their work. Most of the comments related to the providers and how their verbal and non-verbal behavior affects the ability of the interpreter to act as a cultural bridge:

> *If we're looking at staff providers who are ethno-centric and have a view of defense or that everyone has to be treated the same, I know who they are and don't do it because it can create a more hostile environment and not one of mutual understand it.*

The fact that the participant above simply chooses to interject only with providers who are ethno-relative (Bennett, 1993) means that the interpreter is not given the space to address both linguistic and cultural issues. This space is important, as it is the area where the communication is taking place. When the provider does not allow the cultural aspect of the communication to be addressed, through verbal and non-verbal language or behavior, then the space becomes void of cultural competency. It becomes a space only for the provider to discuss what he or she wishes to discuss. A provider who believes everyone has to be treated the same may not appreciate the unique makeup of the patient he or she is treating, and seems to have no understanding of how this makeup may affect the understanding, care, and compliance of such a patient. One interpreter expounds on the concept:

> *Let me tell you something about me as a human being. Some docs assume that parents are not good parents and I have an issue with this, as well as when the perception of the parent with the doctors is negative as well. If you think the parent is not a good parent you start treating the patient differently. This can also happen the other way around. Then the relationship can go down the drain. Parents who are in Medicare or lower fees, they keep going, but don't follow the treatment because of the lack of trust. I have found parents that have a hard time with concise communication, and the parents want the doctor to listen and feel disrespected when the doctor doesn't. Sometimes the questions are not elaborated well and as an interpreter I have to interpret what the provider said, so if you don't want a circular open-ended answer then ask a closed ended question! If you ask HOW the child fell, the parents will elaborate. That is constant.*

There are two issues being addressed in the comment above. First, some providers may not trust their patient's parents' ability to treat their children based on non-compliance. This trust may also be related to not understanding that there are cultural factors that may affect both understanding and compliance of the patient. When there is a cultural and linguistic divide between two people, trust can be an issue, according to this participant. The second issue above revolves around cultural communicative styles. High context cultures tend to have circular communicative styles, whereas low context cultures tend to have linear communicative styles. This poses a clear difference in most intercultural communicative events.

Due to the provider's Q&A diagnostic model and scientific medical culture, providers typically speak with linear communicative style whereas the patients may be using circular communicative style. It seems that the participant doesn't understand why a provider would ask an open-ended question and expect a close-ended response. Sometimes providers ask the interpreter to redirect or get the patient to skip the explanations and go straight to the point. The interpreter will usually ask the provider to ask the patient. However, when the provider asks the patient to get straight to the point, it is seen as rude and erodes the provider-patient therapeutic rapport. Most interpreters are taught that to be culturally sensitive, they must respect different cultural communicative styles, and yet they interpret between direct linear and indirect circular styles often. They see this dilemma constantly; as one stated, *"Hospital staff members, including healthcare providers, dieticians etc., can take care of foreign patients calmly, not upset."*

This statement is alerting to the fact that intercultural care can be challenging and frustrating for providers and that providers can get upset and not be calm, as compared to when they are treating patients they feel more comfortable with. This may signal the need to address cultural training for providers in order for them to feel more comfortable and less stressed when working with patients that are culturally and linguistically diverse. As participants stated:

1.   *If medical providers were more sensitive to the cultural matter, it would be easier to bring the matter up. I would like to add that sometimes it depends on the person at hand—some service providers are more open to cultural gaps. Others are not and they will impose their way of this is how we operate and do it here. I can't advocate at all; I can only clarify what situations I think I can. When they say something that the other party will think is rude, I*

can only convey the message but I cannot change the message, I just make them aware of the situation.

2. *Dr. X, she understands a bit about that, but other doctors don't. She understands the meaning of Zäar. She consults with people in the community and she asks questions that are related to it, so she has better chance to understand and hear the patients. Some doctors are interested but others are not. The doctor I spoke about earlier, Dr. X, she is able to listen, to hear the patient, and reach the issue with the patient. Other doctors think it is rubbish and that it has nothing to do with it, that it is a mental illness; they do not have the patience to listen (Note: Provider name disguised for confidentiality purposes).*

3. *Patient's level of understanding. Provider's understanding of our cultural role.*

4. *I have encountered situations where the provider is more focused on efficiently getting through the call in a timely manner.*

5. *In some instances, the healthcare provider is so worried about following procedures that he/she doesn't care about cultural issues that may affect the care of the patient. I encounter this a lot when the provider is not a U.S.A native. They just stick to a script of their own that many times does not remotely address cultural issues.*

6. *Sometimes providers do not know what to do with the information shared and they simply ignore it.*

7. *Depends on the situation, also, if the provider wants to hear about the cultural issue.*

The first statement denotes that the higher the sensitivity of the provider, the easier it is to address the cultural issue. So here the difficulty rises with the increase of lack of sensitivity of the provider. The second participant statement explains that her ability to intervene will depend on the provider at hand. She is referring to how open the provider is to the cultural divide. The interpreter is acting accordingly and noting that there are cases where she simply may not be able to improve the provider-patient rapport. The third statement again showcases that some providers are more culturally sensitive and aware than others, and that it makes a clear difference in their ability to hear the patient.

> *The personnel perceive that you are staying out of your role. When you address a cultural issue they sometimes feel caught with their pants now, we have new residents every 6 months so that is their reaction. Attendants are*

here for a longer time so they are more open to our cultural suggestions. SWs (Social Workers) get upset as they think it is their role. They do not see us as a cultural bridge or an advocate just as a linguistic bridge.

This comment actually speaks to the misperception of some providers and staff personnel with respect to the role of the medical interpreter. As the participant states, they are only seen as a linguistic bridge, without any say or part in the cultural aspect of the intercultural encounter. Some may feel threatened when they are alerted that they are missing cultural information or that they should know this as part of their role. Others, who have become more accustomed to working with medical interpreters, may be more open to the interpreter's cultural suggestions. This is the first time the term *cultural suggestion* has been used and may connote more than addressing a cultural issue, but actually providing suggestions on how to better serve the culturally diverse patients. According to one interpreter, *"I never have a chance to introduce myself. There is no training for doctors here on how interpreting should work."*

This comment reflects the fact that some providers are not allowing interpreters to even introduce themselves in order to explain how interpreting works. This participant seems intimidated by the provider. However, professionally mature interpreters should have control of what to say about their work, including introducing their role in the medical session. Interpreters may be better served if they always introduce themselves tactfully, and sometimes even forcefully, regardless of whether the provider has simply ignored them and starts to speak to the patient when the interpreter arrives.

It seems some interpreters may feel intimidated, to interrupt a session, to introduce themselves. However, without this action, the interpreter may not be acting in a professional manner. Some healthcare directives from the Joint Commission, for example, requires all working with patients to identify themselves and their role, all in the name of patient safety. Perhaps some interpreters do not feel that their responsibility to introduce themselves is important enough to override the provider's wishes for them not to do so. Most of the times the provider simply is not aware of the importance of the introduction precisely because he or she is not trained on how to work with a professional medical interpreter. More research is needed in this area. The temptation will be to rush through, and coalesce to the providers, need. However, the interpreter has ultimate control of whether or not to follow the tenets of interpreter practice and introduce himself to the patient and the provider appropriately. Without a proper introduction, the interpreter will not be acknowledged as a professional party needed for the intercultural triadic dialogue. One interpreter explained that *"Sometimes providers believe that they are bilingual when they are not, thus, do not value the interpreter's input until confusion happens and we have to intervene."* Other participants seem to work in environments where the institution is more culturally competent:

1. *My place of employment encourages interpreters to bring up any cultural belief that may interfere with treatment or understanding.*
2. *For me the need to intervene is only necessary if the situation requires it. All providers these days have the knowledge about the different cultures and to deal with the patients but that's most of the time.*
3. *Never had any problems when I intervene. Providers, they are always eager to learn about various cultures, and are very respectful towards patients' beliefs and culture.*
4. *The provider is appreciative of the clarification I bring when the issue occurs.*
5. *Hospitals and clinics that I work for are located in Madison, WI, and they also serve as a teaching facility for University of Wisconsin Medical School. In Madison, WI, we do have quite a high amount of foreigners that are here to study, work for University, live here or elderly that reunite with families. In general doctors and medical staff are quite sensitive to patients' backgrounds and are somewhat exposed to various cultures and thus are ready to hear and collaborate with differences.*

The interpreters had varied and diverse opinions about the specific challenges of timing:

1. *I find that addressing the cultural issue offers clarity to the situation and how a person may react during that appointment. The challenge for me is finding an appropriate time to interject and the appropriate vocabulary to match the register and setting for all involved. Cultural mediation is a part of my job as an ASL Interpreter. Sometimes it can be taken care of in the interpretation, and sometimes, additional information to one or both clients is necessary. Deciding which should take place is a challenge.*
2. *Sometimes I feel rushed, like the provider does or sometimes even the patient does not have time and they get easily annoyed when I do this.*

3. *The challenge is whether it is necessary to raise a cultural issue or not and when.*

4. *Cultural issues need to be resolved at the right moment and it comes consequently. It is then the interpreter would intervene and transfer them to a more understandable between the patient and provider.*

5. *Ensuring that intervention doesn't result in an unintended negative outcome . . . time to discern need for intervention vs. letting the situation play out and predict outcomes all while under the pressures of interpreting in the medical encounter.*

6. *It takes time, so sometimes, so it may not be welcomed by the doctor or nurse. Medical personnel are often too rushed or busy to consider there are cultural differences. – I could learn more about medical culture.*

7. *The only challenge I've encountered is to be able to briefly stop the session to insert my comment. Other than that, I have not encountered any challenge so far.*

8. *I have to make a split second decision whether or not to intervene, remaining professional and impartial.*

9. *Sometimes the urgency of the matter (trauma case) doesn't allow for immediate interventions.*

Timing can be a challenge for the interpreter, as it counters the goal of maintaining a seamless flow of communication. Handling and solving demands, that are counter to other equally important demands, is challenging for any professional. Timing of intervention will be further addressed later in this chapter. Another challenge can be selecting the wording to address the issue in a culturally tactful manner:

1. *A challenge is how to avoid offending any party selecting the correct wording.*

2. *The inability of either party to understand the reasoning of the other.*

3. *I prefer to empower the Deaf consumers I work with, to advocate for themselves as opposed to my assuming they cannot discuss their cultural differences with providers directly. Many, however, do not speak up so I do sometimes culturally intervene in subtle ways. I always strive to work in a manner in which not only information is conveyed between provider and patient, but also so that their interpersonal/clinical/therapeutic relationship is fostered. I don't want the focus to be on me as the interpreter, and yet, at times, cultural intervention is necessary. It's a subtle, unique balance*

that I work toward continuously. Over 30 years of professional
experience has brought me wisdom and confidence. But it's still
an ongoing challenge.
4. *My years of experience and judgment come into play, having*
   finesse to mediate cultural differences/issues in an indirect, non-
   confrontational manner.

These statements above denote the high level soft skills needed
to address cultural issues. Finding the right words, being tactful, and
deciding how much to encourage a party to address the issue, and when
to give up and construct and engage in explanatory models of cultural
issues is not something that can be easily done. Discussing cultural issues
in a professional manner requires terminology, knowledge and skills that
are taught to interpreters to varying degrees. Two of the four participants'
comments above mention their years of experience as helpful to gaining
the wisdom and confidence to do it competently. This work is not the
primary or most obvious work of the medical interpreter. It may be,
however, as important as the linguistic work the interpreter provides,
and when interpreters are engaged in cultural matters, they are not just
interpreting the message of others as a conduit for communication, but are
constructing their own professional messages and language, interjecting
professional cultural perspectives and opinions related to the discussion of
the encounter, aimed to assist the matter at hand, and becoming an active
participant in the conversation.

If the interpreter is not as familiar with the patient's cultural background,
this can be a challenge for the medical interpreter. The reality is that the
interpreter can only provide input or even identify certain cultural issues,
if they are indeed familiar with the cultural background of the patient
and the provider. Educating interpreters to equip all with the diversity of
patients they will encounter is as important as educating providers about
the diversity of patients. Likewise, identifying if the situation is cultural
or not may be more challenging than it seems. Maintaining the flow of
communication and not disrupting that flow can also be a challenge:

1. *It is true that sometimes addressing cultural issues takes us away*
   from an important conversation.
2. *The culture of the patient may not be familiar to me when I first*
   encounter someone who is new here in America and I am not
   familiar with his or her country of origin.
3. *The problem is that the barriers may appear to be cultural, but*
   perhaps they are not.

Here is a comment from an over-the-phone interpreter (OPI) showcasing a specific challenge to addressing cultural issues for remote interpreters with no visual cues:

> *I think this issue is very important. I never give up, and try to work through any challenges. The biggest challenge for me as an OPI is that I may not recognize as readily that a cultural issue has come up, since I cannot see body language.*

Focus group participants did not have as much to say about the challenges, but they did speak of the dangers of unqualified individuals addressing cultural issues: *"There can be a problem if the interpreter is biased, like from the culture of the patient. Sometimes, they can have that bias."*

This statement is due to the fact that there are times when interpreters, who have not been acculturated to the local country, enter the field and can only relate with the patient's culture. These untrained and unqualified interpreters have quickly taken the patient's side due to their lack of understanding of medical culture or the way things work in the United States. Two of the focus group participants were also concerned about the ability of the interpreter to remain neutral. Here is a short dialogue to that effect:

1. *You do have to be careful with the role of cultural advocate. You have to be neutral, or what I call 'culturally neutral'. When intervening, you have to preface the information with how you learned that information like, "I lived in Mexico for 5 years, and ..." or, "In this culture, studies show ..."*
2. *It is important that we mention that we are addressing the issues for the patient and the provider, both at the same time, we are helping both, that is what I mean by neutral cultural competency, without personal opinions, but interventions that are professionally based.*
3. *But medicine is not culturally neutral. If something is happening, we need to verify what is going on, and use transparency, and redirect the person in the other direction.*

Online responses on this issue were similar to that of interviewees. Fifteen challenges were listed (based on the interview responses) to see which had the greatest level of agreement with participants. Participants were able to agree with as many statements as they wished and also had a chance to provide comments, as with all the online survey questions. Table

23 shows the level of agreement of each question. As with many questions, they were not required to be answered and could be skipped.

Table 23
Challenges of Addressing Cultural Issues (Survey participants only)

Answer Choices	%
There is no time in the appointment to intervene, so I just interpret.	36.36%
The provider does not want to hear about the patient's culture.	35.95%
The provider does not want me to intervene for any reason.	23.55%
The patient does not want to hear about the country or healthcare culture.	14.05%
The patient does not want me to intervene for any reason.	9.09%
I do not feel equipped to explain the cultural beliefs or values of the patient.	7.85%
I do not feel equipped to explain the cultural beliefs or values of the country of service.	2.89%
I do not feel equipped to explain the cultural beliefs or values of the healthcare system of the patient to the provider.	11.99%
Sometimes it causes more confusion than is helpful to address a cultural issue.	21.49%
Sometimes there is a risk of conflict generated by the cultural discussion, so I avoid it.	13.64%
Sometimes I feel that it is not really that helpful to the provider to address a cultural issue.	10.74%
Sometimes I feel that it is not really that helpful to the patient to address a cultural issue.	10.33%
It is very difficult for the other party to understand the concepts I am trying to explain so I give up.	6.20%
I do not think addressing the cultural issue is that important to my work as an interpreter, so sometimes I do not address it.	4.96%
Other	31.40%

As can be seen above, the top three challenges were the following: (a) lack of time (36.36%); (b) the provider does not want to hear about the patient's culture (35.95%); and (c) the provider does not want me to intervene for any reason (23.55%). The time issue seems to be the greatest challenge to addressing cultural issues, on all data sets. It seems that this issue can be blamed for other aspects of the quality of healthcare, but the fact that an appointment, which relies on consecutive interpreting, requires twice the amount the time, is significant because this has never been discussed or taken into account in medical interpreting research. This challenge will need to be further investigated to see what solutions or cultural adaptations can be made that do not include the provider shortening the level of communication to compensate for the lack of time. This will greatly affect the care received if language minority patients are getting half the time of medical interactions they are paying for.

The second and third highest challenges involved the resistance of providers to the interpreting interjecting or having a voice. These results show that the interpreter has some clear challenges when they are trying to advance the cultural competency in healthcare through their interventions, and yet the providers they are working may provide behaviors and statements that indicate they wish the interpreter to be a voice box only. What they may not understand is that the interpreter cannot be a voice box without the ability to interject questions of clarification to several issues related to the communication at hand, such as grammatical, linguistic, or cultural issues that affect meaning of the message. As stated previously, the percentages of agreement were not high: (a) lack of time (36.36%); (b) the provider does not want to hear about the patient's culture (35.95%); and (c) the provider does not want me to intervene for any reason (23.55%). This means that roughly a third of the participants agreed with these statements of challenges, the majority of participants did not. This means that these challenges, however present, are not significantly high in terms of affecting the majority of medical interpreters with their ability to address cultural issues.

Other comments to this question, as with the interviewee data, included comments about conflicting goals. These include the conflict of following the impartiality and invisibility tenets vs. having a voice and remaining neutral. It also includes the goal of having a seamless flow of communication and having to interrupt that communication to clarify an issue that may be affecting the communication. According to one of the interpreters, there are a myriad of challenges: *"Both parties don't fully understand the job of the interpreter. The code of ethics and the situation at hand are in conflict.*" Another interpreter addressed the organization and communication:

> *Sometimes one has to micromanage the flow of communication in order to get everyone's misplaced assumptions and misunderstandings out in the open. This generally occurs when trust has been breached due to the failure to use an interpreter beforehand. This can be very stressful.*

There are several other cultural-linguistic challenges, according to the interpreters, and they include the following:

1. *Even in the same language not every word has the same meaning in Mexico or El Salvador. These differences we come to learn with experience. A word may be offensive to some of one culture and yet it is a common term in another culture. Also depending on the voice or tone and intonation of utterances, the meaning changes in that sentence.*

2. *You need to relay the cultural phenomena, so you need the examples. It is difficult to translate or explain a term that is culturally bound in Hebrew.*

3. *It may take courage for patient to address cultural issue: after some experiences with labor and delivery of Muslim women, a mother from Muslim country told us that what they say during the labor is not "screaming" but praying, so we should not worry about interpreting those words. And she asked us to just observe if this thing happen to any Muslim women in future.*

4. *People may feel, an interpreter may feel a little self-conscious or insecure as to how to do it or when to do it or if you should do it. Not knowing about a particular tradition, behavior or practice that would be very crucial.*

5. *One of the challenges that happened is that at some point the interpreter steps into the limbo zone. The parent may think we are taking their side or the doctor's side. They may distrust what you are saying because the provider or patient said something that does not seem to make sense. 'Who are you to intervene?' Sometimes it is uncomfortable. There are also many differences between the Spanish speaking cultures, so I need to clarify with the patient first before even addressing the issue, asking for cultural clarification.*

6. *In Japan there are few Muslims so it takes some time for Japanese to understand their habits. Almost all hospitals don't have a prayer room because we don't recognize so much the importance of the prayer.*

7. *Not so much, especially the foreign North Americans; once they find out that I am North American, then they ask me about in Germany we do this what about in America, so I converse to assess their language skills. So many of the cultural issues are addressed there, so they know I can't address all their cultural needs, that they have be their own voice in these issues. It's a challenge for me, if they share with me ahead of me, like outside the office, a little bit about their background, then I know when they speak to the doctor, I know what they are talking about, but if they blurb out some cultural thing that I have not been cued to, I may have to, on rare occasions, I need to ask the patient as I didn't understand what the patient said, and then go over and it solves that whole issue, but it's not pure interpreting as I am sharing what she said vs. interpreting what she said.*

These comments address the same challenges that were addressed by interviewees, where the subtleties of culture can be difficult to explain. The second comment mentions that translating culture-bound terms and concepts need to be paraphrased, and there again, an interpreter has to recreate the message in a manner that makes it clear for those who are not familiar with that concept or message. As stated before, the interpreter does not need to have knowledge of only one culture, but of all the cultures that represent the speakers that they interpret for, which may or may not coincide with the interpreter's own cultural background.

The interviews, focus group, and online survey produced interesting results. There are different challenges that affect the interpreter when addressing cultural issues. The cultural work is difficult, according to participants, as they need to utilize soft skills of facilitation (turn taking and interrupting to clarify and ask if a speaker wishes to clarify an issue) as well as the soft skills of tactful communication about differences of culture, which are in effect differences of opinion or at least worldviews. This may create conflict or confusion and interpreters seem to be aware of that. The conflicting goals in an interaction seem to make the interpreter's work more complex than initially thought of. This study gives light to a part of the interpreters' work that is often invisible and not valued enough by users of the service. Is the medical interpreter a cultural and linguistic mediator to a certain extent, in the healthcare system, or is the interpreter an individual who simply 'interprets' word for word? A participant describes this dilemma very well in this comment: *"The concept that the interpreter should just interpret is unviable. To not intervene at all for anything at any time?"*

Participants have described how their work is truly the work of cultural and linguistic bridges, and mediation is exactly that, being a neutral bridge between two people. This is an aspect of the work of the medical interpreters that requires more research as it addresses the core of the medical interpreter's identity and work.

4.2.6 Strategies of addressing cultural issues.

One of the research questions of this study was to identify the strategies that practitioners are utilizing to address cultural issues. This section will address their responses according to their own perspectives of their work. Participants were very resourceful in providing strategies used. There is no published study or paper that relays the interpreter's thoughts on specific strategies utilized to address the cultural component. This information may help newcomers in the field, as well as interpreter educators to teach these strategies to newcomers in the field. Until the time of this study, there was no previous study that discussed the strategies utilized to address cultural issues. One interpreter discussed body language and debriefing:

> *I will debrief outside the room, but [with] some physicians I just can't. The patients need to feel a willingness. In high context cultures, the body language, all these things that are being communicated, and some cultures are more perceptive than others. A 'hi' across the room is not the same as shaking hands and asking who the family members are, that is what is culturally appropriate. I have to teach by example. Perhaps if the provider sees me do it, they will consider greeting patients in a culturally appropriate manner. It affects the patient's trust. The patient can sense that difference. The patients can evaluate the doctor based on how they were treated rather than on their skills as a healthcare provider. The more they feel comfortable the more they will follow up and do what they need to do.*

Assisting the provider and patient to develop a therapeutic rapport is something that takes finesse and professionalism. Even a culturally competent greeting can have an effect on the rapport, as the first impression is important.

Interpreters can only act according to their parameters as they are understood, yet what they do in their professional behavior, may have an effect on the patient's view of the institution and the care they will receive. The provider may take a cue from the interpreter and consider greeting patients in a manner that is culturally appropriate. Trust has been mentioned many times, and without it there will be a confrontational communication, and not a collaborative one, according to one interpreter. One participant stated:

> Sometimes if I know that the patient has information that I am aware of culturally, I will ask the patient to speak to the health professional, and explain to the provider. Very seldom it happens, but sometimes I have to ask when I feel it will help the provider and the patient. I always speak to both parties.

In this comment above, the participant is stating that asking the patient to speak up is part of her work. Speaking to both parties, signals the participant's commitment to transparency, as one interpreter explained:

> I really believe that the interpreter needs to be sensitive to the cues that the patient or provider is giving, like grimacing, or looking confused, the interpreter needs to be assertive enough to pick up those cues and act on them. Because I train interpreters and observe them when I do assignments, they are hesitant or embarrassed, but I am not, perhaps it is because I'm older. But if I do not understand something I stop and ask. You have to be assertive.

The participant above seems to be describing the professional stance needed to work in this environment. Assertiveness is mentioned twice in the comment, signaling that interrupting a conversation between a provider and a patient, for any reason, requires a certain level of assertiveness and professionalism. Two other comments by different respondents expand on this theme:

> I'm trying to be impartial, so when I'm trying to balance my communication I feel I am stepping out of my role of conduit, but that has to be utilized because I feel that the communication is challenged and we are in an extreme situation, that it would negatively impact the level of service that the patient is receiving. When it is absolutely

*necessary when I feel the explanation will make a big
difference.*

Another respondent emphasized collaboration: "Important thing is
that the both parties make effort to try to understand each other. We have
to be humble that the things we think it is universal is not always common
understanding in other country."

The first comment above speaks to the importance of addressing
cultural issues in an impartial or neutral manner, and shows that it is
possible and that if done correctly there is no conflict with the code of
ethics or the standards of practice. This participant speaks of stepping out
of the role of conduit in order to clarify an issue. This has been the theoretic
framework taught to interpreters, that they can only be in one role at a time,
not realizing that as one may be engaging overtly in one role (conduit), one
may at the same time be assessing a cultural situation (cultural mediator),
even though you are not speaking about it at the moment. The second
speaks to the interpreter's acknowledgement that the parties are the ones
that will need to make an effort to try to understand each other. The reality
is that there will be times when one of the two parties may not understand
the cultural concept easily, or may reject it as not true or not the right way.
There are different ways to interrupt patients, according to the interpreters:

1. *The best strategy is to be very honest. I ask the client to clarify the use
   of the term I am not certain of, just to confirm. I may ask: Please say
   this in a different way, as I don't want to put words into the client's
   mouth. Please rephrase so I understand what you really mean. To
   be very honest, is crucial, the fact is that you need to intervene when
   necessary, it is important that the message is delivered as the client
   meant, not as close as possible, it has to be exact.*
2. *Well, interjecting and stating 'Excuse me, the interpreter… whatever
   it is…" The other one is for example, if the doctor says something
   and the LEP seems completely confused or makes a comment that
   triggers the recognition of something on my part, what I will do is I
   will say 'I believe there is a breakdown in the communication; or 'a
   miscommunication may be taking place'. That would be during the
   session. After the encounter I can also approach them to try to explain
   things in a polite and professional way, so they do not feel less or
   not educated about something, trying to be as professional as you
   can. It boils down to being able to identify when the right moment
   has arisen and not start interjecting in the middle of something but
   waiting for right moment. I think timing is very crucial.*

In the comments above, the participants give cues as to how to interrupt a conversation to interject a professional opinion that a new formulation is required (i.e., please say this in a different way). The second comment also gives script ideas on how to interrupt the conversation to interject, and here the interpreter also discusses that the timing of the intervention needs to be well thought out:

> *I need to explain some information about the culture of the patient. The doctor will give me a perplexed face. I often go outside and ask the patient to go outside to discuss. Or when they have a break I will do it so that the therapeutic rapport improves. I will say, let me tell you what I see as an interpreter, I see this cultural issue interfering with your therapeutic rapport. They want to speak in the hall and I want a more private space. The way questions are asked is so different here than in other cultures and that is an easy thing to correct. I ask the provider to let me clarify with the patient that if it is a cultural thing. Once this happened with the practice of putting a piece of thin thread on the forehead due to hiccup.*

In the description above, the participant gives an example on when an interpreter may call a party to the hallway to have a private discussion with him or her. In the case above the interpreter chose to go outside and have that conversation outside. Some may argue that this is unnecessary, but perhaps the interpreter did not wish to interpret his or her conversation with the provider for a specific reason that we are unaware about. One interpreter explained:

> *When you are a good interpreter you have to have a good sense to try to make yourself part of the other person's inner side. You have to become part of them. If not, you cannot transfer the message. You have to do it in a quick way. You have to know them before you speak. It's not easy but if you can train an interpreter using different people, so that they can see it in action, then that person will do ok. You have to understand the person's feelings too, and situation. In the Asian tradition, these are thousands of years of tradition. All the Asian cultures are somehow tied.*

What the interpreter is saying above is that the interpreter needs to have superior listening skills, to listen to the messages in the context of the intentions of the speaker, in order to be able to reformulate the messages as if they were spoken in the other language, so that the listener understands the message as if it was spoken in their language and culture. The interpreter needs to have the context of the message in order to interpret it correctly. And this needs to be a skill that is learned and done quickly. Emotion is part of intention, and as the IMIA Standards (IMIA & EDC, 2007) state, the interpreter is not only interpreting words but also emotion.

As the dissimilarities between providers' and patients' assumptions increase, however, literal interpretations become inadequate, even dangerous. In such cases, to convey the intent of the message accurately and completely, the interpreter may have to articulate the hidden assumptions or unstated propositions contained within the discourse. Here the role of the interpreter is to assist in uncovering these hidden assumptions, and in doing so, to empower both patient and provider with a broader understanding of each other's culture (IMIA & EDC, 2007, p. 15). As one interpreter explained, *"What I can do is to explain their cultural habits to doctors, nurses etc. In my working hospital they are very generous so they always try to understand them."*

As discussed earlier, whether some agree or not, medical interpreters seem to be filling a need and working as cultural educators. Some believe that interpreters are not cultural experts, and whereas most do not have an anthropology degree, it is clear that they seem to have more cultural information than the providers or hospital staff they are working with, so that is perhaps why they are filling this void. This study will argue that medical interpreters are cultural and linguistic experts to a certain extent, but not cultural anthropologists. Perhaps separate courses and certification in this this area may be needed in order for healthcare organizations to be assured of the level of knowledge and skills medical interpreters have in this area. The level of education that t they are receiving will be further discussed in the training section of this chapter. In the comments below, it seems that the participants are aware of their need to be unobtrusive, yet to ensure that the communication is taking place and that the parties understand each other.

1. *That to me is the art, I don't want to become the focus of what is going on in the room but I want to be sure that the conversation is the best that it can be, recognizing cultural differences, but not trying to fix each one.*

2. *In the debrief, I can also go over some strategies to address the communication better. It really comes with skills, learning about cultures. My way of doing that was going deeper into cultural skills, I used the Intercultural Development Inventory (IDI), by Bennett (1986), which looks at individuals as being ethno-centric or ethno-relative.*

3. *If the provider keeps repeating I think you understand this over and over and the patient just nods, I ask if I can ask a question and ask the patient what the provider said and then I know.*

In the third comment, the interpreter is asking the provider to do a teach-back. A teach-back is the professional communicative strategy to ask the listener to explain what he or she just understood. It is the best mechanism to know exactly to what level the patient has understood. In the United States, providers and hospital staff, including medical interpreters, are being asked to provide teach-back to patients to ensure understanding, a tenet for patient safety by the Joint Commission, an organization that accredits healthcare institutions in the United States and abroad (Joint Commission, 2007, Arocha, 2011). The last comment relates to participants taking it upon themselves to dig deeper in this subject matter, and insinuates that this was not done in the classroom, but on her own study time. The interpreter below reaffirms that each person has a level of cultural competency based on many factors, such as background, empathy, and also contact with diverse patients:

> *There is a lot of learning out there for that in the field of intercultural communication. The more you are around people who are different than you then it is easier to see that you don't do it or believe that, and constantly coming to that awareness, then you can see it and the next step is to learn how to adapt, change the words, it can be more meaningful, it is a long process to develop these types of skills.*

However, another participant said that it is a long process to develop these types of skills. Most experts state that cultural competency is a continuum where one can always grow (Bennett, 1993).

> *I really do not have any strategy as such, but during the consultation I try to, it is more important to be neutral and just say what the doctor says or the parents or patients*

say. I don't really try to step in too much. Sometimes it may not be something some agree with me, but after the consultation in the waiting room I may talk to the parent or family member. I seldom explain anything cultural to the provider.

Neutrality came up in the responses of participants 13 times, and is clearly a concept that they are very familiar and knowledgeable about. Some providers may view asking a provider to explain something to a patient as being outside the scope of the medical interpreter, if the medical interpreter is just viewed as a voice box. As one interpreter recounted, *"I would say ... Dr... In their country, usually they do... or I would say... can you explain... because they may not be familiar with this procedure?"*

According to the data, the vast majority of medical interpreters believe they are there to bridge the cultural and linguistic gap. They may have a greater understanding than the provider, about what the patient may or may not understand, based on their pre-session with the patient or simply the patient's choice of vocabulary and level of language skills during the encounter. Without this information, the provider will not be able to know if an explanation is needed, or helpful or not.

We are told to interpret, so it is hard to have a strategy to ask the physician to say something. He the provider is the one who leads, he is asking the questions. When the food or Zäar issue arises, I only interject if the doctor asks. The doctor will ask me to explain what the food is etc. I only explain, when I am asked, or when there is a misunderstanding that I have to explain.

This participant seems clear on the hierarchy of the session, with the provider being the one who leads the encounter. However, when a facilitator is present in a conversation, in this case it would be the interpreter, the interpreter would actually be the leader of the communication flow, but not of the medical session. This may provide tension between the provider and interpreter, which this interpreter avoids by only interjecting when the doctor asks. One participant explained, *"As a phone interpreter it is more difficult. It is better to interpret face to face to maintain eye contact and analyze the body language; we don't know what is going on in the room. It is better to do it in person."* Another expanded on this theme:

I know if it is appropriate to intervene or explain. The doctor is trying to provide a service but the answer is illogical, so I have to explain the cultural background they believe in, so the doctor understands what is happening. With face to face interpreting, it is easier to react as you see what is happening, you see the patient's gestures, emotions and that provides me more information which facilitates my reaction. With telephonic we only have the verbal information.

The two phone interpreters, who made comments above, as others throughout the study, have mentioned that it is more difficult to engage in their responsibility or task of ensuring understanding via phone interpreting. This is due to the fact that they are not able to see the patient or provider's body language. However, when the information is crucial and must be understood, there are possible verbal strategies, such as teach-back, which can be used by the provider or suggested by the interpreter to ensure understanding regardless of the viewing or not of the ability to view body language. One interpreter talked through her process:

I ask: Is it ok for me to clarify a cultural issue with him? And usually the provider is happy that I am addressing an issue that he may not be able to speak of. It is very important for them not to remove something from their hand, so when they go to surgery they want to remove their bracelet. They are shocked to hear this, but the provider, knowing it cannot be ever removed, may change his mind. When this situation happens I have to intervene, and if it is possible, we adapt to the patient need. This is only in Punjabi. The women wear a knife, this is a specific example, like a sword. Not all, but some strong Punjabis do. It is shocking for the European people here. They lack the cultural understanding. It is a blunt weapon and it is for their protection. These are very common in the Sikh religion. You can't carry that inside the surgery room so we have to explain to those people that sometimes it is necessary to remove or keep under the pillow or on the side, as the sword needs to be with her all the time ... Mostly male, just one female.

When a patient makes such a request, it gives the healthcare organization the opportunity to adapt their service to the needs of the patient. In this case, the interpreter ended up being the go between or mediator of that request, ensuring that the providers understand the reasoning of the patient, and ensuring the patients that the healthcare organization or providers will attempt to heed to the request, but need to work within their constraints.

Another interpreter reflected on the dangers of spending too much time with the patient in a waiting room to avoid patient expectations that go beyond what is professionally accepted:

> *They have these expectations, and because we have a lot of wait time, the hospital asks me not to leave the patient alone, but sometimes I do as I do not want to get too personal, but it helps me assess their ability in English, and because of the things they share I am able to explain that in Japan it doesn't work that way, or I tell the patient that they will have to be the one to initiate that conversation with the doctor, that I will not do it on their behalf, so they know how it will work. So for example in Germany you pay a few weeks later, but in Japan you pay on the time of visit, and then they say it's ok.*

However, the interpreter does use this time to do a cultural and linguistic assessment and provide cultural education to the patient. Other times, being aware of the time investment is important, according to one respondent:

> *Well, usually I let the encounter go on. I won't intervene unless I see that the provider is having problems, or does not understand. I usually handle the cultural issues by interpreting what the patient says, and let the provider find out by listening to what the patient says. I only get involved when I see the situation going around in circles, and then I may intervene. Usually it relates to patients doing things outside the biomedical way of doing things. A good interpreter should allow the doctor to get the information from the doctor. Unless there is no communication going on, there is no understanding, then the interpreter can intervene to get clarification and explain it to the doctor. But if the interpreter keeps interpreting, the misunderstanding*

> *will come out. Doctors aren't dumb: they get it. I think it is*
> *important to have good listening skills and body language,*
> *to have good discernment to know what people are saying*
> *through their body language.*

The strategy of not intervening immediately is an important one. An experienced interpreter, as the one above, will wait to see if a situation or misunderstanding resolves itself between the two parties involved, and only chooses to intervene when the issue is not getting resolved but getting worse. This skill requires finesse and acute awareness of what the issues are. These issues are not being stated but are assumed, based on cultural factors, according to another interpreter:

> *When these situations arise, you can imagine a situation*
> *where there are two people in a dark room who can't see*
> *each and I am trying to link them. Perhaps that person*
> *just immigrated to the U.S. so she is going through*
> *cultural transition, and the provider doesn't know where*
> *Uzbekistan and what the culture is. I know both, I was born*
> *in Uzbekistan, and I have been in the U.S. for 10 years.*
> *Since I have the knowledge of both worlds, I am usually*
> *straightforward. When I see cases where the patient feels*
> *distressed, and she, (most of the times it's a female) and*
> *she is shy and or ashamed, then I step out of my role and I*
> *say 'culturally, let me provide a cultural explanation' and*
> *then I explain. I need to be sure of what I am going to say*
> *before stating it. Please let me explain in Uzbekistan ...*
> *There are other issues, like terminology, there are terms*
> *they can't visualize, as in Uzbekistan they don't have the*
> *advances in technology so for example a simple question,*
> *have you filled a living will, when I translate and say a*
> *document you fill out when you die so they know what to*
> *do, so now they think they may die and are very stressed,*
> *so I have to explain to the provider that the living will is*
> *not usually included in their healthcare, can you provide*
> *an explanation? So my tip is to use common sense, and*
> *if you are sure, then be straightforward and direct. I can*
> *offer the explanation, but ultimately it is the doctor and the*
> *patient who have to decide. So sometimes I ask the doctor*
> *to elaborate more so they have a clear understanding so*
> *they realize what this is about.*

The comment above describes how, after living in the United States for just 10 years, that the interpreter understands both cultures. Regardless of how much or how little he understands of both cultures, and the fact that the provider and the patient are unique individuals with their own cultural makeup, the interpreter is still the person in the room with the most cultural context. His example of the difficulty in translating the term living will goes beyond the need to paraphrase, but also calls for an explanation of how things are done in the United States healthcare system. In most countries one would not discuss a living will unless one is in a life-threatening situation. The stress the patient felt in the example would not be known by the provider unless the interpreter informs both parties to approach this topic with care due to cultural factors.

Focus group participants shared a few strategies. Some were perplexed as they understand addressing a cultural issue as intervening and addressing it, so they were not sure what was meant by strategies. An explanation was given and they were asked what they would say to a newcomer in the field about how to go about addressing cultural issues. This may indicate that medical interpreters are not trained on specific strategies related to interpreting culture. One interpreter responded, "It is important that any intervention to be addressed be interpreted for either party." The other response went into greater detail:

> *The obligation to be transparent in all communication may conflict with a patient's cultural taboo and he or she may feel exposed. Interpreter needs to help build trust towards provider by helping patients understand that this cultural disclosure is part of the medical encounter. Interpreter needs to know when to desist from this if patient is not receptive to this interpreter intervention and let provider know that further conversations may be needed in the future to address a particular topic.*

Transparency is mentioned in these first two comments. It is very important that both parties know what is going on and that the party's wishes are respected at all times. Another comment addressed other considerations: *"I avoid language or behavior that could be offensive to either party."* In this comment, the participant is speaking about using appropriate cultural language and behavior and being culturally competent with all that are served. The IMIA Standards of Practice Tenet B-1 (IMIA & EDC, 2007) further explained this tenet in two parts: (a) observes the rules of cultural etiquette and/or institutional norms (e.g., regarding behavior and language suited to age, gender, hierarchy, status, level of acculturation) appropriate to each party; and (b) adjusts behavior to observe the appropriate rules of cultural etiquette.

The interpreter has to change his or her choice of words or phrasing based on cultural issues. The interpreter has to observe and adjust, in the sense that a culturally competent interpreter will behave and speak differently to people depending on their culture, in order to make them feel more at ease and to establish a rapport and understanding with them.

These comments below discuss the importance of interpreters doing cultural self-assessments and identifying their own biases and challenges in dealing with others who are different. Unless you know what your cultural characteristics are, it would be impossible to recognize a different cultural point of view as culturally bound. Many individuals who have not done self assessments may challenge an idea not realizing that their own belief vs. the other belief has more to do with culture than with their own personal beliefs. Self-study and research are necessary, as most educational programs do not cover this topic in depth. Neutral intercultural mediation is the golden standard, according to participants. One respondent made this suggestion: "*We need to do cultural self-awareness to identify our own biases and them accept them and know how to work them.*" Another added, "*research helps us identify our own biases.*" The other comments were equally illuminating:

1. *It's basically to practice what you are going to say. For example, "This is the interpreter, I would like to tell you... "I ask permission if it needs to be noticed or is important enough to be addressed then I intervene.*

2. *It is important to examine the reactions to see if an intervention is required or needed. Sometimes it is necessary; there is no need to intervene all the time as a way to brag.*

3. *You need to explain what you know but you cannot try to explain what you don't know. Don't take unnecessary time. There is a need to be succinct.*

The last comments speak about working within the time constraints, not to engage in a subject matter unless one is knowledgeable about it, to be attentive to reactions, and to practice interventions so that they can be well presented in a professional manner. Survey participants were given six strategies to mark their agreement level with, and an *Other* field in order to provide other strategies or comments (Table 24). Their responses were as follows:

Table 24

Strategies for Addressing Cultural Issues (Survey participants only)

Answer Choices	%
I include, in my interpreter introduction, that I may need to address a cultural issue.	22.31%
I intervene and mention to both parties that we need to explore a cultural issue that may be occurring and affecting the encounter.	53.69%
I intervene and inform the provider about a value or belief about the patient's culture that is helpful to the provider.	54.51%
I intervene and inform the patient about a value or belief about the healthcare culture that is helpful to the patient.	38.02%
I intervene and inform the patient about a value or belief about the country we live in that is helpful to the patient.	25.21%
Sometimes I do not intervene, but prefer to wait until after the appointment to address a cultural issue with the provider or the patient.	26.86%
Other	8.68%

The top two strategies utilized were related to intervening by informing both parties of the need to explore a cultural issue (53.69%), and to inform the provider about a cultural value or belief (54.51%). It is noteworthy to mention that the other strategies only received agreement levels between 22.31% and 38.02%. This means that participants are not utilizing these strategies liberally and this is surprising when these are all strategies that were mentioned by interviewees. The open-ended responses were reviewed to see if they contained other strategies not mentioned in the list of six strategies given as options. These did include a few other options: "*Sometimes it depends on the case. If I have had exposure to the patient & his care beforehand, it is easier to address their cultural concerns with the provider before the encounter and with the patient & provider after the encounter.*" In this statement, the interpreter can foresee the cultural issue that may take place and address it with the provider. Another participant took a different approach: "*I intervene by re-stating the communication in a culturally appropriate manner and allow all parties to process the information before continuing.*" A third method utilized discretion, according to the interpreter: "*I don't intervene by saying, "I am going to add information now,' or anything so blatant. I interpret the message WITH the unspoken meeting."* In these two statements, the participants are simply using appropriate cultural language by paraphrasing to ensure that the full meaning of the message is maintained in the interpretation, not just the spoken words.

It seems that a reasonable number of strategies were given. However, the online survey responses show a low adherence to those strategies. These are important tools for interpreters to understand how they may address a cultural issue. Perhaps interpreters and the public may think that an interpreter cultural intervention during a medical encounter should be avoided, to ensure the seamless flow of communication. This is perfectly logical, to struggle with two opposing tasks.

4.2.7 Timing of addressing cultural issues.

Interviewee participants were not asked about the timing of cultural interventions. This was not a research question, and was simply added to the online survey. Here are the responses (Table 25):

Table 25
Best Time to Address Cultural Issues (Survey participants only)

Answer Choices	%
Before the medical encounter.	12.70%
During the medical encounter.	60.25%
After the medical encounter.	6.57%
Other	20.08%

As can be seen in the responses, the majority of participants stated it was during the encounter. Perhaps this reflects their practice, even though many interviewees and focus group participants stated that it is best when addressed before or after the encounter, so as to not interrupt the flow of communication unless necessary. However, as discussed earlier, remote and contract interpreters may not have the information or access to approach either party before the encounter is to begin. Some remote interpreters do ask the provider not to hang up, so they do have the option of engaging in a conversation after the encounter; however, the interpreter has no control of whether the patient will or not be present. Comments were enlightening, not because they discussed timing per se, but because participants explained in most comments that it depends on a variety of factors. Here are some of the factors shared by one of the interpreters: *"It depends on the knowledge that the interpreter has of both the patient and provider. Some providers have had more cultural exposure to the patient's specific background than others, and, therefore, understand the patient better."*

It has been stated by other participants that some providers know more than others, and therefore the interventions may decrease as the provider's and patient's knowledge of the other culture increases. Some participants discussed how the severity of the issue, or how it affects the health of the patient, or the encounter, determines if the issue can wait or not until after the appointment. This is reflected in the comments below:

1. *Depends on how addressing the issue will affect the encounter.*
2. *If it's extreme and affecting communication...then during. If it's minor but an opportunity at the end arises, then at the end.*
3. *It depends on the gravity of the issue and also the setting (inpatient vs. outpatient).*
4. *As they arise if needed to provide good patient care, but if not essential, at the end of the consult.*

The issue, of an interpreter requiring permission from a provider to request a clarification, was mentioned by only two participants (0.43%): *"Never unless the provider asks the interpreter,"* and *"any clarification has to be with permission from the client, and as brief as possible."*

Asking the provider to discuss a cultural issue would be very beneficial to reassert the provider's position as the leader of the medical encounter. However, the first participant stated that she would not intervene unless the provider initiates the request. This poses problems to the profession as it goes against the professional standards of practice (IMIA & EDC, 2007) and doesn't address what to do when cultural issues are affecting the communication. The standards of practice include using and adjusting language and behavior to cultural factors, recognizing and addressing those issues (IMIA & EDC, 2007, B-2). It also does not address all the other ways of addressing cultural issues that do not require intervention during an appointment. If neither the provider nor the patient is aware that there is a cultural issue, how are they to resolve it on their own? The second participant states that permission is needed, but doesn't address what to do if the client does not give such permission. Where is the interpreter agency in this perspective? These are only the opinions of two participants, among 458, which indicate that the belief that permission or a request is required represents the views of only 0.43% of participants. Below is a diagram that showcases the domain of each participant of the triadic encounter:

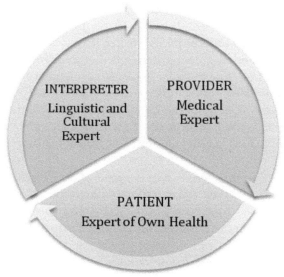

Figure 1. Expertise of each participant in an interpreted communicative event.

Adapted from Margarita Battle's Areas of Power-Clinical Interpreter Training Program. Harvard Community Healthcare Program (HCHP) 1998, with her permission.

In Figure 1, the interpreter is the linguistic and cultural expert. This is due to the fact that the interpreter is the only person that knows two languages and is familiar with two cultures, to whatever extent. Even if the interpreter is not completely familiar with the culture of his or her patient, the interpreter is still the person with the most cultural and linguistic knowledge in the encounter. The interpreter is also the communication facilitator, initiating the introduction and explaining to the parties how to work with the interpreter, providing cues for the other parties to speak and alerting the parties that only one person can speak at a time and intervening when required. Other related domains include positioning in the room, as well which mode to interpret in (simultaneous or consecutive). These are all responsibilities laid out in the IMIA *International standards of practice for medical interpreters* (IMIA & EDC, 2007). The patient is the expert of their own health, being the only person that can provide the other parties with the symptoms felt, the history of the issue, and his or her preferences for treatment. Nobody else can do that for the patient. The provider is the medical expert in identifying the medical issue and relevant treatment. Each party has their own domain of expertise.

In a triadic relationship, the provider loses some ground in terms of decision making of how the appointment discussion will go, when it comes to the communication or flow of the session, it is the interpreter who holds the power. This causes a power struggle sometimes between the provider and the interpreter, and that may be why providers sometimes tell interpreters "just" to interpret, so that they can attempt to control the flow of communication. Unfortunately, when an interpreter relinquishes this power, the interpreter loses control of the flow of communication and the ability to address the nuances, whether cultural or linguistic, may get lost. This would be a great topic for further research to help interpreters and providers work better together. According to the study mentioned earlier, a shared social justice framework provides another opportunity for providers and interpreters to work together, where both can find considerable common ground in their roles of patient advocates, cultural mediators, and social justice workers (Messias, McDowell, & Estrada, 2009).

These participants explained that in medical interpreting each encounter is distinctive so there is no way to generalize when an intervention should occur or even if it should occur, as each case is unique. Some of the responses included the following:

1. *Each encounter is unique; therefore any of the above could apply.*
2. *Again, it depends on the circumstances specific to the situation in question.*
3. *Whenever it comes up - usually during the encounter, but sometimes it is better to do it before or after, depending on the circumstances.*

For telephone interpreters, this is more complicated, as there is usually no pre or post session. There is only the encounter as defined by the caller, as in the comment below. However, the interpreter may ask the parties to stay on the call until the issue is addressed without the stress of mixing it with the previous conversation. Even though an issue is addressed after the main conversation ended, it is still within the call, and if all parties are present, then it is not a new encounter. However, if one party leaves, and the interpreter speaks with the patient or the provider alone before finalizing the call, then another encounter would have started. An encounter is a communicative event that occurs between two or three or more people. Each time a participant changes or leaves, a new encounter commences. The last item brought forward by a participant, in the following comment, relates to the predictability of timing of cultural interventions: *"I only interpret incoming calls. So anything that is addressed will have to be addressed within that call."* Some cultural issues may be predicted, and as the interpreter gains more experience and knows the type of dialogue that will ensure in a particular situation, he or she can alert the provider or patient ahead of time and avoid a difficult situation during the encounter. Likewise, most issues that are related to the healthcare system of the country of care can also be addressed after the encounter, so an interpreter may know before the encounter even starts, that he or she will be giving certain instructions to the patients after. One participant discussed the role of timing in these encounters:

> *For example, when going into a palliative care encounter, it is helpful to brief the provider on any known issues so there is adequate preparation. In these instances, the interpreter would likely be aware of what cultural issues could arise. In the emergency medicine encounter, an intervention during the encounter can allow the provider to proceed with all necessary information at hand. When addressing U.S. healthcare culture with patients, I generally perform that intervention after the encounter and after informing the provider of the intervention.*

The timing of addressing cultural issues is an important one. An issue does not always need to be addressed at the moment it arises, and it may even be intrusive to do so in the middle of an important discussion. The participants shared how they have many tasks at hand that they are preoccupied with prior, during, and after each encounter, and they need to weigh in many factors before deciding what to do, sometimes at the same time that they are interpreting. This showcases the multitasked nature of the medical interpreters practice. Learning different strategies is important for medical interpreters to feel comfortable working in various situations. Professionalism and tact are needed to address cultural issues. Interpreting culture involves assessing cultural backgrounds, conforming and adapting to different cultural norms, acting in a culturally appropriate manner, identifying cultural issues and addressing them before, during, or after an encounter.

4.2.8 Stress of addressing cultural issues.

The interviewees were not asked about the stress level of their work, but this topic came up on the focus group. One member of the focus group mentioned stress. She gave the following statement:

> *There is a lot of stress due to the relationship between the interpreter and the provider. If doing it remotely, not so much with the staff and family, but with providers there is more, particularly if you are in an institution that does not value cultural differences.*

This comment confirms the statement made in the beginning of the study about the difficulties to communicate with someone who does not speak your language, with the assistance of a medical interpreter. Other comments not related to stress did mention providers were sometimes frustrated or even mad, and certainly the loss of control of the communicative process is frustrating indeed. This means that interpreters are not always walking into collaborative and welcoming environments, as some may believe. Sometimes there is great difficulty if a provider does not let interpreters do the work they are being paid to do. Comments about the challenges also referred to the providers' attitude being a challenge sometimes and even affecting the ability of the interpreter to intervene. Therefore, this question about stress was added to the online survey to see if this aspect of addressing culture could be explored further. Here are the results of the survey question (Table 26):

Table 26
Stress Levels Related to Addressing Cultural Issues (Survey participants only)

Answer Choices	%
Extremely stressful	1.65%
Very stressful	5.37%
Somewhat stressful	36.78%
Not very stressful	33.47%
Not at all stressful	19.42%
Other	3.31%

It seems that 43.87% felt addressing culture was *Somewhat* to *Extremely stressful*, with 56.15% stating it was *Not very* (33.61%) or *Not stressful at all* (19.26%). This 43.87% may be considered a high percentage of stress for an activity that is part of the interpreters' work. The *Other* section responses may provide some clarification as to why addressing a cultural issue may be stressful. Of the 15 comments provided, five of them simply said no stress at all, and the other one said "I don't know." The other nine statements are listed below:

1. *It is very stressful, because you want to do it in a way that gets people closer and not apart, and when you want to intervene it's because one party is doing something that is inappropriate culturally, so the communication and treatment really goes well.*

2. *Sometimes I get stuck in a dilemma. Both doctors and patients gave me complaints after the consultation. I was asked to give a message to a patient from a doctor after the consultation.*

3. *It was so stressful for me.*

4. *Feeling empowered in what they are doing vs. being in an organization where they are not part of the healthcare team or supported in that role. People can order a cultural consult and we will go in and help, there are folks that have cultural issues, we assist, to get more guidance to address situations. I think having the knowledge, awareness, and being supportive of your role. If you don't have that support, then you feel that you shouldn't do it or just do it in a limited fashion. Many nurses have an associate degree and they need a bachelor's by 2016, so they are interested now in cultural competency and now feel confident enough to include me in their journeys. I would love to see us get to a point where all providers work from a culturally sensitive point of view and are ethno-relative, but we are not there yet.*

5. *I don't know how stressful. In a way, it is always stressful to interpret between two cultures. But that is my job, and after intensive interpreting I am often exhausted. We always have to make sure that both parties understand each other. So intervention should come naturally and it is our routine work.*

6. *I'm very comfortable being forthcoming with the cultural issues that come up when I need to be. The advantages are huge, but they must know that we all look like Indians, but we come from different cultures. Each person is unique.*

7. *Well, I'm usually stressed, well I think because I have come to experience this more (this person is not from America) when I feel*

I don't understand what they are saying I will basically do flow management, stop the flow and make sure they know it is my issue, that I don't understand a cultural issue, being transparent, and ask for clarification so I can understand to find out what they wish to say and mean, and then I take the floor back to the patient and the doctor.

8. *It's somewhat stressful. Perhaps stressful may be a strong word. It may be less comfortable; it is a bit uncomfortable. I am more comfortable as a conduit, as it is not me speaking, I am just interpreting. When I am a culture broker it is I who speaks, I am the one communicating, but I am a trying to improve the services for the patient.*

9. *One way to cope with the stress of our work is to be able to debrief with supervision.*

There are several interesting statements above that merit further discussion. The first statement infers that on occasion the intervention may be due to a behavior or statement of one of the parties that may be culturally inappropriate. In such a case, an intervention has to be very tactful as to not to make the party feel inadequate. If one of the parties is not understanding and needs a message to be rephrased so that it is more culturally appropriate, an intervention may make that individual have a difficult time. When a patient goes to the doctor, there is already a certain level of stress due to their symptoms or disease. Providers can be uncomfortable with the inability to communicate and need to rely on a medical interpreter. Any lack of understanding by either party may cause stress and that carries on to the work of medical interpreters. The second to last statement also brings to the forefront the fact that when an interpreter is acting as a conduit, or interpreting language back and forth, the interpreter is reformulating other people's messages. When interpreters have to intervene, for whatever reason, they become more visible participants. The interpreters have to have self-agency and speak for themselves as linguistic and cultural professionals to the other parties.

This is not something that interpreting courses can focus on in a short 40-hour course. Most programs focus on the act of interpreting, with little time to address the other roles or tasks of a medical interpreter. This seems to be why Canadian trainers added the caveat of not acting as a cultural advocate, based on their own statement. The last statement provides for a strategy to deal with the stress interpreters feel in their work in general, and probably refers to stressful encounters not only due to a cultural issue but perhaps due to the content of the discussion and gravity of the situation (e.g., end of life discussions, pediatric cancer, confrontational encounters, rape, etc.). There are several studies that discussed the vicarious trauma to medical interpreters due to their proximity to very stressful situations. In conclusion, increased training in this subject is very needed in order to diminish the level of stress interpreters are feeling when engaging in interpreting culture and addressing cultural issues. This topic of education will be addressed further in the next section.

4.2.9   Education received on addressing cultural issues.

Most interpreting programs address culture in their curriculum. However, as stated before, there are many medical interpreters whose education is limited to an intensive forty-hour course. In order to practice and be competent, interpreters need to learn the following topics: medical terminology, consecutive interpreting, sight translation, simultaneous interpreting, note taking, code of ethics, standards of practice, intercultural communication, overview of healthcare system, interpreter roles and tasks, interpreting in different medical areas (e.g., emergency, maternity, oncology, genetic counseling, inpatient, etc.), patient safety, interpreter safety, and more. Due to the limited time of instruction, the interpreter will be lucky to get some terminology, consecutive interpreting, and the code of ethics. Most courses spend the majority of the hours or at least 15 of the 40 hours in consecutive interpreting practice. Otherwise graduates would come out without any ability to interpret consecutively, the most core function of an interpreter. A recent study stated that trained interpreters were more accurate whether they provided services in person or by videoconference. Errors were about twice as common in visits with ad hoc interpreters: 54%, compared to 25% with trained interpreters. These differences remained statistically significant after adjustment for other patient- and visit-related factors (Wolters Kluwers Health, 2015). The fact that trained interpreters are making errors on 25% of their visits is troubling for patient safety. Increasing the education of medical interpreters will certainly reduce the number of interpreting errors. No study has measured the performance of medical interpreters in addressing cultural issues against the standards of practice for the profession. The other topics may be touched upon for an hour or a few hours at the most. This can be verified in the curricula of the courses listed in the International Medical Interpreter Association's Educational Registry at http://www.imiaweb.org/education/trainingnotices.asp.

Those interpreters that were educated in multi-course educational programs at universities have access to a more in-depth program and probably had a course on intercultural communication, as per the listings in the IMIA Educational Registry. Below are some of the comments from interviewees related to the question of whether the participant received enough training on this subject. The first interviewee had an impressive background in this area:

Appropriate, I got a BA in anthropology with a focus in applied anthropology in the medical paradigm. I was trained by and under very highly qualified persons with Doctorates – but most interpreters do not get enough. The training I received as a medical interpreter was cursory and old school, focusing on general health beliefs of a large ethnic group. It was useful, but far from complete. Cultural competency training on specific groups is uncommon among Sign language interpreters—and should be encouraged. Lack of understanding—I did not learn anything new and I believe a linguist should understand cultural issues through language. Understanding language deeply means you understand the perception and ideology of the given culture. Continuous learning is crucial in this area.

This participant above had a bachelor's degree in anthropology and as such seemed to get more education on the subject than most interpreters. However, a bachelor's degree in anthropology will not teach an interpreter the practicalities, limits, and factors that are relevant to know how to address cultural issues in an interpreted medical encounter. The participant above also described that the education she received in the interpreter course she attended was not in depth. Teaching general concepts of health by ethnicity can actually incentivize the stereotyping of patients. Another participant gave another perspective:

I think I was trained. As a matter of fact, after the 40-hour course, not more than 2 weeks after, I can't recall the specific situation, but one of things that I was taught came to be in my interpretation session and I knew exactly how to handle it. I would have to say that the best training unfortunately is the real life experience. No matter how many books, classes and trainings you take, until you get into the pool, you can't really start swimming. I am a firm believer that the real world is what gives us the visual experience to better understand, 'ok there is a misconception here' there is a misunderstanding here, with all said, if you pay attention whether you go through certification or other seminars, you can get a lot of valuable tips and education. Specifically, in the certification process I think there could be a little more training in that aspect, not too much as it can be overwhelming, but yeah at least cover it a little more—I think it is up to each individual to strengthen their knowledge and grow their knowledge of the different cultures that he or she will be dealing with. Through watching videos, talking to colleagues, but I think that it is very important that we understand where our interventions can begin or where they shouldn't begin, because I think that if we look simply at the code of ethics black and white, our role is very clear, and only, and only, I think, when a cultural issue will hinder the communication those are the only times when we should intervene, or obviously if there is danger.

This participant above mentioned the fact that even within 40 hours he obtained tips that were useful. However, interpreting is a practice profession, and as such that it is difficult to teach this topic in the classroom and he also states that it was not enough. Last he tried to explain that cultural competency is individualized and that self-study is part of the process of professional development in this area. Another interpreter complained about the fact that she did not get any training from the interpreting course:

I didn't get it from the interpreting course. I teach courses on working with children of different cultures, and counseling the multicultural client (university prepares school counselors) and so I have a little more knowledge and skills and I learned to put my poker face when needed. As an interpreter I never received any of that. Once the provider asked a question five times, and at the 6th time, I stated to the provider, you have asked this five times; we need to respect the wishes. I have two bachelor's degrees, two master's degrees, and a PhD. Most interpreters will not be as assertive or consistent because of their own professional development. I do believe that those letters by your name do give you credibility. People know who I am now and respect me as a professional. When I speak to them they do not challenge me, I have the background to be a team worker and can I have more education than many of the people I work with and that gives me more validity of my behaviors as a medical interpreter. My education is as follows: bachelors in elementary school; a second bachelor in psychology (childhood trauma), a master's in early childhood education (concentration in guidance) and a PhD in early childhood education—(education research).

This interpreter above explained that all of her training on this topic was done through her impressive academic education and credentials. She is a staff interpreter who does act as a cultural consultant and mediator as needed, even outside her medical encounters, according to her interview. Some may question an interpreter's ability to act as a cultural consultant. Their ability and skills will depend greatly from their own educational and life experience and background, and not only their interpreting training or education. The following participants share how their training on cultural issues did not seem to be sufficient.

I don't think it was at all sufficient; I definitely think this training would be great. There are a lot of possibilities out there. There are folks that are experts in this area. The intercultural communication field is large, and using this would be great for medical interpreters. One of the interviews I had for my thesis, my interviewee said that everything that we learn and how we see these differences comes into play. I think the IDI is a really good tool, as the feedback gives you where you perceive yourself to be and where you are exactly, which is a bit of a slap in the face and a reality check. I can't know everything there is to know about this and that culture, like distances, people are so much more rich than just that.

Another participant expanded on this theme, looking at her own educational experiences and job functions:

I don't know where you draw the line to know if there was enough training or not. I have received training, webinars, which covered the very basics, and of course it was helpful. Each situation is very different. Webinars tend to cover the culture of Hispanics and not Japanese patients. There are not that many Japanese patients in the United States, especially in the East Coast. Most of my assignments are business related, for pharmaceutical and medical device companies. I go to do medical appointments once, twice, or three times a month or maybe 50 times a year. It has been almost 20 years but the number of encounters under my belt is not huge. I do face-to-face mainly. I am very busy. I have done telephonic but almost none.

The next respondent continued in that vein: "*There are so many cultural issues so it would be better that there are programs where we can learn more examples and more stories which include mistakes and failures in each situation, so that, we can learn from them and be better prepared.*"

Another respondent pointed out ways the education and training could possibly be improved upon for interpreters:

I really appreciate the things I have learned, but definitely culture is not really well addressed, and maybe it's because there is an assumption that anyone who takes the course will work in a U.S. setting, and you will have an occasional person like myself, because we prefer the training in English or we happen to be there, or the reputation of training may be more reputable to that of our own country, the programs only seem to assume that we will be interpreting from one particular culture in the U.S. setting and not explore the possibilities that we will deal with individuals from other cultures. Like Spanish includes those from Spain, Mexico, and other countries, I wish they could address this more. If we treat all Hispanics as the same, there is the danger of stereotyping. I don't think people are always aware.

The interpreters above shared that culture was addressed in their basic training, yet more was needed in order to equip them to be more effective in this area. However, participants seemed to understand that all of their goals are interrelated and bridging the cultural gap is but one of many goals. Participants mentioned cultural diversity, as something that needs to be better understood. As they stated, generalizing populations as Hispanic or Asian may not be in the best interest of culturally appropriate patient care. This comment speaks to understanding the patient culture based on experience.

> *I think the fact that I am Latina, even though I was a heritage speaker, I was brought up in a Latino household, so from experience I learned different things. Perhaps an Anglo wouldn't have as much information as I do. It's hard as most of it is learned through life experience.*

According to participants, most of one's cultural knowledge is gained through tacit learning, through experience living in another country, or being raised with cultural values other than the country one lives in. Unfortunately, not all interpreters have or can travel or live abroad. Personal knowledge, therefore, is not enough. Professional interpreters need to understand cultural issues from a more theoretical point of view so that they can describe these differences based on intercultural explanatory models, such as that of Bennett (1993) or Hall (1989). Without learning these concepts, they will be bound to explanatory models that rely on personal experiences and language and not utilizing professionally known cultural terms.

One participant above spoke to the fact that cultural knowledge and skills are complex and that there cannot be strict rules on what to do in each scenario since every encounter is unique:

> *If the guidelines are too strict if the patient says this then do this, you can't create rules for every situation. You have to use your common sense. If you are going to use that right to become a cultural broker, will that improve the communication of the parties? You can have general rules but there will always be exceptions.*

There was one participant who seemed to be the only interviewee who believes she had enough training on this subject matter.

> *I loved my training and they are the best in New Zealand. When we were studying we covered a special area on culture, we had different people doing workshops about different cultures. When it comes to culture, providers are very behind us on this. It is hard to calculate but I can tell you how the training is for us: once a week for 3 hours for 1 year to become a liaison interpreter. For advanced certification we*

> *have to do this for a whole year in three semesters. NAATI*
> *workshops too: We do 5-6 hours each year to sit for exams,*
> *or we do 3 months of full-time training.*

Only three focus group participants had something to say about their training on cultural issues. The three discussed how training has not yet been standardized and varies greatly. One participant explained that interpreters couldn't be considered as cultural experts when some only receive 3 hours of training. However, as we have seen in other participant stories, interpreters do not have to be experts to assist as intercultural mediators, and there are other ways in which interpreters gain that knowledge, and this can be through self-study, travel, or living abroad, or even studying the topic academically. The CMIE *Educational standards for medical interpreting* (2014) do suggest longer training may be needed for medical interpreters, and that the 40-hour minimum training is simply not enough. Until certifying bodies do not require more training, medical interpreters will be undertrained in this area. The Canadian *standards addendum* (HIN, 2007) acknowledged that where training is limited, it is impossible to cover this topic adequately. The last participant below speaks as to the importance of practicums in interpreter education. Some academic and non-academic programs do offer and some even require practicums, but the difficulty of finding host organizations that have the capacity and infrastructure to support practicums has made this a slow practice to become implemented in interpreter education. Respondents had various reactions to this trend:

1. *Medical interpreters receive training in the area of cultural competency to varying degrees. Others do not, as training availability varies widely worldwide and medical interpreter training and education is still unregulated by the government in most countries.*
2. *I received 3 hours of training on this. Often medical interpreters are considered like cultural anthropologists, like experts. Yet the interpreters need help, as they are not experts in culture. Role-plays and scenarios that are cultural can be helpful in training.*

Many consider medical interpreting a practice profession, and as such we need practical supervision, such as a supervised practicum as in other health professions. As the understanding of the profession increases, supervised practicums will become the norm, as with other healthcare-related professions.

Table 27

Did You Receive Enough Training to Address Cultural Issues? (Survey participants only)

Answer Choices	%
Yes	37.70%
No	30.74%
Don't know	18.85%
Other	12.70%

According to the responses, the affirmative answer received the highest concordance, yet it was not the majority of the participants (37.70%). There were also 30.74% who did not agree with this statement. A large percentage of participants did not know (18.85%), and another large percentage of participants (12.70%) decided to answer in the comments section in the *Other* category. There were 31 comments. Of those 31 comments, nine stated they did not learn enough, and 11 comments were related to how they are receiving the education through continuing education. Here are some of the comments:

1. *I would like training on this topic being that I may not know key things that are pertinent during an interpreting session.*
2. *As a trainee, I definitely did not receive enough information or adequate explicit training on mediation skills and the how and when to intervene for cultural reasons. The training I received was the first kind we got in this field, highly interventionist and putting the burden on the interpreter to fix cultural problems and explain cultural information in a way that took the voice away from the speakers. As a trainer, I have had to undo that training and learn how to train others in less interventionist techniques that prioritize the autonomy of the communication between the parties and minimize the disruption I cause as an interpreter.*
3. *I don't think I received "enough" training but the years of practice have given me the experience to decide when and how to intervene.*
4. *Never have received training for this*
5. *There is always a need for more clarification*
6. *I did not receive enough training in my interpreter-training course. But I feel I have sought out information outside the course to support my work as an interpreter (self-study).*

7. *ASL interpreters have 4 years of full time study. Two years are strictly to become fluent and culturally competent with a variety of Deaf persons. However, we don't have much access to formal study in the specialties like medical interpreting. It's a trial-by-error process and we try to pass on our knowledge informally to each other.*

One respondent explained that the approach of her training (high interventionism, as she calls it) is different from the approach she uses (low interventionism): *"Since I do interpreter training, I feel comfortable confronting the issue if I need to, but a 40-hour training is not enough time to equip novice interpreters."* This only confirms that some interpreters have a preference for low intervention whereas others prefer to intervene more. The question is when it is necessary. Participants described they will intervene when it is affecting the communication. One interpreter may believe that the issue is not affecting communication, and another may believe and determine that it is, so the determination of what affects the communication is a relative interpretation that may vary depending on the interpreter's approach (conservative vs. liberal). Interpreters seem to have the professional agency to make that determination in each unique encounter. A few interpreters spoke of the fact that cultural sensitivity is not easily learned in the classroom:

1. *I don't think it's possible to know all the possible cultural issues that could arise.*
2. *Though I hold a master of arts in intercultural studies and have understood enough about what culture is even since I was in high school, I believe I know enough about it to understand that while I do know a lot about it, I don't know everything and therefore when I need to stop and educate myself in an area.*
3. *Too much black and white training. Cultural sensitivities cannot be addresses by a book or even a training, seminar. Cultural sensitivities are either understood based on previous experiences in encounters with the public in general or within an organized setting and based on those cultural encounters issues that arise can be competently addressed by the language professional*
4. *I belong to intercultural medical associations; we have conferences, role playing education for health workers. In the U.S.A we have Native Americans, rural, gypsies, Afro communities, that even they are not LEP, some cannot read or write and in my hospital U.S. interpreters also work with them. The key is self-educating.*

5. *I believe I have, but necessarily during interpreting training. Life experiences such as traveling and interacting in multicultural environments have enhanced my cultural awareness and competence.*

6. *I don't think this is a matter of training. It's part of your general knowledge.*

7. *Not from my training but from my personal experience.*

8. *Yes, but this is never done!!!!!*

9. *Cultural issues are so diverse and intertwined with regions and levels of education that to label one training as such is to have be short sighted.*

10. *Unfortunately, I do not feel there is a book of rules about solving cultural misunderstandings; it is mostly a matter of practice and life experience.*

11. *Probably not, but I do have a lot of personal background experience.*

12. *I know the culture, but for interpreters who are English Speaking there should be a little more information in regard to the culture of LEP patients they are interpreting for.*

13. *I relay a lot on my own experience living in different countries and sharing their culture and language than on training material.*

These interpreters were very clear on the fact that most of their learning has been achieved through life experience, work experience, and self-study. They also mention that it is a work that is never accomplished as one can learn more and that in effect one is never completely culturally competent, but can rather have a high level of competency. However, the majority is speaking of their patient's culture(s) and not of the other cultures that also influence the medical encounter, such as medical culture, or the organization's culture and level of cultural competence.

There were two other questions that were only asked of online survey participants (Table 28 and Table 29). These involved asking interpreters if they received training on the patients' culture(s), and if they received training on the medical culture.

Table 28
Did You Receive Specific Training on the Patients' Culture(s)? (Survey participants only)

Answer Choices	%
Yes	44.78%
No	55.22%

Table 29
Did You Receive Specific Training on the Medical Culture? (Survey participants only)

Answer Choices	%
Yes	56.76%
No	43.24%

This data is quite surprising, as it seems that almost half of the respondents have not received any training in either the patient's culture(s) or the medical culture. It seems evident that medical interpreters are simply not receiving enough information about these topics. Whereas several interpreters are from the culture of some patients they serve, clearly providing them with more in-depth information and skills about interpreting culture in a medical setting will be useful to their practice.

The last question asked of the survey participants was whether they had any other comments about addressing culture issues. These were some of the options given:

(a) I believe we need a white paper or guide on this topic in the field. (12.77%)
(b) This could be useful information for the future training of medical interpreters. (51.91%)
(c) I hope we see more on this controversial topic. (22.13%)
(d) Other (13.19%)

The comments shed more light to the topic of the study. The first set of comments relates to the need for more training on this topic:

> *This is still one of the most difficult and under or misaddressed issues in our field. Interpreters don't receive enough training in general and definitely not in the process of becoming culturally aware enough of our own cultural biases and responses first to then be able to filter those out and address any culture issue that needs attention in the communication between provider and patient.*

Medical interpreting is only partly addressed by training interpreters in modes and terminology and knowledge about the healthcare system. In healthcare settings, decision-making is just as important, especially the specific mechanics of how we behave when we do decide to step out of the interpreting role and intervene for some reason:

1. *More education and training will only serve to benefit those of us in the field.*
2. *We need in the U.S.A to think of LEP not based on their language but where they come from, because cultures are very different for people from Central America, each South American, PR, Cuba, etc. They cannot be lumped together, also educate about indigenous populations, there are many books related to health with this population.*
3. *Culture is ever changing there's a need for continuous training*
4. *Training on cultures on both sides a must! Training on dealing with difficult subjects within different communities.*
5. *Addressing cultural issues during the session requires tact, diplomacy and should be apply only for the benefit of proper communication.*
6. *We need more written about the topic of HOW to be a culture broker. A white paper based on the assumption that the interpreter is a respected and valued member of the healthcare TEAM.*

The comments above speak of the need for a more articulate and sophisticated level of training in cultural competency. Since there are no standards for the qualifications of individuals teaching interpreting, intercultural communication is a topic that is not necessarily taught by someone who is specifically educated in this area any more than most medical interpreters are. Even those trainers and educators who have taken a Train the Trainer course could not have covered teaching this topic in detail, since these trainings are intensive 40-hour trainings. These programs attempt to teach an interpreter everything they need to know to teach interpreting in 40 hours. There is not only a need for more training in this area, but mostly that interpreters be trained using the standards of practice available for the profession. In addition, there is a strong need for educational materials in this area. To this date there is no comprehensive educational material for interpreters to learn to interpret culture, which would cover interventions, timing, strategies, and more specifics on how to handle these. The only materials available are case studies of a cultural dilemmas, or stereotypical descriptions of large minority groups.

The need for further research was brought up by one of the participants, specifically learning about the providers' and patients' perspectives: "*Provider input on topic is also essential.*" Another participant continued more in-depth:

> We need more formal research and study on the topic, as well as consistency in expectations regarding the interpreter's role in this regard. Interpreters need more training on best practices on interventions: how do to so, when to do so, all while keeping in the scope of practice and not creating more harm by applying generalizations to individuals, especially when the generalization may not apply. "Do no harm" applies to medical interpreters as well.

The following comments below refer to the importance of all the different stakeholders in a healthcare setting environment learning about cultural competency. Medical interpreters tend to be the most culturally aware and competent in the healthcare organization, and yet they realize that all who have contact with the patient need to become culturally competent in order for care to be truly patient-centered:

1. *Cultural differences and issues are very important in every aspect of life. It is more so important in medical field. Not knowing or underestimating cultural differences can bring unfortunate results in medical treatments. Not only interpreters, but all employees should be getting an appropriate training.*
2. *We need a white paper, or a series of papers that explain cultural barriers to communication as part of the larger network of social determinants of health, and highlight the necessity of controlling them effectively as a means to improve patient safety, patient experience and health outcomes. I'd be willing to collaborate in such an effort.*

3. *I think providers have learned a lot and still have to learn a lot more about cultural competency. Technology for example is of great help, but those doctors using laptops all the time should take time to look at the patient once in a while...just an example.*

4. *There should be education of both interpreters and medical staff, pointing out the value of such intervention (interpreting agencies also, if they see this as an undesirable practice).*

5. *I think the healthcare system can only do better in being regularly and properly educated about language, culture and how both are powerful factors in the quality of care patients may receive.*

6. *Japanese medical providers are either very helpful and cooperative to foreign patients relating to cultural issues, or they refuse completely and don't even open their doors by making various excuses. Of course for people trying to build a good system where multicultural understanding is available at any medical facilities, it must be essential to educate all that are involved. But as an interpreter at service right now, I would only try to guide the foreign patients to the former type of medical institutions since at our service the first contact from the patients will often be "Will you find for me a medical facility for so and so symptoms?" Since where I belong is not a hospital, but a volunteer group, this is what I do.*

7. *I understand the provider's concerns, but I feel most definitely that the tendency of some providers to suppress interpreters' cultural facilitation interventions is just a gross disservice to the whole system. If that is what they really want, tell them to get a computer translation. Most definitely, more discussion is needed about this topic.*

The last two comments above speak to the fact that some providers are far from being culturally competent, to the point of not allowing the interpreter the room to practice cultural facilitation. Suppression is a strong word, yet the data shows that on several occasions interpreters have spoken about how they have been instructed only to intervene if the provider allows or instructs them to do so. Others have shared how the provider's lack of understanding in this area limits their ability to provide culturally appropriate services:

1. *What I have learned in all this years, is that every person, every encounter, every culture is unique. We just have to be human, be professionals, be connected without taking sides.*

2. *This is part and parcel of our work: an integral part.*

The comments above relate to the fact that interpreting culture is an integral part of the interpreter's work, and the practitioner aspect of the work means that interpreters have to make decisions on the spot based on the unique circumstances of each case. Standards of practices and guidelines need to be consistent for medical interpreters working in North America. At present, the Canadian guidelines and the standards and those of United States and IMIA on cultural advocacy are not the same.

The last comment speaks to the fact that there are differences of approach between the standards of practice. Earlier in the study, all standards of practice were discussed and compared and clearly all but the Canadian address culture in a more comprehensive way. Even the Canadian standard admits that interpreters must convey cultural nuances. However, it is followed by the caveat "without engaging in the cultural advocate role" (HIN, 2007, p.19) Therefore, it is recommended that this ambiguity in the Canadian standards need to be reviewed. The IMIA Standards are international and have already been adopted internationally, to a certain extent, in the countries where the standards are available in that language (Spain, Italy, Brazil, Japan, and Israel). As more languages become available, greater adherence to a more comprehensive scope of work may be seen.

Chapter Five

COMPARATIVE ANALYSIS

This chapter will include a comparative analysis of the survey data against certain variables, such as gender, general education, interpreter education, certification, years of experience, and country of practice of respondents. Since most of this demographic data (except gender and age) were asked only of the survey participants, the comparisons will be made of the survey participants, and not the others. It is important to review whether or not these variables affected the quantitative results, which may shed some light as to why interpreters think the way they do, and whether these variables may affect their beliefs and behaviors related to interpreting culture.

5.1 Gender

As stipulated before, survey participants were 81.07% female participants, and 18.13% were male. Are women more in tune with cultural issues than men? Are opinions going to differ on this research topic? Since the focus group and interviews involve only qualitative data, it is less evident if there are strong differences, so this comparative analysis section will compare only the survey results.

According to the data, there is no significant variation of the gender data with other demographic data, which includes the following areas: age, general education, interpreter training, and professional experience. There were slight variations with regards to highest level of education, as

8.06% of male interpreters had a doctorate degree vs. 3.16% for the female participants. Female participants had a slightly higher certification quota, with 49.25% of male participants stating they were certified as medical interpreters, vs. 64.97% of females. There were other areas where there was no significant variation, such as the importance or timing of addressing cultural differences, as well as strategies, challenges, advantages or disadvantages. The data is remarkably similar.

There are areas of opinion that show some variation. For example, male participants seem to be more confident in their intercultural abilities as they reported higher percentages of feeling *Extremely knowledgeable* of patient and medical cultures (46.03% and 44.44% respectively) vs. female participants who reported lower percentages (37.77% and 25.18% respectively) for the same question. Likewise, when asked if they received specialized training in the same topics (patient culture(s) and medical culture) male participants reported higher margins (57.14% and 59.68%) vs. female participants, who reported lower margins for the same question, (41.73% and 55.96%). When participants were asked when to intervene, male participants reported different margins for two possible responses, one being conservative following the invisibility model: (a) the interpreter should intervene only when there is a communication problem (77.78% male participants vs. 66.33% female participants), and one that is more liberal, and (b) allowing the interpreter to intervene whenever there is a cultural issue (42.22% male participants vs. 55% female participants). These data suggest that male interpreters may be more reluctant to intervene than female interpreters. This is congruent with general stereotypes of males being more objective than females, and cultural issues entail more subjective qualities, rather than objective qualities.

5.2 General Education

The data was divided into two groups: interpreters with a bachelor's degree or higher, (here called graduates), and interpreters without a bachelor's degree (here called undergraduates) to see if there are any differences of opinion between these two groups. There were no significant differences in all other demographic areas. There were also no significant differences in certain aspects of interpreting culture, such as importance, frequency, advantages, disadvantages, and timing, or level of confidence in their knowledge of patient or medical culture. Small differences in data were noticed in the perceived confidence in the intercultural skills of addressing cultural issues. The situations to intervene and the stress related to cultural intervention also denoted differences of opinion between the two groups.

Graduates had a higher level of certification (49.42%), when compared to non-graduates (37.35%), although both certification programs for medical interpreters do not require a bachelor's degree in order to get certified. When asked about their knowledge of the patient cultural group(s) and medical culture, graduates and undergraduates were equally confident. When asked about their training in medical culture, there was practically no difference (56.20% for graduates vs. 56.63% for undergraduates). However, when asked about their training in patient culture(s), more graduates reported receiving such training (46.31%) vs. undergraduates (38.55%). The perceived competence in the intercultural skillset of addressing cultural issues was lower among the graduate group when answering if they were *Extremely* or *Very competent* (79.22%) vs. the undergraduates (86.41%). However, when asked how stressful intervening for cultural reasons was, graduates reported less stress, with 43.82% reporting *Some* to *Extreme stress*, compared to 50.01% of undergraduates.

Differences in when to intervene included conflictive data. Some of the questions were conservative (only intervene in very specific situations) and other statements were liberal (intervene every time there is a cultural issue), indicating a wide range of approaches in both educational groups. Of all participants, 3.13% of graduates related that one *should almost never intervene for cultural issues,* (conservative view) whereas 6.90% answered the same in the undergraduate group. When comparing the data regarding the statement that one should *intervene only when there is a communication barrier,* (conservative), 70.22% of graduates answered this in the affirmative, and only 62.07% of undergraduates did. When asked if interpreters should intervene when it affects the healthcare of the patient, (liberal) graduates agreed 50.56% of the time, compared to 37.93% undergraduates who agreed with this statement. Last, when given a statement that they should intervene whenever he/she notices a cultural issue, for whatever reason (liberal), 49.44% of graduates agreed, with even more undergraduates agreeing (65.52%). These were all similar results to the general population. In conclusion, the differences between graduates and non-graduates are not very significant.

5.3 Interpreter Education

Medical interpreter education varies by region and is not regulated. There are multiple opportunities to get educated on the intricacies of medical interpreting. Some interpreters attend an intensive course to practice, and others undergo a multi-course educational program at a college or university. Others simply attend workshops at conferences, and some have higher levels of interpreting education, such as a bachelor's, master's, or PhD in interpretation. Because of this widely distributed variation in educational opportunities, this study planned to compare participants with academic vs. non-academic education, and those with fewer than 100 hours of specialized training in medical interpreting, vs. those with more than 100 hours of specialized training.

5.3.1 Academic vs. non-academic education.

Interpreter education varies significantly between countries and regions, and as stated before, the spread of types of education included these three major categories: 31.16% had certificates of education in one medical interpreting course, whereas; 16.43% had attained multi-course medical interpreting certificates, and 16.15% had been educated through conferences and workshops. Since the data is too distributed among many different categories, and could be academic and non-academic, it was not possible to compare or group these results in any significant manner. More research is needed in this area, as most professionalization efforts involve the move to a more academic professional development.

5.3.2 Participants with fewer vs. greater than 100 hours of instruction.

The study also asked participants the question of how many hours of specialized medical interpreter education they had received. There were 66.48% ($n=294$) of participants who responded that they had received less than 100 hours of training, specifically in medical interpreting, and 33.52% ($n=67$) responded receiving over 100 hours of training specifically in medial interpreting. Therefore, data was compared between these two groups. These two groups had comparable general education ratios (73.79% of the group, with under 100 hours of training, were college graduates vs. 74.58% for the other group, with 100 hours or more of training who were also college graduates). For purposes of this discourse, they will be described as the group with more specialized training and the group with less specialized training, keeping in mind that the benchmark is under or over 100 hours training.

There were no significant differences in responses of these two groups regarding adherence to certification, or agreement with the challenges, advantages, disadvantages, or strategies to address cultural issues, listed on the survey. However, there were areas of more noticeable differences (over 5%) in other areas. For example, those with over 100 hours reported having graduated from a multi-course medical interpreting program at a college or university at a higher level (34.75% vs. 7.23% for the group with less specialized training). This makes sense as interpreters that received less than 100 hours or training typically graduate from a single workshop or medical interpreting course, and not an educational program of instruction. The group with more specialized training had more experience (46.28% with over 10 years' experience) when compared to the group with less specialized training (31.36%) for the same number of years of experience. The group with less specialized training also seemed to have a higher group with less experience (15.68% with under 2 years of experience) vs. the group with more specialized training (3.31% with under 2 years of experience) and the same difference was found for those with 2-5 years' experience with the group with less specialized training (24.58% with 2-5 years of experience) when compared to the group with more specialized training (19.01%) for the same time frame. This may be an additional variable (higher experience for group with higher specialized training) that may affect the data comparison between these two groups. Having exposed this, there are other areas of differences between these two groups.

When asked about their confidence level of knowledge about patient and medical cultures, the group with more specialized training seemed more confident, stating they were *Extremely knowledgeable* or *Very knowledgeable* at (90.52% and 88.79% respectively) vs. the group with less specialized training at (83.11% and 72.44% respectively). When asked about whether they received any training in patient and medical cultures, the group with more specialized training answered at higher levels (53.31% and 72.17%) than the group with less specialized training (39.56% and 48.66%). These results would confirm the logic that with more confidence comes a higher perception of knowledge about a subject matter.

When asked about the importance of addressing cultural issues as medical interpreters, the group with more specialized training felt it was more important than the group with less specialized training. There were 50.60% of those with more specialized training who answered that it was *Extremely important,* and the percentage rose to 96.38% when combining the responses for the categories of *Extremely important* and *Very important.* This is a higher rate than for those with less specialized education, which answered at 43.48% for *Extremely important* and 86.34% for the category of *Extremely important* and *Very important.* When responding about the frequency of addressing cultural issues in their work, 85.54% of those with more specialized training answered that they address cultural issues somewhat often to extremely often, as compared to 77.64% of the group with less specialized training.

When asked about their competency in addressing these issues, the group with more specialized training was more confident, with 85.54% stating that they were *Extremely competent* or *Very competent*, as compared to 73.91% of those with less specialized training. Congruently, the stress levels of those with more specialized training were lower at 40.96% stating that it was *Somewhat* to *Extremely stressful* to address cultural issues, when compared to the group with less specialized training at 45.34%. Strategy statements were given to participants and there were only two strategies with noteworthy differences. The first related to the strategy of *mentioning to both parties the need to intervene*, a very important protocol of transparency, an ethical tenet that places on the interpreter the responsibility of keeping all parties informed of any intervention, side discussion, or comment that has to be made, before it is made by the interpreter, when the interpreter needs to have a voice. There were 60.24% of the group with more specialized training that agreed with this statement as opposed to 50.31% of the group with less specialized training. When the advantages of addressing cultural issues were asked, 77.10% of the group with more specialized training agreed with the statement: *The delivery of services is more culturally competent when we are able to address these cultural issues.* By comparison, 63.98% of the group with less specialized training agreed with this statement. This was the only statement that spoke to the direct benefit of the interpreter's work in the healthcare organization's ability to provide culturally and linguistically appropriate services. The group with more training also had a higher level of agreement with this statement: *The parties I interpret for learn something new about each other's culture.* 46.99% of participants with more specialized training agreed with the statement above, whereas 40.99% of participants with less specialized training agreed.

When discussing the disadvantages, the fact that interventions delay the appointment was listed as the primary disadvantage and challenge to addressing cultural issues: 60.24% of participants with more specialized education agreed when compared to 52.80% of participants with less specialized training. This may be due to the fact that they intervene less often, as per frequency data comparison previously presented. Causing confusion was listed more as a disadvantage by the group with less specialized training (44.72%) vs. 37.35% of the group with more specialized education and training in this area. It could be that once an interpreter is better trained, competent, and skilled in addressing cultural issues, that he/she may know or have better strategies to avoid the confusion that can be caused by unqualified and inappropriate interventions in the interpreter's attempt to address a cultural issue. When asked if they received enough training to address cultural issues, 51.81% of interpreters with more specialized training agreed, and only 30.43 of the group with less specialized training agreed.

It seems that the amount of specialized training participants received does matter. The comparisons showed a direct correlation with the number of hours of training and the level of perceived knowledge, skills, and ability to address cultural issues. Likewise, interpreters with more specialized training seemed to have a higher understanding of the advantages and disadvantages, as well as the importance of addressing cultural issues within the larger framework of healthcare sector's goals of becoming more culturally and linguistically competent to address a growing diverse patient base. The data also seem to suggest that the group with less training believe addressing cultural issues is less important and also address these issues less frequently. The level of training does seem to affect the level of commitment to providing culturally appropriate care. More training in this area would seem to equip interpreters better in this area, as well as helping interpreters feel less stress with this part of their work. However, since the differences are not very significant, more research will have to be done to establish if greater differences in education make a greater difference. Under and over 100 hours is still not the same as comparing non-academic programs with academic education.

5.4 Certification

The research examined whether being certified made a difference in the responses of participants. As previously stated, 168 participants were certified in medical interpreting, and 186 participants were not. There was no significant (over 5%) difference in most demographic areas such as gender, general education, or country of practice except when related to interpreter education. There was a larger group of uncertified interpreters (46.47%) who had been trained solely by taking one course in medical interpreting when compared to certified interpreters (28.96%). Certified participants (22.35%) were more likely to engage in multi-course programs of medical interpreting than their uncertified counterparts (10%). The same was true when the hours of training were compared. Certified participants (43.51%) had over 100 hours of training, whereas uncertified participants (23.40%) had over 100 hours of training. Uncertified interpreters had a higher number of inexperienced interpreters (16.67%) vs. certified interpreters (5.85%) who had less than 2 years' experience.

There were some other opinions that did not show differences, and that included timing of interventions, importance and perceived competency of addressing cultural issues, their perceived knowledge, and training about the patient culture(s) that the participants served. However, there were differences in the level of perceived knowledge of the medical culture, with 85.03% of certified interpreters stating that they were *Extremely* or *Very knowledgeable,* as compared to 71.26% of uncertified interpreters. It seems that in all comparisons, there are smaller differences with the participants' knowledge of patient culture, which can be learned through life experiences, whereas medical culture needs to be studied, unless one comes from another medical profession, and in that case it could be learned through healthcare related work experience. However, if you are not already a healthcare professional entering the field of medical interpreting, it seems one would need to receive training on medical culture to appreciate the concepts behind patient care, and the unspoken norms and protocols of behavior within the healthcare system. When asked about receiving any training about medical culture, 62.05% of certified participants responded that they did receive some training, as opposed to 51.45% of uncertified participants. This may explain why the certified participants were more confident about their knowledge of medical culture. Stress was less reported by certified participants (40.84%) vs. uncertified participants (50.81%) during the intervention for a cultural issue. It seems that the perceived knowledge is tied to training and stress levels when performing these tasks.

The interpreters that were certified also seemed to have more experience. Only 5.85% of participants had less than 2 years of experience, when compared to 16.67% of uncertified interpreters with less than 2 years' experience. When asked about strategies used, participants agreed with most, but certified interpreters agreed more with the statement about mentioning an intervention to both parties (60%) vs. uncertified participants (47.58%). This has been the trend with previous comparisons of general education, and specialized training. The certified group also had a higher level of agreement with the strategy of informing the provider about a cultural issue (58.33%) vs. the uncertified group (50.81%). Informing the provider may be more challenging and stressful than informing a patient for the simple reason that the provider may not welcome cultural information, whereas the patient is in the healthcare setting to receive medical health and information. The strategy of *not intervening and waiting until after the appointment,* was listed by uncertified participants (28.84%) at a higher rate, as compared with their certified counterparts (24.17%).

With respect to challenges or deterrents, certified interpreters listed *the lack of time* as a major challenge (39.17%) vs. uncertified participants (33.87%). Providers and patients can have an effect on interpreter behavior. Certified interpreters had a higher rate of agreement with *patients do not want me to intervene for any reason* (16.67%) vs. uncertified participants (11.29%). The opposite was true for the agreement with the phrase: *providers do not want me to intervene for any reason.* There was a higher level of agreement for the uncertified participants (26.61%) than for certified interpreters (20.83%). When asked if they agreed that *the delivery of service is more culturally competent when I am able to address cultural issues,* 72.5% of certified participants agreed whereas 54.52% uncertified participants agreed. These differences, however, do not seem to be very significant.

5.5 Years of Experience

Perhaps the number of years of experience will affect the opinions and perspectives of a professional. Therefore, comparisons were made with participants with fewer than 10 years ($n=224$) and participants who had over 10 years of experience ($n=126$). In order to see if there were greater differences when the groups were the outliers, participants with fewer than 2 years of experience were compared with participants with over 20 years of experience. Each comparison will be done separately.

5.5.1 Participants with fewer vs. greater than 10 years of experience

Perhaps the number of years of experience will affect the opinions and perspectives of a professional. That is why comparisons were made with participants with fewer than 10 years and those who had over 10 years of experience. In most professions, certain knowledge, confidence, and competence tend to improve with experience. However, that is not always the case with certain skills. For example, an interpreter who does not have a high level of proficiency in one of their languages, will continue to make the same grammatical mistakes 10 or 20 years later, unless that individual takes classes or focuses on improving grammar. Or, if an interpreter was taught to never intervene, that interpreter will never intervene, irrespective of their experience. However, practitioners who are working on improving themselves with continuing education and attending conferences and workshops may have a perspective that is always in flux, having a professional stance that changes over time.

The age of participants is lower in the group with less experience. This is to be expected, with 50.61% for group with under 10 years of experience being under 44 years of age, when compared to only 25.40% of the group with over 10 years of experience. There was a small difference in gender distribution, with the group with less experience having a female/male ratio being 83%/16%, whereas the group with more experience had a 78.46%/21.54% ratio. There is no significant difference in general education. However, there were differences when comparing specialized education. There were 28.64% of those with less experience having received over 100 hours of specialized education, when compared to 43.07% of those with more experience. This would demonstrate shorter courses for those entering the market, at least with the study sample. Certification showed a small variance, with 46.26% of those with less experience being certified, when compared to 50.77% of the group with more experience being certified. This makes sense, as national certification for spoken language interpreters is relatively new, as the National Board started testing in 2009. When participants were asked if they were born in the country of practice, 38.71% of participants with less experience answered so, compared to 49.17% of participants with more experience.

The area of knowledge and training related to interpreting culture showed some differences. Knowledge of the patient culture(s), medical culture(s), and training(s) data exhibited the pattern of practitioner perceived knowledge and training to be lower in the group of participants with less experience, than the participants with more experience. Knowledge of the patient culture(s) rated at 85.26% for those with less experience, compared to 87.5% for those with more experience. Knowledge of the medical culture showcased a larger difference of 73.73% for those with less experience, compared to 85.83% for those with more experience. When asked about whether they received training related to patient culture(s), 37.79% of those with less experience received any training on patient culture(s), and 56.67% of participants with more experience received the same training. With respect to receiving training about medical culture, 52.78% of those with less experience received any training, whereas 63.87% of those with more experience received the same training.

There were no significant differences when comparing the level of importance or frequency or competency of addressing cultural issues, and/or the stress associated with doing this task. There were also no significant differences when discussing strategies, advantages or disadvantages of addressing culture. The data shows that there are minor differences when comparing medical interpreters with less than 10 years of experience to those with more than 10 years of experience.

5.5.2 Participants with fewer vs. greater than 20 years of experience.

Because the data was inconclusive when comparing those with less or more experience, a comparison was made between those with less than 2 years of experience (n = 41) with those with over 20 years of experience (n = 41). Both groups represent 9.70% of all participants. These may be the outliers. These results may showcase larger differences that were not visible when comparing interpreters with fewer than 10 years of experience with those over 10 years of experience. As predicted, more significant differences were found. We will call the group with under 2 years' experience the inexperienced participants, and the group with over 20 years of experience, the very experienced group.

Inexperienced participants had a lower level of general education and specialized education. For example, 44% of the inexperienced participants were college graduates and 4.88% had received over 100 hours of specialized training, whereas 84.61% of participants were college graduates and 24.39% had received over 100 hours of specialized training. There was also a greater number of inexperienced participants (29.27%) who entered the field with just 8 hours of specialized training, vs. the very experienced group of participants (4.88%). The rate of certification is 24.39% in the very inexperienced group, as compared to 43.34 in the very experienced group. Certification is not a requirement for practice anywhere but the state of Washington in the United States. These data suggest perhaps entry parameters for medical interpreters to enter the field have been lowered, possibly due to increased demand.

The difference in gender distribution of the two groups is also more accentuated than with the first experience comparisons with a benchmark of 10 years. The very inexperienced participants had a 90.24/9.76% male/female ratio, whereas the very experienced group had a male/female ratio of 78.05%/21.95%. It seems that through the years the profession has become more female dominated, perhaps due to the erosion of working conditions for medical interpreters recorded in IMIA salary surveys (IMIA, 2008). When asked if they lived in the country of practice over 20 years, 50% of those with less experience answered yes, as compared to 97.44% of very experienced participants. There were 26.32% who had lived less than 5 years in the country of practice, as compared to none in the very experienced group. These data suggest that very inexperienced participants have a higher ratio of having recently immigrated to the country of work where they interpret as compared to very experienced interpreters. Only 39.47% of very inexperienced participants were born in the country of practice, as compared with 58.97% of very experienced participants.

With respect to their perspectives on addressing cultural issues, variations were more significant. Of the very inexperienced participants, 78.95% stated being *Extremely knowledgeable* or *Very knowledgeable* on patient culture(s) and 57.89% said the same when discussing their knowledge of medical culture. When compared to 89.74% for patient culture(s) and 94.87% for medical culture for the very experienced group, there is a perceived difference of over 10%. With respect to having received any training on patient culture(s) and medical culture, 31.58% and 36.84% of the less experienced participants had received such trainings, respectively. On the other hand, 64.10% and 79.49% of the more experienced participants had received such trainings. Competency in the area of addressing cultural issues was lower in the very inexperienced group of participants (72%) reporting to be *Extremely competent* or *Very competent* when compared to very experienced participants (84.38%), and stress levels followed at 76% stating it was *Somewhat* to *Extremely stressful*, when compared to 43.25% of the very experienced participants. Less experienced participants gave a lower importance of *Extremely important* or *Very important* (76%) and reported a lower frequency of *Somewhat often* to *Extremely often* (36%) given to addressing cultural issues, when compared to very experienced participants, who reported 93.76% and 46.88%, respectively.

Several listed strategies also had differences in perspective. Only 16% of very inexperienced interpreters include a phrase about addressing cultural issues in their professional introduction to the parties involved, 34.38% of their very experienced counterparts do so. Does this mean that training is not focusing on this skill as it used to? Further research is needed in this area. The strategy of mentioning to both parties the need to explore a cultural issue also had a lower adherence by very inexperienced participants (32%) when compared with their very experienced counterparts (59.38%). On the strategy of not intervening, and leaving the discussion on culture to after the encounter, 16% of very inexperienced participants agreed, while 25% of very experienced interpreters agreed. Perhaps the data show that as participants gain experience, they are better able to ascertain when to intervene to address a cultural issue that is the least disruptive to the medical encounter at hand. For the next section, a chart will be more helpful to compare both groups.

Table 30
Agreement with Strategies to Address Cultural Issues

Agreement with the Strategies of Addressing Cultural Issues as a Medical Interpreter	Participants with under 2 years of experience	Participants with over 20 years of experience
I include in my introduction that I may have to address a cultural issue, if needed.	16.00%	34.48%
I intervene to mention to both parties that we need to explore a cultural issue that may be occurring and affecting the encounter	32.00%	53.13%
I intervene and inform the patient about a value or belief about the medical culture that is helpful to the patient.	32.00%	43.75%
Sometimes I don't intervene, but prefer to wait until after the appointment to address a cultural issue with the provider or the patient	16.00%	25.00%

Of the six strategies listed, less experienced interpreters had lower score on all of them, but in the four categories above, it was greater than 5% (Table 30). The level of agreement with these strategies can be considered low in general, as it is fewer than 50%. When reviewing responses in the other category, few novel strategies were shared. This showcases that medical interpreters perhaps do not have a wide range of tools to handle addressing cultural issues with the involved parties. The very inexperienced group had lower levels of adherence to most strategies, when compared to their very experienced counterparts. When discussing the advantages and disadvantages of addressing cultural issues as a medical interpreter, variances existed in almost every survey item, so these are again laid out in Table 31 and Table 32 for easier comparison.

Table 31

Agreement with the Advantages of Addressing Cultural Issues

Agreement with the Advantages of Addressing Cultural Issues as a Medical Interpreter	Participants with under 2 years of experience	Participants with over 20 years of experience
The rapport between the interpreter and the provider improves.	52.00%	40.63%
The rapport between the interpreter and the patient improves.	48.00%	25.00%
The rapport between the provider and the patient improves.	52.00%	65.63%
There is a better understanding of the reasons behind the participant(s) ideas and opinions.	48.00%	62.50%
There is an opportunity for the provider to adapt the service to the patient's cultural preferences.	56.00%	62.50%
There is an opportunity for the patient to adapt better to the healthcare system serving him/her.	44.00%	59.38%
The delivery of services is more culturally competent when we are able to address these cultural issues.	48.00%	71.88%
The parties I interpret for learn something new about each other's culture.	36.00%	50.00%

This data showcases significant differences in all eight advantage-categories. In general, there is a lower agreement with virtually every advantage except the two related to the interpreter's relationship with either party, which had higher levels of agreement with the very inexperienced participants. It seems that very inexperienced participants were more in tune with their relationship with each party and how their actions affect that relationship, than with the relationship between the provider and patient. Very experienced interpreters had a lower level of agreement with these phrases being listed as advantages. Perhaps they see them more as mere consequences of their work, but they do not seem very preoccupied with it. One of the main goals of the medical interpreter is actually to act in a way that will improve the rapport between provider and patient, and, thus, many of the activities, such as encouraging direct eye contact, or direct speech, are activities and protocols to that effect. It is not surprising that a group with a lower level of perceived importance, knowledge, training, or competency in addressing cultural issues, will also have a lower level of understanding of the advantages of such interventions. This will have to be discussed further. When looking at the disadvantages, a similar pattern arises.

Table 32

Agreement with the Disadvantages of Addressing Cultural Issues

Agreement with the Disadvantages of Addressing Cultural Issues as a Medical Interpreter	Participants with under 2 years of experience	Participants with over 20 years of experience
Sometimes it does delay the time of the encounter.	56.00%	56.25%
Sometimes it causes more confusion than clarity as the parties really cannot conceptualize or accept the ideas being put forth about the other culture.	48.00%	37.50%
I can end up being reprimanded for getting too involved with the patient and healthcare provider interaction.	28.00%	21.88%
The patient may not appreciate what I have to say about their culture.	20.00%	15.63%
The provider may not want me to address cultural issues and if I do the provider may get upset with me.	8.00%	28.13%

When comparing the disadvantages on the Table 34, three of the five disadvantage sub items had a higher rating for the very inexperienced group vs. the very experienced group. Both conceded almost equally (56.00% vs. 56.25%) that the time it takes to address cultural issues is a disadvantage. However, there was one statement which had a lower level agreement of the very inexperienced participants, and that was the statement about the provider not wanting the interpreter to address the cultural issue and the fear that the provider may get upset with the interpreter if they do intervene. Only 8.00% of the very inexperienced participants agreed with that statement, as opposed to 28.13% of the very experienced participants. Earlier in the survey, both the very inexperienced participants, and the very experienced participants had similar adherence rates to the strategy of informing the provider of a value or belief about the patient's culture that is helpful to the provider, with 56.00% and 53.13% adherence, respectively. The challenges of addressing cultural issues were the next item to be compared (Table 35).

Table 33
Challenges for Those Under vs. Over 10 Years of Experience

Agreement with the Challenges of Addressing Cultural Issues as a Medical Interpreter	Participants with up to 10 years of experience	Participants with over 10 years of experience
There is no time in the appointment to intervene, so I just interpret.	41.56%	27.27%
The provider does not want to hear about the patient's culture.	33.77%	40.91%
The provider does not want me to intervene for any reason.	22.73%	26.14%
The patient does not want to hear about the country or healthcare culture.	12.99%	13.64%
The patient does not want me to intervene for any reason.	9.09%	7.95%
I do not feel equipped to explain the cultural beliefs or values of the patient.	8.44%	6.82%
I do not feel equipped to explain the cultural beliefs or values of the country of service.	3.25%	2.27%
I do not feel equipped to explain the cultural beliefs or values of the healthcare system of the patient to the provider.	7.14%	6.82%

I do not feel equipped to explain the cultural beliefs or values of the healthcare system of the patient to the provider.	4.55%	4.55%
Sometimes it causes more confusion than is helpful to address a cultural issue.	22.73%	19.32%
Sometimes there is a risk of conflict generated by the cultural discussion, so I avoid it.	15.58%	9.09%
Sometimes I feel that it is not really that helpful to the provider to address a cultural issue.	9.74%	12.50%
Sometimes I feel that it is not really that helpful to the patient to address a cultural issue.	9.74%	12.50%
It is very difficult for the other party to understand the concepts I am trying to explain so I give up.	6.49%	5.68%
I do not think addressing the cultural issue is that important to my work as an interpreter so sometimes I do not address it.	6.49%	2.27%

The comparison of challenges generated inconsistent data relationship. According to Table 34, most (13 out of 15) challenges had a higher agreement by very inexperienced interpreters (time delay, the perception that the provider or patient does not want the interpreter to intervene, not feeling equipped to address cultural issues (all four sub items), causing more confusion, risk of conflict, not that helpful to provider or patient, difficulty of parties to understand the interpreter regarding these issues, and lack of importance). The challenges where the very experienced participants had a higher concordance were two: the provider not wanting to hear about the patient's culture, and the patient not wanting to hear about the country or medical culture(s). It is safe to say that the table that follows showcases that very inexperienced participants perceive more the challenges than the very experienced group.

Table 34

Challenges for Those Under 2 Years vs. Over 20 Years of Experience

Agreement with the Challenges of Addressing Cultural Issues as a Medical Interpreter	Participants with up to 2 years of experience	Participants with over 20 years of experience
There is no time in the appointment to intervene, so I just interpret.	48.00%	18.75%
The provider does not want to hear about the patient's culture.	16.00%	56.25%
The provider does not want me to intervene for any reason.	32.00%	31.25%
The patient does not want to hear about the country or medical culture.	16.00%	18.75%
The patient does not want me to intervene for any reason.	20.00%	6.25%
I do not feel equipped to explain the cultural beliefs or values of the patient.	16.00%	9.38%
I do not feel equipped to explain the cultural beliefs or values of the country of service.	4.00%	3.13%
I do not feel equipped to explain the cultural beliefs or values of the healthcare system of the patient to the provider.	16.00%	6.25%
I do not feel equipped to explain the cultural beliefs or values of the healthcare system of the patient to the provider.	12.00%	6.25%
Sometimes it causes more confusion than is helpful to address a cultural issue.	32.00%	12.50%
Sometimes there is a risk of conflict generated by the cultural discussion, so I avoid it.	16.00%	6.25%

Sometimes I feel that it is not really that helpful to the provider to address a cultural issue.	12.00%	6.25%
Sometimes I feel that it is not really that helpful to the patient to address a cultural issue.	12.00%	9.38%
It is very difficult for the other party to understand the concepts I am trying to explain so I give up.	8.00%	3.13%
I do not think addressing the cultural issue is that important to my work as an interpreter so sometimes I do not address it.	12.00%	0.00%

When comparing the advantages, disadvantages and challenges of addressing cultural issues, it is clear that the very inexperienced participants had a more negative perception of different aspects of addressing cultural issues. Likewise, their importance and frequency of addressing cultural issues was lower than very experienced interpreters. Here are some of the qualitative responses provided in the *Other* section included the following comments from very inexperienced interpreters:

1. *Sometimes I feel rushed, like the provider does or sometimes even the patient does not have time and they get easily annoyed when I do this.*
2. *It is my understanding that I am to interpret and not to be personally involved. So I have to walk that fine line in terms of involvement. However, in order for me to do my job effectively I have to advise the provider about the patient's dialect.*
3. *I have never done this, I was unaware I could, so I did not know all the challenges and difficulties that would arise.*
4. *When you work in the emergency department the providers are rushing all the time. Even when there is no trauma, they tend to just speed speak and really don't care to stop or slow down. Sometimes they don't wait for me to interpret the response because they think they understand all the responses. I have had situations where they have cut me off to the next questions thinking the first was fully asked and answered and when I have stopped to clarify they have said that I have already asked the question and I have said that I haven't and they have insisted that I have. I intervene*

regardless because it is unethical not to do so, but there is never enough time to interpret let alone intervene.

These comments point to the fact that the challenges can greatly impede the interpreter's ability to address cultural issues. One of the interpreters believes that a professional cultural intervention equates to becoming personally involved. In this case, the interpreter seems to be limiting himself/herself to disclosures of dialect, which can interfere with the linguistic work of interpreter. There was another comment that stated that the interpreter did not know he/she could address a cultural issue. This points to very poor training for this particular interpreter, as the majority of training programs do address acting as a cultural interface, clarifier, broker, or mediator. The last comment points to a lack of respect for the interpreter by the provider. Even when lack of time is an issue, proper etiquette requires the providers to wait for the interpretation before proceeding. Here are some of the qualitative responses of provided in the *Other* section from the very experienced participants:

1. *The patient is embarrassed about admitting to using or preferring a traditional home remedy and may not want the interpreter to tell the provider.*
2. *Sometimes the patient asks to let the provider know about cultural issues without her husband knowing, after. When a woman wants a hysterectomy and does not want her husband to know.*
3. *On the contrary, I don't think I have ever had any problems and the patient and medical staff are very receptive and grateful for the intervention, as it usually clears the path to mutual understanding. I feel that if you do it right, have the knowledge and feel confident, it works every single time.*
4. *If necessary, I intervene because it may avert problems for the patient in the future.*
5. *My years of experience and judgment come into play, having finesse to mediate cultural differences/issues in an indirect, non-confrontational manner.*

In these comments, it seems that the participants provided new challenges that were not in the list, and also seemed to have a positive attitude about it. One explains that often consumers do not speak up, forcing her to address the issue, and two participants mentioned how experience affects their confidence in their ability to address cultural issues.

In conclusion, the data comparison results between participants with less or more than 10 years' experience were inconclusive. However, the comparison between participants with less than 2 years or more than 20 years, generated a stronger variation of responses. The inexperienced group reported lower levels of perceived knowledge, competence, frequency and importance given to these aspects of addressing culture than in those with more experience. Inexperienced interpreters reported higher levels of stress, challenges, and disadvantages, indicating a more negative outlook on addressing cultural issues as part of their work as medical interpreters. This could have indicated a possible training trend for less intervention, as very inexperienced were just trained as medical interpreters, when compared to the very experienced. However, the former group had a lower level of general education and specialized medical interpreter basic education, which means that the group had less formal information on the topic to go by when relaying their perspectives about the topic. It could also mean that as time goes by, with experience, interpreters are able to better understand the role culture plays in their work. It is also possible that their confidence and these very high level soft skills improve mostly with experience.

5.6 Country of Practice

Does the country of practice have an effect on the responses to the survey questions about addressing culture? Since there are differences in training and standards from country to country, this study is comparing two groups. The first comparison is between participants who work in the United States (65%) and those who do not (35%). The second comparison will be between participants who work in Canada with those who do not.

5.6.1 Working in the United States vs. other countries.

Participants reported working in 10 countries other than the United States. However, 276 (65.2%) of participants reported working in the United States, and 147 (34.80%) worked in other countries. Are the practices different between interpreters working in the United States vs. those working in other countries? Demographically, age and experience are very similar, as well as time living in the country of practice, with no significant variation over 5%. Gender distribution was slightly more pronounced for those not working in the United States, with a female/male ratio of 86.30%/13.70%, whereas in the United States it is 80.21%/19.79%.

Table 35

Non-U.S. Countries Where Participants Practice

Canada	12.10% (51)
Japan	5.91% (25)
United Kingdom	4.26% (18)
Australia	3.55% (15)
Italy	2.84% (12)
Spain	2.60% (11)
Mexico	1.89% (8)
Israel	0.95% (4)
Language India	0.47% (2)
New Zealand	0.24% (1)
Total	34.81 % (147)

With regards to general education, 90% of the non-U.S. participants were college graduates, whereas only 70% of the U.S. participants were college graduates. With respect to their specialized medical interpreting education, both groups had similar ratios for having taken a course in medical interpreting (non-U.S., 31.88%, U.S., 30.99%)). However, fewer non-U.S. participants had participated in multi-course medical interpreting programs (4.35%) vs. their U.S. counterparts (19.37%). However, both groups had the very close ratios of participants who had received over 100 hours of specialized instruction (non-U.S., 23.27%; U.S., 24.21%). There were 27.40% of non-U.S. participants who were nationally certified, vs. 53.13% of the U.S. participants.

Regarding opinions about their knowledge and training regarding patient culture(s) and medical culture, non-U.S. participants scored *Extremely* and *Very knowledgeable* at 80% for patient culture(s) and 71.43% for medical culture. U.S. participants answered at a lower rate for patient culture(s) at 54.94% but higher for medical culture at 79.71%. This may be due to the specialized nature of the work of interpreters in the United States as compared to other countries with more generalist interpreters. With regards to training in those subject matters, only 27.14% of non-U.S. participants claimed to have been trained in patient culture(s) and 40% in medical culture, when compared to U.S. participants who were trained at 49.08% and 60.97% respectively. U.S. participants scored the importance of addressing cultural issues at 92.27% vs. 80% for non-U.S. participants. Likewise, they also scored higher on the frequency of addressing cultural issues, at 92.47% vs. 72% for non-U.S. participants. Interestingly, non-U.S. participants had a higher perception of competency, where 74% stated they were *Very* or *Extremely competent,* vs. 78.87% for U.S. participants. There was no significant variance in stress levels. When challenges were presented in the survey, there were four areas of variance. Only 30% of non-U.S. participants claimed that providers do not want to hear about the patient's culture, as compared to 37.63% of U.S. participants. Fourteen percent of non-U.S. participants agreed that they were not equipped to explain about the healthcare system of the patient to the provider, compared to 5.67% of the U.S. participants. Risk of conflict was listed by 20% of non-U.S. participants, when compared to 11.86% for U.S. participants. When asked when an interpreter should intervene, 62% of non-U.S. participants agreed, whereas 70.10% of U.S. participants agreed with this phrase: *I only intervene when it is affecting the communication between the provider and the patient.*

When advantages and disadvantages were listed, there were only a few sub items that had variance in each category. For the eight listed advantage sub items, there were two with variance over 5%. The phrase: *Opportunity for the provider to adapt the services to the patient's cultural preferences* engendered a 60% agreement from the non-U.S. participants, as compared to 65.98% from the U.S. participants. The other phrases stated: *The delivery of services is more culturally competent when we are able to address these cultural issues.* It engendered a 60% agreement from the non-U.S. participants, as compared to 70.62% from the U.S. participants.

For the five disadvantage sub items listed, there were three where there were three sub items with a variance over 5%. These included the delay of time, with 42% of non-U.S. participants agreeing, and 58.76% of U.S. participants agreeing. The fact that intervention can cause confusion was listed as a disadvantage and non-U.S. participants agreed at a rate of 36%, when compared to their U.S. counterparts at 43.81%. Last, there was a disadvantage listed whereas the interpreter can end up being reprimanded by the provider, and 28% of non-U.S. participants agreed, when compared with 16.49% of U.S. participants. In general, there were no significant differences that point to major differences in approach as to the participants' perspectives, when comparing non-U.S. participants with U.S. participants.

5.6.2 Participants working in Canada vs. other countries.

Are there any differences of opinion between interpreters who practice in Canada vs. those practicing everywhere else? Since the Community Interpreter Standard of Canada (HIN, 2007) has restrictive language on the topic of addressing culture, this would be a comparison worth checking. In section 8 of the Standard, entitled Role and Responsibilities of Interpreters, point 6 specifies that: "The interpreter must be able to understand and convey cultural nuances without assuming the role of advocate or intercultural mediator" (NSGCIC).

As explained in the literature review, this phrase is ambiguous at best. If one must be able to convey cultural nuances, how is one to do that without assuming the role of advocate or culture broker? Nonetheless, the purpose of comparison is to see what Canadian interpreters' perspectives are on this subject as compared with non-Canadian participants. As expected, demographic differences were noticed. Age wise, Canadian participants had a higher age than non-Canadian counterparts, with 88% being over 44 years of age, compared to 61% of non-Canadians. Canadian participants also had a higher female/male ratio, with 84%/16%, as compared with non-Canadians at 81.44%/18.56%. Canadian participants had a lower rate of college graduates, at 56.52% when compared to non-Canadians at 74.06%. However, they did have a higher rate of individuals having taken a medical interpreting course (56%) when compared to non-Canadians (31.16%). Last, the Canadians had a lower rate of having passed multi-course medical interpreting educational programs (8%) as compared to non-Canadian counterparts (16.43%). The same is true for the number of hours of training, with 24% of Canadian participants having received over 100 hours of training, as compared to non-Canadian participants at 33.52%. Canadian participants had more experience, with 48% with over 10 years of experience, as compared with 36.41% of non-Canadian participants. There were more Canadians that were certified (52%) than non-Canadians (47.92%). A lower percentage of Canadians were born in the country of practice (20.83%) as compared to non-Canadian participants (42.52%). This may reflect the fact that Canada is a country of immigrants and has recently received a large influx of immigrants.

When Canadian participants were asked how knowledgeable they were about patient culture(s) and medical culture, 79.16% responded that they were *Extremely* or *Very knowledgeable* about patient culture(s) and 75% responded the same for the same question on medical culture. Non-Canadian counterparts responded at higher levels at 85.30% and

78.01%, respectively. When asked about whether or not they had been trained on patient or medical culture, Canadian participants responded at 37.50% and 45.83%. Non-Canadian counterparts responded at 44.57% and 56.64%, respectively. Canadian participants and non-Canadian participants felt similarly about their competency to address cultural issues, at 81.25% and 77.87%, respectively. There were 75% of Canadians participants who believed it was *Extremely* or *Very important* to address cultural issues, as opposed to 89.75% of non-Canadian participants. Frequency of addressing cultural issues showed interesting results. There were 43.75% of Canadian participants who stated they addressed cultural issues *Extremely often* or *Very often*, where as 36.48% of non-Canadians answered that they agreed with the same categories. When asked about their level of stress when addressing these cultural issues, 31.25% of Canadian participants had a higher level of stress when compared to non-Canadian participants, at 7.38%. Could this be due to the fact that they believe that their standards do not want them to intervene? More research is needed in this area.

When asked about strategies, of the six strategies, there were only three where they had lower scores and one with a higher score. It is important to note that they had no significant difference in the strategy of mentioning to both parties that there may be a cultural issue that needs to be explored as it may be affecting communication. Canadian participants had lower scores on the interventions that could be helpful to patients and providers, but perhaps utilize the post session to address them, since they had a higher score on interventions after the encounter. It is expected that they would have lower scores. However, the differences are still not markedly different, considering that the Canadian Standards are against interpreters acting as advocates or intercultural mediators.

Table 36

Strategies: Canadian and Non-Canadian Participants

Agreement with Strategies of Addressing Cultural Issues as a Medical Interpreter	Canadian Participants	Non-Canadian Participants
I include in my introduction that I may have to address a cultural issue, if needed.	18.75%	22.54%
I intervene to mention to both parties that we need to explore a cultural issue that may be occurring and affecting the encounter	50.00%	53.69%
I intervene and inform the provider about a value or belief about the patient's culture that is helpful to the provider.	43.75%	54.41%
I intervene and inform the patient about a value or belief about the medical culture that is helpful to the patient.	12.50%	38.11%
I intervene and inform the patient about a value or belief about the country we live in that is helpful to the patient.	18.75%	25.41%
Sometimes I don't intervene, but prefer to wait until after the appointment to address a cultural issue with the provider or the patient	37.50%	27.05%

However, in order to understand better, the other category allowed for an explanation, and five participants chose to comment on this aspect of addressing cultural issues. These are the comments provided by five Canadian participants:

1. *I am bound by the Canadian standard for practices and interpreters' guidelines that I CANNOT act as a cultural advocate for non-English speaking patients. However, I am caught in a dilemma*

that my certification for medical interpreters (issued by National Board for Certification of Medical Interpreters in U.S.A) has a component with regards to cultural advocacy in the American standard of practices.

2. *Never intervene. IT IS NOT OUR JOB TO DO.*
3. *I inject a brief comment that there is a cultural issue. I allow the provider to pick it up, and talk about it if he or she wants.*
4. *Briefing before the encounter to understand the goals of the encounter.*
5. *Don't intervene as its not comes under my role & responsibility.*

One participant does not clarify enough whether or not she or he interprets culture, as the response conflicted about this and cited the Canadian Standards. It seems that only two of the 453 participants in the study (comments 2 & 4) explained that they simply do not intervene as it their understanding and belief that it is not their job, role, or responsibility to do so. This represents 0.43% of all participants. One participant speaks of her dilemma as she sees there are two approaches, and she is caught in the middle. The other two participants' comments speak about their own strategies about addressing cultural issues.

Other data point to the impressions that Canadian interpreters are knowledgeable, competent, and believe it is important to address cultural issues. However, their data states that they received less training on the topics of patient and medical culture, and feel more stress when addressing cultural issues. When asked about agreement with what situations they should intervene on, they answered in the following manner, illustrated in Table 39.

Table 37

Interventions: Canadians vs. Non-Canadian Participants

Agreement with What Situations Call for Cultural Intervention	Canadian Participants	Non-Canadian Participants
The interpreter should almost never intervene, as we are there to interpret language, and not to address cultural issues.	18.75%	4.51%
The interpreter should intervene only when it affects the communication between provider and patient.	75.00%	68.44%
The interpreter should intervene only when it affects the health of the patient.	37.50%	47.13%
The interpreter should intervene only when the provider asks for it	12.50%	12.70%
The interpreter should intervene only when the provider allows it, after being asked for permission to intervene.	25.00%	14.34%
The interpreter should intervene only whenever she/he notices that there may be a cultural issue for whatever reason.	43.75%	53.28%

It seems that the responses of Canadian participants do point to a more conservative approach to addressing cultural issues. However it cannot be considered a significant difference. There was a 75% agreement from Canadian participants that interpreters should intervene only when it affects the communication, which is the standard worldwide. Intervening just because it is helpful to one or another party would be considered intrusive to the primary goal of the medical encounter, and to the provider, who is there to treat an ailment. It seems that this study challenges the notion that Canadian interpreters do not interpret culture. One Canadian participant added this comment after this survey item:

> *I have come to the point of refusing to work for providers that are not allowing intervention: I feel I am doing a disservice by following strict "word for word" interpretation*

instructions. My job is to make sure the parties understand each other, to facilitate the situation, not to behave like a machine.

It seems that the participant is describing a scenario where the provider wants a word-for-word interpretation with no intervention, which is an impossible task for an interpreter who wishes to be accurate in his work. This scenario is a good example of why Canadian participants may feel more stress when addressing cultural issues.

When comparing advantages and disadvantages, Canadian participants had a lower level of agreement on the advantages of addressing cultural issues than non-Canadian participants. They also had a higher level of agreement with the disadvantages of addressing cultural issues when compared to non-Canadian participants. These, however, are not significant differences:

Table 38
Advantages: Canadian vs. Non-Canadian Participants

Agreement with Advantages of Addressing Cultural Issues as a Medical Interpreter	Canadian Participants	Non-Canadian Participants
The rapport between the interpreter and the provider improves.	12.50%	37.30%
The rapport between the interpreter and the patient improves.	12.50%	31.97%
The rapport between the provider and the patient improves.	56.25%	70.90%
There is a better understanding of the reasons behind the participant(s) ideas and opinions.	43.75%	66.80%
There is an opportunity for the provider to adapt the service to the patient's cultural preferences.	56.25%	64.75%
There is an opportunity for the patient to adapt better to the healthcare system serving him/her.	43.75%	57.79%

The delivery of services is more culturally competent when we are able to address these cultural issues.	56.25%	68.44%
The parties I interpret for learn something new about each other's culture.	31.25%	43.03%

As expected, in the table above, Canadians had a lower level of agreement with all the advantages listed. When asked if they had any comment, four interpreters responded with the following:

1. *Not in interpreting.*
2. *I feel I am hired as a general facilitator, that includes conveying ALL the concepts and meanings that need to be conveyed.*
3. *I can explain the trauma suffered by the patient and the resulting behavior.*
4. *I don't see any.*

It appears that one (1) out of 51 participants (1.96 %) did not see any advantages with addressing cultural issues. The other participant explains that the role includes all concepts and meanings. Perhaps the participant is referring to the cultural concepts and meanings that may become evident in an encounter but not evident linguistically in the language used by one of the speakers.

Table 39
Disadvantages: Canadian vs. Non-Canadian Participants

Agreement with Disadvantages of Addressing Cultural Issues as a Medical Interpreter	Canadian Participants	Non-Canadian Participants
Sometimes it does delay the time of the encounter.	37.50%	55.33%
Sometimes it causes more confusion than clarity as the parties really cannot conceptualize or accept the ideas being put forth about the other culture.	31.25%	42.21%

I can end up being reprimanded for getting too involved with the patient and healthcare provider interaction.	25.00%	18.75%
The patient may not appreciate what I have to say about their culture.	25.00%	15.98%
The provider may not want me to address cultural issues and if I do the provider may get upset with me.	37.50%	23.77%

Again, as expected, Canadian participants had a higher level of agreement with three of five of the disadvantages of addressing cultural issues, hovering between 25% to 37.5% level of agreement. This is not a high level of agreement, but is slightly higher than their non-Canadian counterparts (Table 41). However, there were two disadvantage listed that Canadians had a lower level of agreement than with their non-Canadian counterparts. Canadian participants had a lower level of agreement with the disadvantages of the delay of time of the encounter or the fact that addressing cultural issues can cause confusion. Canadian participants provided the following comments:

1. *Liability.*
2. *It depends on the providers' values and appreciation of our role and conduct.*
3. *It may upset the patient even further.*

Challenges were compared between both groups. Of the 15 challenges presented, Canadian interpreters had a higher level of agreement on all but three sub items: the time constraint, the provider does not want to hear about the patient's culture, and sometimes it causes more confusion than is helpful.

Table 40

Challenges: Canadian vs. Non-Canadian Participants

Agreement with the Challenges of Addressing Cultural Issues as a Medical Interpreter	Canadian Participants	Non-Canadian Participants
There is no time in the appointment to intervene, so I just interpret.	31.25%	36.48%
The provider does not want to hear about the patient's culture.	31.25%	36.07%
The provider does not want me to intervene for any reason.	31.25%	23.77%
The patient does not want to hear about the country or healthcare culture.	18.75%	13.93%
The patient does not want me to intervene for any reason.	12.50%	9.02%
I do not feel equipped to explain the cultural beliefs or values of the patient.	12.50%	7.79%
I do not feel equipped to explain the cultural beliefs or values of the country of service.	12.50%	2.87%
I do not feel equipped to explain the cultural beliefs or values of the healthcare system of the patient to the provider.	25.00%	7.38%
I do not feel equipped to explain the cultural beliefs or values of the healthcare system of the patient to the provider.	25.00%	4.51%
Sometimes it causes more confusion than is helpful to address a cultural issue.	18.75%	21.72%
Sometimes there is a risk of conflict generated by the cultural discussion, so I avoid it.	25.00%	13.52%

Sometimes I feel that it is not really that helpful to the provider to address a cultural issue.	25.00%	10.66%
Sometimes I feel that it is not really that helpful to the patient to address a cultural issue.	18.75%	10.66%
It is very difficult for the other party to understand the concepts I am trying to explain so I give up.	6.25%	6.15%
I do not think addressing the cultural issue is that important to my work as an interpreter so sometimes I do not address it.	12.00%	4.51%

Four Canadian participants presented some comments on this question about the challenges encountered:

1. *There is a potential risk that individual interpreters may have different perspectives and interpretation of certain cultural practices observed by their patients. By being a cultural advocate, the interpreter may not be providing services that are in the best interest of patients.*
2. *There is a risk of conflict generated by the cultural discussion, so I avoid it, I do not address it.*
3. *Dismissal by the care provider.*
4. *None of the above.*

It is interesting to note that one of the Canadian interpreters did not believe any of these were challenges to interpreting culture. With regards to timing, 50.00% of Canadian participants stated *during the encounter,* vs. 60.25% on non-Canadian participants. These are the comments made by Canadian participants regarding the training they are receiving:

1. *It would be beneficial, without training we have to rely on our own experience and have to keep up with any new development by travel to "home" country and following new developments on our own.*
2. *The medical culture that I work in has little knowledge about the patient cultural group. Also, medical professionals have limited familiarity and understanding of interpreter's roles, expecting*

them to speak for patients or their groups. Also, patients have limited knowledge of and familiarity with the medical systems through which they access healthcare services. The support system for interpreters is almost non-exist, leaving interpreters more or less in standard positions. A lot of work needs to be done in this area.
3. *What is the medical culture?*
4. *I did not receive training about medical culture although got one about country culture.*
5. *Mostly, I have learned through observations and reading.*

It is interesting to note that one participant did not know the definition of medical culture (comment 3). It seems Canadian responses were more conservative on the issue of interpreting culture, yet they do not indicate a significant difference of practice with their non-Canadian counterparts. As stated before, perhaps the Canadian stakeholders may benefit in reading this study and learning more about the practitioners' perspectives about interpreting culture. This study will help dispel two myths about medical interpreting in Canada: (a) That the Canadian standards forbid interpreting culture (since understanding and conveying cultural nuances is an activity of interpreting culture); and (b) That Canadian professional medical interpreters are not interpreting culture, nor intervening for cultural reasons. The differences were less evident in the qualitative data, suggesting that the perceptions and values about interpreting culture are generally similar. It seems that the vast majority of participants value and engage in intercultural mediation. Interpreting culture is part of their work, just as interpreting language is.

5.7 Spoken vs. Sign Language Interpreter Perspectives

Sign language interpreters have developed their profession separately from spoken language interpreters in most countries for several reasons, primarily because their services are usually a result of each country's efforts, initiatives, and laws to address those citizens with disabilities. In contrast, spoken language interpreters usually serve individuals who do not speak the language of service, typically immigrants or tourists. The spoken language community interpreter profession (which includes medical, legal, educational, and other social service interpreting) emerged from different national efforts, initiatives, and laws to address discrimination, equality of services, and/or the provision of cross culturally competent care. It is interesting to note, however, that many Deaf and hard-of-hearing communities do not see themselves as disabled, but rather as a distinct cultural group within the country they live in. Comparing the results of spoken and Sign language interpreters will be a way of learning if their views are different or not on the subject of interpreting culture. Interpreters who work in some languages and cultures may have a higher rate of cultural issues to handle than interpreters who work in other languages and cultures. However, it would have been unattainable to compare all the 77 languages in this study. The excerpts in this study showcase that there were several instances in the interviews and focus group where interpreters mentioned that in some languages they have to address cultural issues more often than others. The data indicates that certain languages, representing certain culture(s) may have a greater variance from the culture of service.

What were the differences of opinion between Sign language interpreters vs. those with spoken working languages? There was one Sign language interpreter interviewed and no Sign language interpreters in the focus group or essay. The survey generated 39 Sign language participants. This totals 40 Sign language participants of the 458 total numbers of participants of the online survey, comprising 8.73% of all participants.

As expected, some demographic differences were noticed. Regarding the age of participants, Sign language participants had a higher age average than their non-Sign language counterparts, with 70.26% being over 44 years of age, compared to 61.67% of non-Sign language participants. Sign language participants had no significant variation (> 5%) for female/male ratio or general education, when compared with non-Sign language participants.

The results for specialized medical interpreting education were mixed. Most Sign language participants received most of their specialized training in workshops and conferences (45.95%), compared with non-Sign language participants (16.83%). Fewer Sign language individuals had taken a medical interpreting course (5.41%) when compared to non-Sign language participants (28.48%), or a multi-course medical interpreting educational program, (8.11%) when compared to non-Sign language participants at 7.80%. This may be due to the fact that most Sign language interpreter educational programs are generalist programs. Sign language interpreters had a higher rate of having a bachelor's degree in interpreting, at 10.81% when compared to non-Sign language participants at 0.65%. Regarding the number of hours of specialized medical interpreting training, 16.22% of Sign language participants received over 100 hours of training, as compared to non-Sign language participants at 21.52%.

Sign language participants had more experience, with 61.51% with over 10 years of experience, as compared with 36.86% of non-Sign language participants. There were fewer Sign language interpreters who were certified in medical interpreting (5.41%) than non-Sign language participants (37.66%); however, more had other certifications (91.89%) when compared with non-Sign language participants. This is because most Sign language certification programs are generalist programs. A higher percentage of Sign language participants were born in the country of practice (97.22%) as compared to non-Sign language participants (42.09%). This may reflect the fact that the majority of Sign language interpreters are not immigrants.

There was no significant variation on their perception of knowledge of patient cultures. When Sign language participants were asked how knowledgeable they were about medical culture, 61.11% responded that they were *Extremely* or *Very knowledgeable* on medical culture, whereas non-Sign language counterparts responded at 76.77%. When asked about whether or not they had been trained on patient or medical culture, Sign language participants responded at 88.89% and 75.00%, respectively. Non-Sign language counterparts responded at 44.11% and 55.25%, respectively. Sign language participants and non-Sign language participants felt similarly about their competency to address cultural issues, frequency, and importance of addressing culture issues. When asked about their level of stress when addressing these cultural issues, 67.86% of Sign language participants had a higher level of experiencing stress (*Somewhat stressful* to *Extremely stressful*) when compared to non-Sign language participants, at 45.19%.

When asked about strategies, of the six strategies, there were only two strategies where Sign language participants had lower scores than non-Sign language participants. Sign language participants had a lower score on explaining to the patient something about the country where services are obtained, probably because most Deaf and hard-of-hearing patients are born in the country of service and are not immigrants or visitors. They also had a lower score on the intervention related to mentioning to both parties the need to explore a cultural issue (Table 41).

Table 41

Strategies: Sign Language vs. Non-Sign Language Participants

Agreement with Strategies of Addressing Cultural Issues as a Medical Interpreter	Sign Language participants	Non-Sign Language participants
I include in my introduction that I may have to address a cultural issue, if needed.	28.57%	22.54%
I intervene to mention to both parties that we need to explore a cultural issue that may be occurring and affecting the encounter	46.43%	53.69%
I intervene and inform the provider about a value or belief about the patient's culture that is helpful to the provider.	50.00%	54.41%
I intervene and inform the patient about a value or belief about the medical culture that is helpful to the patient.	60.71%	38.11%
I intervene and inform the patient about a value or belief about the country we live in that is helpful to the patient.	14.29%	25.41%
Sometimes I don't intervene, but prefer to wait until after the appointment to address a cultural issue with the provider or the patient	53.57%	27.05%

However, in order to better understand the responses, participants were allowed to explain, and five participants chose to comment on this aspect of addressing cultural issues. These are the comments provided by Sign language participants:

1. *Empower the individual: I ask the patient if they want to explain the cultural differences or if I may address the concern.*

2. *I tell the provider they need to explain to the patient what_____ means specifically to them.*
3. *Briefing before the encounter to understand the goals of the encounter.*
4. *I don't "intervene" by saying. "I am going to add information now" or anything so blatant.*
5. *I interpret the message WITH the unspoken meaning.*

It seems that in the statements above, one of the comments empowers the parties involved to provide explanations in order to enhance the patient provider relationship, as the standard of practice calls for. The other two participants discuss the strategies: reformulating the communication in a culturally appropriate manner or requesting the provider to do so. Rephrasing, or embedding a cultural message in another in order to make it culturally appropriate seems to be a less intrusive way of addressing the issue according to the last comment participant, but it can also be considered less transparent, as the "other" party not receiving this information is not aware that it is being added for understanding. Others may argue that in order to interpret the message appropriately the cultural explanation would have to be included in the interpretation. In translation, translators often add at the footnote of a document a translator's note, where they explain whatever needs to be explained, just as an author's note would do. This rephrasing could be a means to convey cultural nuances without acting as a cultural mediator, advocate, or overt intervention. However, even if it is a strategy that foregoes the need for intervention, it is important to note that the interpreter is still acting as a cultural mediator; perhaps not overtly, but implicitly in his or her actions and decisions of what and how to interpret.

One comment discusses the strategy of using the briefing before the encounter to understand the goals of the encounter. It is safe to assume that the participant implied and is speaking of speaking to the provider about the medical goals, not the communication goals. It is important to note that on several occasions the medical interpreter is concerned and focused the health of the patient.

When asked about agreement with what situations they should intervene on, they answered in the following manner, illustrated in Table 42.

Table 42

Interventions: Sign Language vs. Non-Sign Language Participants

Agreement with What Situations Call for Cultural Intervention	Sign Language Participants	Non-Sign Language Participants
The interpreter should almost never intervene, as we are there to interpret language, and not to address cultural issues.	3.57%	4.51%
The interpreter should intervene only when it affects the communication between provider and patient.	71.43%	68.44%
The interpreter should intervene only when it affects the health of the patient.	46.43%	47.13%
The interpreter should intervene only when the provider asks for it	3.57%	12.70%
The interpreter should intervene only when the provider allows it, after being asked for permission to intervene.	14.29%	14.34%
The interpreter should intervene only whenever she/he notices that there may be a cultural issue for whatever reason.	67.86%	53.28%

It seems that the responses of Sign language participants do point to a somewhat more liberal approach to addressing cultural issues, however slight, and not a significant variance with non-Sign language interpreters. There was a 71.43% agreement from Sign language participants that interpreters should intervene only when it affects the communication, which is the standard worldwide. However, the option to intervene whenever one notices a cultural issue for whatever reason, Sign language interpreters were again in greater agreement, with 67.86% agreeing, vs. 53.28% of non-Sign language participants. Intervening just because it is helpful to one or another party may be considered intrusive to the primary goal of the medical encounter, which is to treat an ailment. The responses that required the request or permission of the provider received low scores, pointing to the fact that Sign language participants may not see the provider as the decision maker party for interpreter cultural interventions. One Sign language participant added this comment after this survey item: "*The interpreter may intervene when the mental capacity of either consumer, Deaf or hearing, is unable to do so. To the maximum degree possible, I prefer the two parties to negotiate their own communication strategies but that isn't always possible or effective.*"

The comment above is congruent with a mediation role and what the majority of the participants of the study emphasized: their objective to enhance the patient provider therapeutic rapport by allowing them to be the primary parties of the discussion. It seems that the participant is describing the reality of having a goal of having the parties negotiate their own communication strategies, which is not always attainable for a variety of reasons. The participant does not explain why it isn't always possible or effective. This may be due to the fact that the parties involved may not be aware of the "other" cultural view or even be able to identify or understand a cultural difference to address it. If an ethno-centric individual sees their culture as reality, they do not know the other reality to form a comparative explanatory model. Further research is needed on the difficulties encountered by providers and patients to provide cultural explanations.

When comparing advantages and disadvantages, Sign language participants had a higher level of agreement on the advantages of addressing cultural issues than non-Sign language participants, and a lower level of agreement with the disadvantages of addressing cultural issues when compared to non-Sign language participants.

Table 43
Advantages: Sign Language vs. Non-Sign Language Participants

Agreement with Advantages of Addressing Cultural Issues as Interpreter	Sign Language participants	Non-Sign Language participants
The rapport between the interpreter and the provider improves.	46.43%	37.30%
The rapport between the interpreter and the patient improves.	42.86%	31.97%
The rapport between the provider and the patient improves.	85.71%	70.90%

There is a better understanding of the reasons behind the participant(s) ideas and opinions.	85.71%	66.80%
There is an opportunity for the provider to adapt the service to the patient's cultural preferences.	85.71%	64.75%
There is an opportunity for the patient to adapt better to the healthcare system serving him/her.	67.86%	57.79%
The delivery of services is more culturally competent when we are able to address these cultural issues.	89.29%	68.44%
The parties I interpret for learn something new about each other's culture.	50.00%	43.03%

In Table 43 it is clear to see that Canadians had a higher level of agreement with all the advantages listed. It seems that Sign language interpreters value their relationship with each party to a higher level than non-Sign language participants, and they seem to understand the larger benefits of providing culturally and linguistically appropriate and competent services. There was only one comment made in this regard, and it stated: *"Delivery of services is just more satisfactory for patient and provider and successful."*

It appears that Sign language participants had higher level of agreement with all five of the disadvantages of addressing cultural issues on the list, and had a very high level of agreement with the challenge of how it does delay the time of the encounter at 71.43%

Table 44

Disadvantages: Sign Language vs. Non-Sign Language Participants

Agreement with Disadvantages of Addressing Cultural Issues as a Medical Interpreter	Sign Language participants	Non-Sign Language participants
Sometimes it does delay the time of the encounter.	71.43%	55.33%
Sometimes it causes more confusion than clarity as the parties really cannot conceptualize or accept the ideas being put forth about the other culture.	46.43%	42.21%
I can end up being reprimanded for getting too involved with the patient and healthcare provider interaction.	28.57%	18.75%
The patient may not appreciate what I have to say about their culture.	25.00%	15.98%
The provider may not want me to address cultural issues and if I do the provider may get upset with me.	35.71%	23.77%

Sign language participants provided the following comments:

1. *I have not had a negative outcome when addressing cultural issues.*
2. *I don't think any disadvantage overrides the importance of cultural sensitivity.*
3. *That's why it's important to let the two cultural perspectives work themselves out whenever possible.*
4. *Both parties don't fully understand the job of the interpreter, the code of ethics, and the situations are in conflict themselves.*

Challenges were compared between both groups (Table 45). Of the 15 challenges presented, Sign language interpreters had a varied level of agreement on all sub items, when compared to non-Sign language interpreters.

Table 45
Challenges: Sign Language vs. Non-Sign Language Participants

Agreement with the Challenges of Addressing Cultural Issues as a Medical Interpreter	Sign Language Participants	Non-Sign Language Participants
There is no time in the appointment to intervene, so I just interpret.	21.43%	36.48%
The provider does not want to hear about the patient's culture.	60.71%	36.07%
The provider does not want me to intervene for any reason.	32.14%	23.77%
The patient does not want to hear about the country or healthcare culture.	7.14%	13.93%
The patient does not want me to intervene for any reason.	32.14%	9.02%
I do not feel equipped to explain the cultural beliefs or values of the patient.	10.71%	7.79%
I do not feel equipped to explain the cultural beliefs or values of the country of service.	0.00%	2.87%
I do not feel equipped to explain the cultural beliefs or values of the healthcare system of the patient to the provider.	14.29%	7.38%
I do not feel equipped to explain the cultural beliefs or values of the healthcare system of the patient to the provider.	10.71%	4.51%
Sometimes it causes more confusion than is helpful to address a cultural issue.	28.57%	21.72%
Sometimes there is a risk of conflict generated by the cultural discussion, so I avoid it.	14.29%	13.52%

Table 45 cont'd

Sometimes I feel that it is not really that helpful to the provider to address a cultural issue.	21.43%	10.66%
Sometimes I feel that it is not really that helpful to the patient to address a cultural issue.	21.43%	10.66%
It is very difficult for the other party to understand the concepts I am trying to explain so I give up.	10.71%	6.15%
I do not think addressing the cultural issue is that important to my work as an interpreter so sometimes I do not address it.	7.14%	4.51%

The largest level of agreement (60.71%) was related to the provider not wanting to hear about the patient's culture. It seems this can be a major challenge for the majority of Sign language participants. Other Sign language participants presented comments on this issue:

1. *I find that addressing the cultural issue offers clarity to the situation and how a person may react during that appointment. The challenge for me is finding an appropriate time to interject and the appropriate vocabulary to match the register and setting for all involved. Cultural mediation is a part of my job as an ASL interpreter. Sometimes it can be taken care of in the interpretation, and sometimes, additional information to one or both clients is necessary. Deciding which should take place is a challenge.*
2. *Medical personnel are often too rushed or busy to consider there are cultural differences. - I could learn more about medical culture.*
3. *The culture of the patient may not be familiar to the provider. Occasionally, there are just ignorant healthcare providers who appear to want to remain that way.*
4. *My years of experience and judgment come into play, having finesse to mediate cultural differences/issues in an indirect, non-confrontational manner.*
5. *I check with the patient or the patient's family first, to see if they want the cultural issue addressed, and proceed according the wishes of the patient. It's their appointment, not mine.*

6. *Time constraints in brief encounters. Medical emergencies prioritize information exchange over cultural exchange.*
7. *Dismissal by the care provider.*
8. *Not equipped is not the right phrase. I am capable, that is equipped, yet it is not my role. What we need and only occasionally have is an advocate.*
9. *Sometimes (often) neither group knows I was mediating the cultural information.*

After examining the data above, note that two of the participants mention how provider attitude affects their thoughts about intervention. Two of them imply the difficulty of this work, with one discussing how challenging it is to know when to intervene, and the other discusses how his or her experience have helped finesse her skills. One participant discusses how sometimes neither party knows or is aware that the interpreter is mediating the cultural information. This is another instance where interpreters acknowledge that not all of their cultural mediation work is visible to all parties. One participant mentions it is not his/her role, yet that what "we need and only occasionally is an advocate." It is difficult to infer what the participant meant by this utterance, other than perhaps that the interpreter only needs to act as an advocate occasionally.

In reviewing the data, one can see that there were four sub items that started with '*I do not feel equipped...*' and they referred to the interpreter's self-perceived ability to explain cultural issues to the provider and the patient. It is interesting to note that not one of the sub items had over 15% agreement for Sign language interpreters, and was even lower for spoken language interpreters. As stated before, usually the Sign language interpreter is not Deaf (although there is a rise in the number of Deaf interpreters in the United States), whereas the spoken language interpreters usually identify with at least one cultural group they interpret for.

In general, Sign language interpreters are more liberal in their approach to interpreting culture than their non-Sign language interpreter counterparts. The difference is less evident in the qualitative data, suggesting that the perceptions and values about interpreting culture are generally similar. It seems that the vast majority of participants value and engage in intercultural mediation. Interpreting culture is part of their work, just as interpreting language is.

5.8 Comparative Analysis Conclusion

Most demographic comparisons did not yield significant differences. However, there were some noticeable patterns. When participants reported lower perceptions of knowledge, training, competence, frequency, importance, and advantages in addressing cultural issues, these were combined with higher perceptions of stress, disadvantages, and challenges. The groups that responded with a slightly lower value to addressing cultural issues included those with less general education, less specialized education, and less experience (outliers only). When comparing participants by experience, comparisons between the group with under 10 years of experience and those with over 10 years of experience did not yield variance. However, these differences became more pronounced, as expected, when the outliers were compared (participants with under 2 years of experience vs. participants with over 20 years of experience).

The groups with higher general education, specialized education, and experience tended to have a slightly higher perception of knowledge, training, competence, frequency, importance, and advantages related to addressing culture. Likewise, they had lower perceptions of stress, disadvantages, and challenges related to these cultural activities. These differences were not pronounced, yet are significant in that they indicate that as the professional's level of education and experience increases, the tendency was for interpreters to recognize the positive aspects of addressing culture to a greater extent. According to the majority of participants, the data seem to indicate that training and experience affect and improve the knowledge and skills necessary to address cultural issues. Increased training in this area will aid in giving more context and relevance to the interpreter's work from the onset of their practice. According to participants, addressing cultural issues makes for a more culturally competent environment and delivery of services.

There were two specific survey data comparisons where greater differences existed; however, they were not pronounced differences. These involved the last two comparisons of Canadian vs. non-Canadian participants, and the Sign language vs. non-Sign language participants. After a closer look at the survey data, one can state that Canadian interpreters tend to have a somewhat more conservative approach to addressing cultural issues, and that Sign language interpreters tend to have a somewhat more liberal approach to addressing cultural issues when both are compared to the rest of the population of participants. Further study of this issue is needed. While most agree that standards and education affects one's practice, ultimately each individual professional will develop their own approach to their practice based on a multiplicity of factors. Until this project, there had been no studies comparing the approach of interpreters on addressing cultural issues. It is important to note that these differences were also observed in the qualitative data, albeit with a low number of participants in either comparative group.

In general, the comparison study of this chapter suggests that the general perceptions and values about interpreting culture are similar across all groups. Most importantly, the vast majority of participants (99.56%) value and engage in intercultural mediation in their practice. Does this make them professional intercultural mediators? Not necessarily, but it does mean that they are engaging in the role of intercultural mediator within their practice. Interpreting culture is clearly considered part of their work, just as interpreting language is.

Chapter Six

THEORETICAL DISCUSSION

This work uses the premise that practitioners are the ultimate experts in their own craft. This study produced a large number of self-reported data from interpreters (N = 458) through a qualitative-quantitative mixed methodology research from four data sources. They described the different aspects of interpreting culture (i.e., advantages, disadvantages, stress, challenges, strategies, timing, and more) eloquently. This is the first in-depth exploration of the practitioners' point of view in a doctoral study about the cultural component of the work of healthcare and medical interpreters. The results reviewed shed light into the thought patterns, objectives, and decision-making processes medical interpreters attest to making in their work to interpret culture. These data, including the latest research, raise questions about traditional theoretical models of invisibility and detachment. According to participants, the invisibility approach does not meet the healthcare demands they are facing in their day-to-day work.

First and most importantly, according to practitioners, addressing a cultural issue during an interpreted session is but one task related to interpreting culture. Participants explained how culture affects communication styles, understanding, and, mainly, the therapeutic rapport between a provider and patient who do not share the same language or culture. Even the linguistic aspect of the act of interpreting is affected by culture, as messages may include terms, symbolisms, narrative expressions, or concepts that are unknown or unnamed the other language and culture. Most studies in the field analyze the interpreter's behavior via methods such as ethnographic observation or interpreting discourse analysis. The self-reporting method utilized in this study explored their objectives and reasons for acting or not acting in certain ways. For the first time ever, the perspectives of interpreters about this aspect of their work is explored in a doctoral study. Based on the rich data presented, this chapter will provide new theoretical models and frameworks for conceptualizing the work of interpreting culture in healthcare.

6.1 Provider and Patient Cultural Dissonance

How does the work of the interpreter decrease the cultural gap between providers and patients? The provider and the patient each have their own cultural and linguistic backgrounds. Culture is affected many factors: one's level of education, acculturation to current health delivery environment, profession, religion, knowledge, beliefs, and customs of each other's culture, cultural awareness of own culture and other cultures, appreciation for cultural competency, the ability or not to see multiple points of view (ethno-relative worldview), and more. The provider and the patient have different worldviews. This could be said of any provider and patient relationship, as one's cultural makeup is different for each individual. However, it is safe to assume that those individuals requiring medical interpreting may have a greater cultural gap than those who speak the same language, as language acquisition requires some learning of the culture of the learning language. The medical interpreter is the professional who enables the intercultural communication of these parties to take place. The diagram to follow shows the provider and the patient with two different worldviews. The term *gap* does not express the depth of differences at hand, as often patients and providers are not aware of their differences, or may have completely different views, as if looking in different directions, which may also be in opposition. According to participants, providers and patients are not necessarily antagonistic, but could be. However, their worldviews point to different directions, as if each person was looking in a different direction, not being able to see the other person's point of view. Cognitive dissonance is the state of having inconsistent thoughts, beliefs, or attitudes, especially as relating to behavioral decisions and attitude change. *Cultural dissonance* may be a better expression of the cultural differences, when referring to intercultural communication.

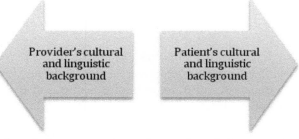

Figure 2. Cultural dissonance in an intercultural therapeutic rapport.

Sometimes these cultural beliefs, views, or practices, are in complete opposition to each other, and sometimes they are just skewed slightly. Interpreters are attempting to do more than just address a cultural gap that needs to be closed. There may be opposing views on how to act (e.g., communication styles, deference to the provider, autonomy, health practices of hot vs. cold treatment, mobility etc.). The lack of knowledge about the other cultural value, or the opposite belief, or practice, generates a communicative space of mistrust, to a certain degree, according to interpreters. For example, a participant described a case where the provider wanted the patient to use cold therapy, but the patient was from a culture where cold is never applied as a treatment for fever, only heat. However, the patient came from a culture where one does not contradict authority, so he did not tell the provider he did not plan to follow the instructions given. Since the provider did not know this, he has no idea that this is an issue that will be a barrier for patient compliance and patient safety. In this case, even though linguistic communication occurred, cultural communication and agreement did not occur. As self-reported, the interpreter had to intervene to ensure treatment would be followed. When one party is unaware of the motivations and thoughts of the other, the therapeutic rapport is weak, if existent at all. A therapeutic rapport cannot exist without trust. If the provider and patient are from different religions, or if one is Western and the other is not, these differences may be even greater. As explained by participants, educational differences or lack of familiarity with Western medicine may also become an aggravator. For example, the technical register and terminology of the language used by the provider, may pose some difficulty in understanding by a patient who speaks a dialect that does not count on such specialized terminology.

There were occasions described by interpreters where there were misunderstandings caused by conflict or conflicting beliefs, some requiring management or intervention (See Case Studies in Chapter 4).

The Standards of Practice published by the IMIA and EDC (2007) describe many of these activities, such as addressing discomfort (A-4), encouraging direct communication (A-7), ensuring understanding (A-8 and A-9), managing the flow to build rapport between the provider and the patient (A-10), managing the dynamics of the triad (A-11), and managing conflict (A-13). These activities, published in the standards and described by participants, demonstrate that in addition to linguistic interpretation, medical interpreters are actively facilitating communication, and to do so they need to redirect providers and patients towards an optimal therapeutic rapport. The primary intention and objective of participants was to provide improved patient care to culturally diverse patients.

Working logistically with a medical interpreter can be uncomfortable and difficult. Providers and patients do not always know how to work with a professional medical interpreter. The patient has to work with the odd situation of hearing someone speak for someone else and having to wait for an interpretation before the other party can engage in a response. As stated before, communicating with the assistance of an interpreter is not comfortable, and can even be stressful for both parties. Not understanding half of the communication when it is being uttered is uncomfortable. Time limitations add to that stress. As stated by participants, providers are very stressed for time, and have to do all the work in half the time when an interpreter is involved, due to the time utilized for the interpretation during the same allotted time for all patients. This creates a set of parameters that interpreters need to work within. Participants mentioned putting patients and providers at ease as one of their goals. Finding ways to make the communication flow is important to ensure that providers and patients communicate and understand each other from a cultural and a linguistic perspective.

Figure 3. Interpreters redirect & approximate the intercultural therapeutic rapport.

When an interpreter comes into a medical encounter, they immediately start working on enhancing and redirecting the provider-patient therapeutic rapport. This is accomplished through the many activities (including but not limited to linguistic interpreting) described by participants. In other words, participants reported that they are not just providing linguistic interpretation services, but in fact, according to practitioners themselves, they are providing intercultural mediation services as well. Cultural and linguistic mediation services include the variety of tasks described in the results section of this study. These may include setting up the stage for cultural and linguistic mediation, the constant reminder for the parties to look directly at each other and speak in the first person, and others. There are also continuous actions on the part of the interpreter to ensure understanding, such as analyzing body language, or requesting teach-back. When a cultural issue is identified, the interpreter will then process several factors and decide if, when, and how to address the issue. The interpreter cannot engage in these activities without professional agency and autonomy. Conduit interpreting alone is not sufficient to ensure the patient a satisfactory visit, or ensure all parties that the patient is being treated in a culturally competent manner. It would also not allow for the interpreter to convey cultural nuances. The reasons cited for improving the therapeutic rapport were directly linked to increasing cultural competency in healthcare, providing quality patient-centered care, and improving patient compliance. *Intercultural interpreting*, a practice that addresses cultural and linguistic issues, allows the provider and the patient to understand each other in broader terms, from a linguistic and a cultural perspective.

6.2 The Medical Interpreter Macro Roles

The diagram to follow is the most known framework diagram to describe the 4 most common medical interpreter roles. It is still utilized in many medical interpreting training circles. The Cross Cultural Healthcare Program, the most prolific medical interpreter-training program in the United States and abroad, introduced this model back in the 1990s. This diagram was later adopted and used by most trainers in the United States. It is important to note than none of the standards of practice contain this diagram a de facto theoretical framework for medical interpreters. However, the CHIA standard uses similar roles (message converter, message clarifier, cultural clarifier, and patient advocate). These have been primarily used in trainings, whereas academia has studied practice and extrapolated a significantly larger number of roles that interpreters undertake, already described in this study (Angelelli, 2004; Hsieh, 2006; Wadensjö, 1998; Wilcox & Shaffer, 2005). Unfortunately the plethora of roles described in the literary review are not shared with interpreter students of intensive occupational training programs.

Figure 4. Medical interpreter roles.

Bridging the Gap (BTG), Cross-Cultural Healthcare Program, 1999.

This traditional pyramid is often the only framework presented to medical interpreters trainees. It has been instrumental in the development of medical interpreter education and has helped conceptualize the work of medical interpreters for decades.

However, more current research in the field demonstrates that it no longer is able to represent the complexity of the interpreters' work or address the multiplicity of roles found in the research literature. It reflects the theoretical paradigm of the medical interpreter as primarily a conduit through the symbol of the triangle with the conduit role as the largest area, and prominently at the base of the triangle. According to this framework, the conduit role is the foundation where the interpreter is to stay grounded in, most of the time. The word *conduit* refers to a medium, a channel, and a means of transmission.

This diagram has also been used to showcase the incremental intervention model. When the need to speak for self arises, the interpreter engages in the other three roles. This diagram describes the essential roles for a first time learner of the art and science of interpreting, followed by a deeper study of the complexities present in interpreting. The goal of the incremental intervention model is to provide guided freedom to an interpreter to exercise his judgment in 'facilitating communication between two people who don't speak the same language.'(Bridging the Gap, 1999)

This summarizes the incremental intervention model, which showcases the linguistic roles (conduit and clarifier) as taking the majority of the space of the triangle, and the last two roles (cultural broker and advocate) taking a much smaller space of the triangle of practice. The emphasis on linguistic roles does not address the interpreter as an autonomous professional, but rather as a mechanism or channel to get information from one language into another between two parties. This traditional model also promotes the idea that the interpreter needs to leave the 'conduit' role in order to ask for a clarification or act as a cultural broker (speak for self). It therefore implies that the interpreter can only have one role at a time, since the interpreter can only be observed doing one thing at a time. It is also a model that describes the interpreter within an interpreted communicative event. It reflects the interpreter's work in interpreted communicative events, but not outside this scenario. This model does not describe the work of the interpreter who is working with only one party. This occurs when the interpreter works with the patient alone, or the interpreter communicates with a provider, or when the interpreter has to engage with other stakeholders such as administrators or families.

The work of an interpreter goes beyond that of a conduit (Arocha, 2007), since the interpreter is not simply a conduit to interpret words, but ultimately is a professional acting as a cultural and linguistic mediator. As the study data suggests, the intercultural tasks are performed before, during, or after the communicative event, and may be occurring simultaneously with the linguistic interpretation itself. The only thing the interpreter is believed to not be able to do simultaneously is to speak for self and interpret at the same time. However, if one considers the fact that when the interpreter speaks for self the interpreter also has to interpret that utterance to both parties, one can say that the interpreter actually never really stopped interpreting. Interpreters can and do act in multiple roles simultaneously (Pöchhacker, 1995). The idea that an interpreter can go through most of a session simply as an interpreting conduit channel without any authorship or agency in the triadic discussion is limiting and not representative of actual practice.

The pyramid schema shows the times when interpreters act in their own voice, or have agency, by giving these other roles names such as clarifier, culture broker, and advocate, with each trapezoid representing the level of activity, in the pyramid. The visual messaging of this schema portrays these other roles come up only occasionally. The incidence of the role diminishes with the size of the trapezoid. Unfortunately, this triangle may inadvertently infer a greater level of importance to the conduit and clarifier roles than to the broker and advocacy roles. The interpreter remains as an invisible conduit with no agency for most of the time, only engaging in the other roles, when necessary. Therefore, this pyramid may be seen to symbolize the paradigm of invisibility.

This role pyramid has been very useful to the field and it's simplicity and clarity have helped advance the profession of medical interpreting. However, it is too simplistic to portray the medical interpreters' work at a macro level as we know it today. The theoretical framework that interpreters must step out of one role in order to engage in another does not fit the reality of the tasks being described by the study participants. It assumes that the interpreter will jump from one role to another, as required. It does not take into account that the interpreter may undertake some tasks, in each of those roles, concurrently. The role pyramid framework refers and describes only the overt and visible tasks of the medical interpreter, not reflecting the synchronous nature of their many roles in the delivery of culturally and linguistically competent healthcare services.

Perhaps this is an appropriate time for a new model, as a variety of approaches strengthen the profession. The study described in this book showcased that interpreters are constantly thinking about and analyzing several factors (e.g., cultural, communication, medical), at the same time that they are interpreting. Interpreters described objectives, actions, and behaviors that went beyond linguistic interpreting and these cognitive activities and skills need to be recognized as an important part of the healthcare interpreters' work. Some examples include: to enhance the patient-provider rapport, to enhance provider cultural competency, to enhance patient understanding, patient compliance, and their integration into the host healthcare system. The interpreter does not need to leave one role or task to get into another role or task.

It is important to note that according to participants, interpreters can simultaneously process additional information to that of the linguistic content being interpreted. Interpreters may need to ask for clarification as a conduit, as an intercultural mediator, or as an advocate, or even in the other roles described in the research literature. Interpreters may advocate for several factors: linguistic accuracy, cultural sensitivity, accommodation and competency, meaningful communication, effective therapeutic rapport, and patient safety, among other factors. In that case the advocacy role can be applied in different situations, not just as a patient advocacy role related to ensuring the patient's safety and dignity. Lastly, one can address a cultural issue at the same time as acting as a conduit (within the linguistic interpretation), as a clarifier (requesting clarification of a cultural issue), and/or as an advocate (advocating for cultural competency), in any specific situation, and within as well as outside an interpreted communicative event.

This study selected verbal reporting as the qualitative methodology for a reason. The value of verbal reports is that they use a cognitive psychology point of view, where the data can be considered as an accurate representation of the happenings of one's mind as one completes a task (Ericsson & Simon, 1993). In introspective analysis, as opposed to protocol analysis, the goal is for subjects to express out loud the thoughts that occur to them naturally. Researchers use these data in conjunction with logical theoretical premises to generate hypotheses and to draw conclusions about cognitive processes, in other words, studying what cannot be observed.

This study provides the first insights into their thought processes about the important work of interpreting culture. As demonstrated by the results, sometimes interpreters could not act the way they would like to. Most reported having to adapt their approach due to demands that they faced, such as the providers' attitude, time constraints, employer's instructions, and other factors. They also described an enormous number of unobservable tasks that they undertake in addition to consecutive or simultaneous interpreting. The participants also described their goals and these were very revealing in explaining the interpreters' cultural actions.

If the need for medical interpreters arises from the healthcare's mandate to provide culturally and linguistically competent healthcare services, then the overriding role of a medial interpreter within the healthcare system is to act as an intercultural linguistic mediator between providers and patients to meet that overall need. Within the healthcare system schema to provide culturally and linguistically competent care, the interpreter is a healthcare linguistic and cultural agent. When compared to other healthcare professions, the healthcare interpreter is the principal advocate and agent of cultural competency and language access. From a healthcare organization's perspective, medical interpreters are the essential piece of the puzzle in providing culturally and linguistically competent care to diverse patients. Are interpreters being utilized by the system at the highest level possible? Are hospitals taking advantage of interpreters as cultural agents? Do they understand or view interpreters as linguistic agents?

After reviewing the results of this study, a new view of the macro roles an interpreter undertakes within a healthcare organization follows. Look at the roles of the interpreter from a macro approach, within the framework of the healthcare environment demands. The results of this study describe three primary and simultaneous professional roles and identities undertaken by medical interpreters within the healthcare system.

Figure 5. Medical and Healthcare interpreters' macro roles.

A medical interpreter operates in all three macro roles, and acts, according to the data, as a professional with three primary areas of expertise: intercultural communication, language, and healthcare. In each of these three macro roles above, an interpreter may need to engage in the tasks of interpreting, clarifying, advocating, assisting, redirecting, explaining, educating, or mediating, in addition to others. These areas of expertise, or macro roles, involve synchronous cognitive processes in the medical interpreters' mind, all with the same level of importance.

The most important aspects of this new macro role paradigm include:

(a) These three macro roles are of equal importance (regardless of frequency of incidence) and reflect the three-faceted professional identity of medical interpreters;

(b) These three macro roles are constantly in the medical interpreter's mind, interchanging rapidly or engaged in simultaneously;

(c) Medical interpreters will have varying degrees of competency (knowledge and skills) in each of these roles, depending on their educational background, employment or contractor status, specialized training, and experience.

(d) Each situation or communicative event is unique and will require varying degrees of each macro role.

All medical interpreter tasks can be classified within these three major professional macro roles, distinguishing the three main areas of knowledge and skills of medical interpreters.

The first, and most taught and well known, is the role of a language professional. This role encompasses all the skills interpreters need to attain in order to provide optimal and accurate interpretation services from a linguistic perspective. When an interpreter holds a preconference with a patient before the interpreted session to ascertain the patient's language and communication style and register, the interpreter is acting in the linguistic domain. These tasks include, but are not limited to, note taking, consecutive and simultaneous interpreting, sight translation, grammatical clarification techniques, paraphrasing, etc. This also includes advocating for the patient's linguistic rights. For example, when an interpreter insists that the patient does not understand enough French, and needs to be served by a Haitian interpreter instead, she is acting as a linguistic advocate, identifying with the linguistic professional role. Another example is when an interpreter explains to a provider the differences between Portuguese and Spanish and how interacting without an interpreter will certainly cause miscommunication at some point. Last, an interpreter may request from a hospital department to translate a particular consent form into a particular language. These are all examples of interpreters acting as linguistic agents or linguistic professionals. When an interpreter is engaged in this role of linguistic professional, he or she will on occasion be simultaneously engaged in the other roles as well.

The second macro role is the interpreter's role as a healthcare professional. Some stakeholders, such as employers, educators, and even patients, may believe that this domain is limited to healthcare clinical providers, such as a doctor or a nurse, but healthcare professionals may be ancillary healthcare professionals. This macro role is not limited to their extensive knowledge of medical terminology in two languages and/or learning about the host healthcare system. The interpreter is not a clinician or a medical professional, but is a non-clinical healthcare professional and as such is part of the medical team and is engaged in patient care. Being very well versed in medical terminology in most medical specialties (health services are provided in large part by specialty in Western medicine) is but one small aspect of this role. The interpreter has to learn to interact in the healthcare environment, being exposed to diseases, difficult patients, and healthcare tasks that go beyond medical interpreting. These range from, for example, activities of assisting patients to book appointments, way finding, to even assisting with referrals within the organization.

The majority of participants discussed their concern, commitment, and advocacy for the health of the patient, just as all healthcare professionals are expected to. This healthcare professional macro role is more developed in the interpreters who work as hospital staff, and are on site, as opposed to contractor interpreters who may or not specialize in healthcare. Those interpreters who have had a prior clinical profession (clinician, nurse, etc.), before engaging in medical interpreting, seem to have this macro role well developed. Interpreters participate in ongoing healthcare workforce trainings, such as those for emergency preparedness or patient safety. These hospital in house trainings relate to the healthcare ethics, protocols, knowledge and skills needed for all those working in a healthcare setting. As healthcare professionals, they need to follow these protocols, patient safety standards, correct protective gear, or for example provide timely and appropriate language access documentation for statistical purposes (A-17) (IMIA & EDC, 2007, p. 38). Some even participate in disaster responsiveness drills and other such trainings. Other healthcare tasks may include documenting linguistic and cultural care in the patient's electronic medical records, providing incident reporting, or other tasks related to their role as healthcare professionals who engage in direct patient care. Whereas the majority of participants were concerned with the patient's health first and foremost, this role may explain why medical ethics may on occasion trump the interpreter ethics. For example, the ethical precepts of do no harm, or patient safety as it is called today, may trump the ethical precept to not become an active participant in the dialogue between the provider and the patient. This is also the role where an interpreter gauges whether or not a cultural issue may lead to a negative health outcome.

Patients may ask for services that an interpreter is not able to provide. In this role, the interpreter may need to ask for clarification from the healthcare organization, in order to be able to know how assist the patient, following the boundaries of such a role as the organization they work for deem appropriate. The interpreter may also need to act in the advocacy role for the patient's well-being. This could include several tasks: addressing discrimination of either party (C-7) (IMIA & EDC, 2007, p. 48), advocating for translated materials in the patient's language, or helping the patient by taking the patient to a professional patient advocate who handles formal complaints, should the organization have such a position. This is not an exhaustive list of tasks. Interpreters, therefore, may address a cultural issue from the perspective of the healthcare professional role. When an interpreter is engaged in the macro role of intercultural communication professional, he or she will, on occasion, be engaged simultaneously in the other macro role(s) as well.

The third macro role involves the roles and tasks where the medical interpreter is acting as the intercultural communication professional or expert. It is of the same importance as the other two roles and has, as its primary concern, facilitating and navigating an intercultural interpreted communicative event. Several tasks can be undertaken simultaneously with interpreting during the encounter, as well as outside an encounter. A typical task related to culture is educating the provider or others in the healthcare organization of the cultural issue a patient is describing, or educating the patient on how the healthcare system works, acting as an integration agent. This role includes tasks such as facilitation or overseeing turn taking of all the parties, ensuring understanding of each party, managing conflict (A-13) (IMIA & EDC, 2007, p. 34), and asking for clarifications or teach back as necessary to ensure understanding and that the there is no miscommunication. Other tasks may include the cultural assessment of the patient at the pre-session, addressing patient comfort needs, predicting and/or identifying cultural issues, and engaging in culturally appropriate behavior with each party. A few more tasks include: adapting messages to be more culturally appropriate, cultural rephrasing, and reformulation (Table 1), engaging in clarification of cultural behaviors or norms, engaging in explanatory models to assist the parties, educating the provider in a post-session, advocating for a cultural adaptation for the patient, or the general advocacy related to cross cultural competency within the organization. This is not an exhaustive list of tasks, and when an interpreter is engaged in this role of healthcare professional, he or she will on occasion, simultaneously be engaged in the other roles as well:

When the interpreter is engaging or thinking about an intercultural communication issue, handling medical and/or language demands at the same time.

When the interpreter is engaging or thinking about the patient's health or the provider's expectations related to the provision of healthcare, handling medical demands, in addition to the language and cultural demands at hand.

When the interpreter is engaging or thinking about a linguistic issue, such as the need to clarify a meaning or handling other linguistic demands, handling medical and intercultural communication demands simultaneously.

Figure 6. Macro role variation within a communicative event.

The activities utilized to address cultural issues, or interpret culture, may occur within the context of intercultural communication needs, the interpretation needs, and/or the healthcare needs. Interpreters may vary from one thought to the other, so it is truly a shifting process, where each domain is enhanced at every moment the interpreter analyzes a demand or situation. These macro roles can be described as expertise domains, professional identities, domains, or scopes of service. The interpreter comprises all three domains in one, as a trinity where you cannot have one without the other. How well versed an interpreter is in each of these three roles will depend on the interpreter's general education, specialized training, background, and experience. Interpreters who are or were medical professionals before becoming medical interpreters will have a stronger understanding and skills for the healthcare professional role. Bilingual employees who were trained to work as medical interpreters are in this category and will have a higher level of healthcare professional knowledge and skills. Likewise, interpreters who have a strong linguistic proficiency, background or experience in a language field such as language education or translation, prior to interpreting, may be more competent from a linguistic standpoint. Like so, an interpreter who has a strong intercultural background, education, or experiences, such as an individual who has lived in many countries, comes from a culturally mixed family, or has studied intercultural studies or anthropology, may have a stronger set of skills and knowledge in this area. This applies to on site or remote interpreters, as well as staff or freelancers. The important factor to keep in mind is that these three macro roles act as the three primary manifestations of the medical interpreter's professional identity and role within the healthcare system.

The pervasive view is that the language professional role is the most important, or crucial, since the primary task of the interpreter is to provide linguistic interpretation. This is understandable as without this skill, interpreters would not be able to perform at a minimum level of accuracy. Language conversion is where the majority of study hours occur in intensive educational programs. However, the data portrays the interpreter as a linguistic and cultural mediator, and not primarily a linguistic interpreter per se. The (invisible) conduit model creates a paradigm that, when taught, may mislead novice interpreters to believe that word for word equivalents, with the least amount of intervention, are their only responsibility as healthcare interpreters. This goes directly against the provision of culturally competent care and the precepts in published standards to ensure meaningful communication, among other important tasks (IMIA & EDC, 2007).

The training received influences the decisions participants make about the interpretation renderings and interaction. It is worth pointing out that academic programs are more balanced in their curriculum, providing courses on intercultural communication, advocacy, professionalism, public speaking, teaching other non linguistic aspects of the interpreter's work. However, intensive programs, due to the low number of instruction hours, barely have time to focus on the linguistic macro role. Most 40-hour programs for example, do not even have enough time to teach basic techniques adequately. These would include note taking techniques, sight translation, and/or simultaneous interpreting. These topics are usually provided only in an introductory manner, and are addressed more in depth in continuing education classes, after interpreters start practicing (See the IMIA Education Registry at http://www.imiaweb.org/education/trainingnotices.asp).

Some interpreters are being taught, for example that interpreters should not intervene without the provider's request. As shown by the data, 12.70% of interpreters believe that the interpreter should only intervene if the provider asks for it, even though this requirement is not published in any standard of practice. This small minority of participants (12.70%) may be limited by beliefs that were taught to them. Limiting a professional's practice in training may not beneficial to meaningful access to healthcare services. This belief is in sharp contrast to more current views of discourse and interaction that have led to a more liberal philosophical stance for the profession based on evidence that meaning is being co-constructed by all discourse participants (Angelelli, 2004; Arocha, 2007; Hsieh, 2006; Wädensjo, 1998; Wilcox & Shaffer, 2005).

The provision of flawless linguistic interpretation is not possible without addressing culture. Interpreters already utilize several linguistic strategies within the language professional macro role to address cultural issues. These include transportation, transportation plus translation, replacement, gloss, or dispensation, according to the specific situation (Shirinzadeh, Sepora, & Mahadi, 2015). When the information is not well understood by the recipient, as if spoken in the recipient's language, the interpretation does not achieve semantic accuracy. These cultural meanings, if left unresolved, could have repercussions and contribute to fall short of an accurate interpretation, but more importantly, can also prevent a positive health outcome (IMIA & EDC, 2007) if left unchecked. In effect, a negative or even sentinel event can ensue if the parties do not understand each other culturally. Without the ability to intervene from an intercultural communication or healthcare perspective, in addition to the linguistic perspective, the interpreters would remain limited and ineffective in meeting their specialization's objectives within the healthcare system. Participants described they need to be able to adequately engage in their healthcare system's mandate to treat the patient in a culturally competent manner. It is true that other patients and providers, who do not require interpretation services, may not have the benefit of someone engaging in cultural mediation or improving the therapeutic rapport for them. However, when an interpreter is present, why should they negate the parties the ability to ensure quality healthcare? In some countries, the concept of cultural mediators has been promoted for congruent language patient provider interactions. In addition, if medical interpreters did not engage in all the tasks requested to them in their standards of practice and as healthcare professionals in their own right, they would themselves be guilty of not providing culturally competent services to patients.

Academic research has demonstrated that interpreters act in more roles and even face role confusion or overload (Pöchhacker, 1998). The new macro role model funnel diagram conveys the interpreter as a professional with three main areas of domain: linguistic, healthcare, and intercultural communication. This framework better explains how medical interpreters are unique in their specialization. They rely on the expertise of the macro roles needed for the moment, and engage in a multifaceted range of tasks that go well beyond linguistic interpreting. This new paradigm does not attempt to minimize the linguistic work of the interpreters. It simply creates a broader framework that includes the context of the demands or intercultural communication needs as well as the healthcare needs to better understand this particular specialization of interpreting in a more sophisticated manner. This new framework, obtained via verbal reported methodology, acknowledges and incorporates the non-linguistic objectives that medical interpreters, as the practitioners, reported as an integral part of their practice. It also acknowledges the interpreter as a bona fide professional with professional agency and decision-making skills that go beyond word choice or when to intervene.

Asking the interpreter to forego any of these macro roles, or to focus on only one macro role, limits the professional agency and effectiveness of medical interpreters in providing culturally and linguistically competent services in any specific given situation. It also limits the perception of what interpreters do and the macro roles they engage in within healthcare field.

6.3 The Medical Interpreter's Intercultural Tasks

As has been revealed from the verbal reporting data described by participants, addressing cultural issues goes beyond an intercultural intervention during an interpreted communicative event. There are many tasks interpreters have described as that address intercultural mediation. The diagram that follows does not list all the possible cultural tasks, only the most common.

Figure 7. Intercultural tasks during an interpreted communicative event.

Medical interpreters are engaging in all of these tasks at different times to mediate or act as an interface of culture. When an interpreter intervenes and takes the floor with a clarification statement such as: "The interpreter would like to clarify an issue that may be cultural..." this message is also interpreted to the other party, to maintain the trust of the parties. All the messages need to be interpreted, including the messages from interpreter to the provider or patient to clarify any issue, be it communicative, linguistic, cultural, or medical. Therefore, the interpreter never really "takes off" his interpreting hat. In order to be totally transparent, all conversations are interpreted in all directions at all times. The interpreter is therefore in effect interpreting for three parties: the provider, the patient, and self. This confirms that there are three participants in the medical encounter that require interpretation, and not two.

Whenever an interpreter intervenes for any specific reason, he or she becomes a visible and active part of the conversation. When interpreters interpret their own renditions, they continue to wear their interpreter linguistic role while engaging in a non-interpreting task. However, others may argue that these interventions, linguistic or not, are an integral part of an interpreter's work. Often literature speaks of the interpreter interpreting for the provider and the patient, when in the act of interpreting. Further research is needed on the interpreter's co-construction of meaning, and on the interpreter's task of interpreting for self. Interpreters execute many tasks simultaneously. Medical interpreters will engage in interpreting language and at the same time will engage in interpreting culture and handling other healthcare demands. Intervention is but one of the options or possible actions for the interpreter.

As per the verbal reported data, tasks that are performed before or after a session, outside the interpreted session, with only one party (provider or patient) are showcased in the diagram on Figure 8. This does not list all the possible cultural tasks, only the most common.

Figure 8. Intercultural tasks outside the interpreted communicative event.

The work of the medical interpreter cannot be reported as limited to his time in interpreting communicative events. The intercultural work outside these communicative events needs to be discussed. The tasks described above, are cultural mediation tasks, and are not linguistic tasks. Professional intercultural mediators, who do not interpret, also engage in these tasks. According to this study's data, the medical interpreter's working status (contractor vs. staff, or remote vs. face to face) will affect the level of agency or autonomy given by the employer, the healthcare institution, and/or the provider. Contract interpreters, as well as remote interpreters, are more limited in their professional agency within the healthcare organization and may not be able to speak with either party before the triadic encounter begins, for example. This is an important limitation of contract and remote interpreting. When interpreters cannot interact with providers or patients outside the triadic encounter, with a pre or post sessions, this limits the interpreter's ability to assess the participants' cultural backgrounds or have context on what type of interaction they are about to participate in. An interpreter who does not have regular contact with the healthcare institution, due to their status as a consultant, will not have the professional access or agency hospital interpreters have to speak with others in their healthcare organization about cultural issues. The recent increase in contract and remote interpreting service models may in fact be limiting the interpreter's ability to have professional agency and impact within the healthcare organization to provide services that are culturally and linguistically competent. Some participants stated that they could still address cultural issues remotely, but that it was more difficult. Others stated they did not let that limit them when they were engaged. However, further study is needed on the effects of remote interpreting on agency and all non-conduit roles and tasks.

6.4 Medical Interpreting Research Trends

Traditional research on interpreting was described as primarily being related to conference interpreting, where typically the interpreter interprets the speaker's messages into one language through a booth and technical equipment. This research has been challenged since the late 1980s (Pöchhacker, 1995) by those who have been studying dialogic interpreting, where interpreters are involved in interpreting into two languages, and are typically interpreting a conversation between a professional and a client or consumer who do not share a language or culture. Several researchers have proposed a model of interpreting based on visibility (Angelelli, 2004; Dysart-Gale, 2005; Hsieh, 2006; Jacobs, 2002; Kaufert, 1990; Putsch, 1985; Solomon, 1997). Hsieh (2006) proposed a mediator model for medical interpreters, arguing that by recognizing interpreters as active participants, researchers will have the opportunity to go beyond the conduit model.

The visibility model recognizes interpreters to be active participants with professional agency and as co-constructors of messages and concepts with the other two parties. The visibility model may require renaming *dialogic interpreting* into *triadic interpreting,* since interpreters are also interpreting their own messages to either party. Why is there some resistance to the visibility model? Where is it coming from? Participants stated that the visible interpreting model poses a problem for some providers who want to maintain full control of the encounter, and may prefer the interpreter to simply be a mouthpiece. This was relayed by several participants of this study: that the attitude of the provider affects the interpreter's ability to intervene and do the job the way the interpreter would like to do it. Their behavior is affected by the dynamics of the encounter. This is explained well in the excerpt below, from an interpreter's point of view:

> *If we're looking at staff providers who are ethno-centric and have a view of defense or that everyone has to be treated the same, I know who they are and don't do it because it can create a more hostile environment and not one of mutual understanding.*

How can this participant manage his ethical and professional responsibility to engage in whatever activity is needed to in order to provide linguistic and culturally competent services when the provider dissuades culturally competent behavior? Unfortunately, some interpreters have been trained to "just interpret," or "never intervene," or "only intervene at the request or approval of the provider," as is described by a few participants.

However, it does not seem to be the view of the majority of participants, (99.96%) who are engaging in interpreting language and culture in the best way they possibly can, within the working conditions, limitations, and sometimes conflicting healthcare demands faced. Interpreter educators need to familiarize themselves with the latest research regarding the visibility paradigm in order to better reflect what researchers have been observing for decades now in the medical interpreters' practice. In essence, the invisibility paradigm does not reflect what professional interpreters are doing in the field (Angelelli, 2002).

Interpreters have been traditionally trained and viewed as language professionals, focusing their attention to provide accurate interpretation services. However, medical interpreters are a specialization that works within the demanding healthcare context. Conference interpreters focus on the preparation and interpretation of the specific conference material mostly in one direction, in the form of presentations or speeches. Medical interpreters are specialized to work within the medical context as practice professionals, interpreting mostly intimate yet difficult intercultural conversations with individuals who need to understand a health ailment and agree on a proposed health recovery plan. In order to understand the dynamics of the healthcare conversations to be interpreted, interpreters need to have a very solid background in understanding the culture or medicine to be truly effective. The fact remains that many medical interpreters work in hospitals as employed staff. This changes their professional identity to one that incorporates the fact that to some healthcare organizations they are seen more as healthcare professionals than as linguists. Interpreters who are freelancers or work remotely may experience more limited scopes of work due to their professional status, as with any other profession. The three macro role theoretical framework shows an interpreter who has an expanded set of skills and abilities in addition to accurate interpretation. That is simply one of the tools he or she utilizes in order to mediate language and culture.

Culture affects the understanding, belief, and practices that are health related. Therefore, intercultural communication brings another level of complexity to the interpreter's work that is not there in an unspecialized or non-triadic practice environment. Recent research on medical interpreting, is demonstrating the unique work of medical interpreters involves addressing aspects of culture, and communication, in addition to providing interpreting services (Angelelli, 2004; Dysart-Gale, 2005; Hsieh, 2006; Jacobs, 2002; Kaufert, 1990; Putsch, 1985; Solomon, 1997). The work of approximating two individuals from different cultures is truly more the work of a mediator than a conduit (Figure 9). Hsieh (2006) pointed to the fact that the interpreter is more of a mediator than a bridge, channel, or medium of communication, actively participating to improve the rapport and communication of each medical encounter. In fact, one can be a linguistic professional without addressing intercultural communication, while one cannot address intercultural communication without addressing language.

Figure 9. The move from linguist to cultural and linguistic mediator.

In a visible model, the medical interpreters are an integral part of the communicative event, and not necessarily in the background. The medical interpreter will not be participating orally to the extent of the other two parties. However, the medical interpreter is still a participant and must be acknowledged as one who has autonomy, ideas and concepts that may be helpful in 1) deriving meaning (semiotics) 2) facilitating the intercultural communication and 3) improving the therapeutic rapport of the other two parties. Interpreters are active participant when they engage in a pre-session with the patient, or when they explain to both parties how to work with a professional interpreter, or when they interject, requesting the parties to look at each other or speak directly to each other, or when they request a clarification or a teach back from the patient.

Separate - an observer who speaks the voice of two participants

Part of - a participant who has a voice and also interprets her voice

Figure 10. The move towards active participation within an interpreted event.

All utterances from the patient, provider, and interpreter fall into the space where all three converge. The diagram (Figure 11) shows the space where the intercultural communication happens.

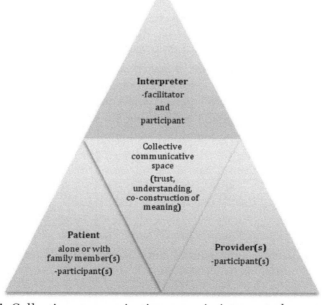

Interpreter
-facilitator
and
participant

Collective communicative space

(trust, understanding, co-construction of meaning)

Patient
alone or with family member(s)
-participant(s)

Provider(s)
-participant(s)

Figure 11. Collective communicative space in interpreted event.

The cultural competency level of the communicative space is affected by the expectations and cultural worldview and cultural competency of each participant. When the provider does not allow the cultural aspect of the communication to be addressed, through verbal and non-verbal language or behavior, then the space becomes void of cultural humility and competency. As participants have mentioned, the space is usually void of trust until trust is established. The interpreter will act in such a way to make this a comfortable and trustworthy communicative space in order to establish or enhance the provider-patient therapeutic rapport. The new theoretical models presented in this chapter may assist in the reformulation of the medical interpreters' professional identity as a practice professional, in contrast to a technical professional identity. Understanding their scope of work beyond that of being a non-participatory technical language conduit can improve the cultural competency of this communicative space.

In conclusion, study participants have described their work in a very concrete manner. This study provides insight into their thinking and perspectives about their work demonstrating a broader professional scope of work than needs to be acknowledged and better understood. The data demonstrate that to medical interpreter practitioners, interpreting culture is as important as interpreting language, one that cannot be done without the other. Interpreters are engaging in linguistic and cultural mediation tasks that go beyond that of accurate linguistic interpretation. As explained before, professional mediators act as an impartial but active party who attempts to assist two other parties to understand each other. As an active party, the interpreter can be, and is impartial. While the conduit model addresses language conversion, a broader linguistic and cultural mediation model addresses the interpreters' autonomy, active participation, and goals and tasks of managing and decreasing the linguistic and cultural dissonance between providers and patients. The mediator model not only allows the interpreter to provide culturally competent services within the healthcare system, but also to act as important intercultural agents within the healthcare system.

According to the data, there are actually more cultural influences at play than the known three (interpreter, provider, medicine) in an interpreter-mediated healthcare. Participants described how they had to be cognizant of all these very different cultures, as each influenced the particular encounter. Previous research has only acknowledged three cultures, the interpreter's, the provider's, and medical culture. In the model below, the interpreter has two cultures at play. One is the interpreter's personal cultural background (where they were born, raised, etc.) and the other is the interpreter's professional culture. What is meant by the professional culture is related to the interpreter's professional background, training, and experience. An interpreter who was a doctor in her previous country will see things differently from one with a greater linguistic background. Likewise, an interpreter who took an intensive course that focused on the conduit model will have a different professional culture than one who studied interpreting at the university level. More research is needed in this area to explore how all of these multiple cultural influences affect patient-centered care.

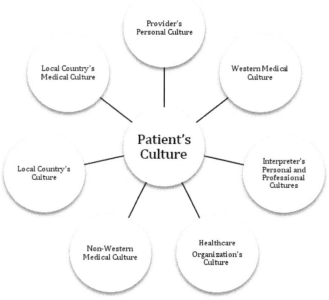

Figure 12. Cultures influencing an interpreter-mediated patient-centered care.

Interpreters described how their need for intervention diminishes as the organization and/or the providers they are working with are more culturally competent: *"Hospital staff members may depend on interpreters too much. We may have to take care of patients, everything sometimes. It's a big burden for us."* This shows the higher need for intervention. Another interpreter discussed the time factor: *"For me the need to intervene is only necessary if the situation requires it. All providers these days have the knowledge about the different cultures and to deal with the patients but that's most of the time."* This shows less need for intervention. Figure 13 shows this relationship, to be further discussed in the Conclusion chapter.

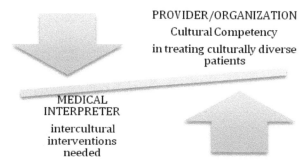

PROVIDER/ORGANIZATION
Cultural Competency
in treating culturally diverse
patients

MEDICAL
INTERPRETER
intercultural
interventions
needed

Figure 13. Relationship between provider cultural competency and intercultural interventions.

Participants described how some organizations are respectful of their scope of work and how others are not. One of the factors that affect the medical interpreters' behavior is the level of cultural competency of an organization or provider, as stated earlier. In culturally competent organizations, all healthcare professionals are responsible and are working together towards patient-centered care, and that involved care and treatment that is centered in the patient's preferences, including cultural and linguistic preferences. In such environments, the shared model of social justice prevails. There are no turf wars between providers and interpreters, and providers welcome the interpreter's input on culture and communication. If the organization is culturally competent, the interpreter will be able to intervene without being told that they are going beyond their scope of work. As the level of cultural competency of the organization increases, so does the interpreter's ability to intervene and act as a cultural competency agent. However, it is likely that providers are more versed in treating culturally diverse patients, and therefore will not require as many interventions.

Chapter Seven

RECOMMENDATIONS

The data revealed a certain disconnect between what interpreters are thinking and claim they are doing and what certain stakeholders expect them to do. There are many actions and initiatives different stakeholders can make in order to better support medical and healthcare interpreters. In addition to the public, some stakeholders with a vested interest in healthcare interpreting include: 1) educators, 2) healthcare providers 3) interpreters 4) researchers, 5) administrators, 6) policy makers, and 7) patients. Certain recommendations were constructed based on the data collected, and are presented in this chapter by stakeholder group.

7.1 Recommendations for Educators

7.1.1 Improvements needed in interpreter education.

Clear healthcare policies and directives towards the provision of linguistically and culturally competent services are in place in several countries. The data show that medical interpreters would benefit from in-depth cultural competency and intercultural mediation education from educators that are themselves qualified in these areas. Interpreter educators may wish to bring qualified guest speakers to their courses to teach cultural competency and intercultural mediation, topics that require a different set of knowledge and skills to interpreting.

Guidelines on interpreting culture are published in the various standards of practice for the specialization (CHIA, 2002; IMIA & EDC, 2007), with the IMIA & EDC standard being the standard that speaks to the greatest extent on this issue. However, according to the qualitative data, it does not seem that the intricacies of this topic are being taught in detail. One of the participants even stated that she did not know she could intervene due to a cultural issue. Clearer standard guidelines are needed. For example, the Canadian standard of practice is ambiguous, as it does not explain how one is to convey cultural nuance without assuming the role of cultural advocate.

Participants also conceded that most of their cultural knowledge was tacit as it was learned through life and professional experiences. This is not an easy subject to teach as it is subjective and only certain cultures are relevant to certain interpreters, so it is quite complex to teach a diverse group of interpreters about an even more diverse number of cultures. Most have resorted to teaching cultural humility and competency paradigms to aid interpreters to be able to be flexible and alert to the situations that may arise and how to handle them. Tacit education is just as valid as explicit education. However, there were many comments about the fact that the instruction on this topic is not in-depth or theoretical. Most participants felt confident of their cultural knowledge of medicine and the patient group(s) they interpret for. However, they were not as comfortable with intervention techniques and expressed a high level of stress when engaging in these activities.

There are academic based educational programs where students undertake multiple courses within a program, and typically one of the courses covers intercultural communication or a similar title. Other titles may include the following: "Addressing cultural issues as a medical interpreter"; "Intercultural communication"; "Intercultural mediation"; or "Interpreting culture." Without a specific course on this subject, interpreters are learning mostly from personal experiences and from their professional experience after they are in the field. The Commission for Medical Interpreter Education (2014) has recommended that this be a required topic in order for an interpreter educational program to be accredited, but has not dictated how many hours need to be taught.

Most intensive programs include this topic in their syllabus. However, they have an enormous number of subjects and skills practice listed to cover in 40 to 60 hours, so the time covered in each topic area is introductory, and not necessarily in-depth. Some educational programs even claim to offer in-depth education in 60 hours, but the amount of information and skills required to educate an interpreter makes it quite impossible to substantiate this claim, as organizations such as NCIHC and IMIA have already published that 40 hours is not enough.

7.3.2 Intercultural inventories needed in interpreter education.

The utilization of cultural inventories is needed to help interpreters have the ability to self-assess their own culture and cultural competency. Most of these inventories are best when taken before a course, and after a course, to see the changes in perception and effectiveness of the course or educational intervention. There are several inventories in the U.S. market. The researcher was not able to verify the existence of inventories in other countries. However, the probability of their existence is high since these inventories are used in a variety of markets, in addition to the healthcare sector. The Intercultural Development Inventory (IDI), for example (Hammer, Bennett, & Wiseman, 2003), assesses *intercultural competence*—the capability to shift cultural perspective and appropriately adapt behavior to cultural differences and commonalities. Intercultural competence has been identified as a critical capability in a number of studies focusing on overseas effectiveness of international sojourners, international business adaptation and job performance, international student adjustment, international transfer of technology and information, international study abroad, and inter-ethnic relations within nations. There are other cultural competency inventories available in the field, such as the Cross Cultural Adaptability Inventory (CCAI) (Kelly & Meyers, 2014). There are no inventories specifically designed for medical interpreters. This doctoral study designed and tested a cultural competency inventory specifically for medical interpreters. The focus group participants acted as pilot testers for the inventory and have provided feedback for improvement. Further development is needed to make it a suitable cultural competency inventory for practicing medical interpreters. Cultural competency education that does not include intercultural inventories misses a very important and necessary component of cultural competency education. Without it, students are not able to assess their own cultural profile to be able to identify one that is different from theirs.

7.3.3 Control-Demand Schema needed in interpreter education.

As previously discussed in this study, there are few specific scientifically validated theoretical models for interpreters to help them address cultural issues. The DC-Schema is one of them, and is very useful as an evidence-based interpreter pedagogical strategy for educators. It is important for educators to use theoretical models that have been validated and tested.

Karasek and Theorell (1990) theorized that occupational stress arises from the relationship between the difficulties (demands) presented by work responsibilities with respect to the interventions (controls or strategies) that professionals have to respond to in their daily work requirements. Dean and Pollard (2001) used this occupational research theoretical framework to examine the nature of demands and controls in the interpreting profession. The DC-Schema is the only validated interventionist model for interpreters that include cultural issues as one of the demands or difficulties of the work. The CHIA Standards (2002) include ethical principles of intercultural sensitivity, and a section on the cultural clarifier role. However, the latter section does not describe all possible intercultural activities described by participants, as the focus is on the specific task of intercultural intervention when there is a miscommunication between the parties. The DC-Schema was developed to be an instructional tool to address all intercultural demands, and interpreter educators may find it useful to learn and become licensed to teach the DC-Schema.

7.3.4 Jezewski model needed in interpreter education.

Study participants described the activities they believed were related to intercultural mediation, but none of the participants actually mentioned being familiar with any theoretical model utilized for intercultural mediation. The only model they have been exposed to is the incremental intervention model that utilizes the role pyramid described earlier in this book. This model explains and assumes that all intervention is related to leaving the conduit model. It is not a mediation model. Interpreters need to learn specific theoretical models on intercultural mediation, to be able to inform the public of what intercultural mediation is. The Jezewski model of intercultural mediation was not developed for medical interpreters. However, it is one of the few theoretical on intercultural mediation in any fiels, and as such, may be helpful to interpreters.

Jezewski's theoretical model is simple and effective. As described earlier, the model has three stages: problem identification, intervention strategies, and outcomes. Specific elements of these cultural mediation strategies are the following: advocating, mediating, networking, negotiating, innovating, intervening, and sensitizing. Most interpreter educators are not familiar with this model, yet it provides for a clear mediation framework that is specific to intercultural mediation, and not a generalist intervention model, as the DC-Schema that can be applied to culture. As established by the model, mediators are impartial and neutral. Mediators are also not the ones who own the main content of the conversation; it is the main parties that determine the messages they wish to send to each other. Mediators act as facilitators, bringing together individuals with different cultural views. Educators may wish to review this model and include it, as well as other theoretical models of intercultural mediation in medical interpreter education.

7.2 Recommendations for Healthcare Providers

7.2.1 Medical interpreters provide intercultural mediation.

The verbal report data expressed disappointment at the fact that some providers are not culturally competent, and that these providers are the ones challenging the interpreter's intercultural role. Interpreters understand their role as one to assist providers in their work with diverse populations. The providers with less cultural competency usually have greater difficulty in handling diverse patients and may require more help. Unfortunately, they may also not value cultural competency. On the other hand, the more culturally competent a provider is, the easier it is for the interpreter as fewer interventions are required. However, no matter how culturally competent providers become, they will never be as versed as a medical interpreter in the culture(s) of the patients they serve due to a variety of reasons. Unless they were born or raised in the patient's culture, for example, or speak the patient's language, they will not be able to identify verbal and non-verbal cues and cultural nuances to the level of a medical interpreter. Interpreters, as with any other profession, will vary in their ability to provide intercultural mediation services. However, the fact remains that they will continue to always be the only ones within the triadic or multi-person encounter who understand both cultures and languages to a greater extent than the other parties. According to the data, interpreters seem to be well versed in the healthcare culture of the country of practice, as well as the institutional culture of the organizations they work for.

More cultural competency education is needed for providers to learn how to work with diverse patients, but more importantly for them to learn how medical interpreters can help them work better with diverse patients. This requires allowing them to act as cultural and linguistic mediators. Most trainings on this topic are logistical, explaining how to call interpreters, hours of operation, languages, speaking in the first person, etc. Trainings often portray interpreters superficially, as the bilingual person who interprets, vs. the professional who mediates culture and language. According to interpreter practitioners, the different expectations providers, patients, and interpreters have of their role affects the interpreted communicative event. The older paradigm of assimilation demanded that the minority culture adapt to the majority culture, and it is still as such in many countries. However, the new paradigm of cultural competency and patient centered care expects both parties to adapt. It actually places the stronger burden on the healthcare system and the providers to adapt explanatory models and treatments to the patient's cultural preferences and understanding, in order to improve patient care, safety, compliance and satisfaction. Medical interpreters remain the most qualified professionals to improve the cultural competency of the healthcare delivery system.

7.2.2 A shared social justice framework.

As described earlier in the study, the medical interpreter specialization was born of the need to provide equitable care to all patients. A social justice framework sees all professionals working with the patient to be invested in social justice as part of their healthcare delivery. This social justice framework is one of the drivers of healthcare policies that encourage cultural competency initiatives to improve the treatment of culturally and linguistically diverse patients. According to a shared social justice framework, it provides another opportunity for providers and other healthcare workers, such as interpreters or others, to work together, where both can find considerable common ground in their roles of patient advocates, cultural brokers, and social justice workers (Messias, McDowell, & Estrada, 2009). Promoters of a more involved role for the interpreter usually cite patient empowerment issues as the reason to support their argument. When provider and interpreter are working together to better serve the patient, patient-centered care will take place. When providers attempt to control all aspects of care, without addressing culture, culturally diverse patients are ultimately not well served. Study participants demonstrated in many of their comments that some providers do not give them the space to work with agency, and as such, do a disservice to patients. The tension between who controls the flow of communication (provider or interpreter) is an issue described by many participants in the study as one of the main difficulties. When providers understand that an interpreter is a practice professional who improves the patient-provider rapport and not merely a conduit technical professional, they will be able to use the interpreter's skills and abilities to their advantage. As providers learn to see interpreters as multi-faceted facilitators and mediators, versus technical linguists, they will better understand the need for the interpreter to manage the flow of communication, as any facilitator would. The full scope of work of medical interpreters needs to be better understood, including the difficulties that intercultural communication presents to the professional attempting to close the language barrier. Current provider education on this issue seems to be lacking, according to participants.

Hsieh (2009) studied the providers' and interpreters' perceptions of their competition in controlling the content and process of provider–patient interactions, and the challenges to providers' and interpreters' collaboration in bilingual healthcare. Hsieh developed themes in areas where providers and interpreters compete and assert their expertise. Results indicated that providers and interpreters experience conflicts over their expertise and authority due to their practice in (a) adopting different speech conventions, (b) controlling the other's narratives, and (c) overstepping expertise and role boundaries. According to Hsieh (2009), authority in bilingual healthcare should not be established through pre-existing categories or expertise but negotiated and coordinated during the interactive process, which allows individuals to be adaptive to the issues emerged in the communicative process. This is what participants of this study shared, that they need to adapt to the demeanor and work style of providers and patients. Interpreter introductions that clearly establish and negotiate better the expertise and role boundaries of each party may be helpful in coordinating this interactive process that occurs in interpreted sessions. How interpreter introductions affect the triadic encounter is another topic that requires further study.

7.3 Recommendations for Medical Interpreters

Data from this study points to a move from the invisibility paradigm into the visibility paradigm. The table that follows demonstrates the characteristics of this continuum. The traditional transparent, passive, neutral, linguistically focused, and detached approach may not be applicable to the highly contextualized needs of the healthcare setting. Professional standards and ethics have framed that interpreters address cultural issues primarily to avoid a cultural miscommunication. The data shows however, by the cases given, that they are also engaging in intercultural mediation guided by healthcare related objectives, such as improving the patient-provider therapeutic rapport, and also guided by the guidelines to provide culturally competent services as healthcare professionals.

Table 46
The Invisibility-Visibility Continuum

INVISIBILITY	CONTINUUM	VISIBILITY
Scope of work limited ⬇	Conflicting scope of work	Scope of work expanded ⬆
Black box Machine Voice box Conduit role	Conflicting roles	Intercultural Mediator Co-diagnostician Patient representative Cultural informant
Provider expectation: "Just interpret word for word. Help me understand the language."	Conflicting provider expectations	Provider expectation: "Help me communicate and understand this person."
Patient expectation: "You are here only to address my inability to speak the language."	Conflicting patient expectations	Patient expectation: "You are here to help me navigate the system, and advocate for my rights."
Institutional support: Interpreters seen as language technicians	Conflicting institutional support	Institutional support: Interpreters seen as cultural and linguistic mediators
Interpreter training: Linguistic paradigm	Conflicting paradigms	Interpreter training: add Social/Medical paradigm
Linguistically competent services	Conflicting Purpose of services	Culturally and Linguistically competent services
Language professional	Conflicting professional identity	Multi-faceted professional (language, culture, healthcare)

Professional autonomy is a status that results from a profession's deep conceptualization of the professional acts and professional practices of its members and the agreement of its members to behave and act in a manner that is similar to each other. However, adhering to such a cohesive paradigm can be challenging. The degree of decision latitude afforded to interpreters working in various settings is also impacted by a wide range of internal factors as well, such as their educational background, ethnicity, familiarity with the institution, professional standing, and presence, to name a few. These differences in the professional agency and decision latitude of practitioners in different work settings have significant implications in their work. The more balanced the autonomy is expressed by all participants, the more likely the interpreter will exercise appropriate choices. The less balanced the autonomy expressed by participants, the more likely the interpreter is to exercise inappropriate choices.

7.3.1 The healthcare interpreter specialization is unique.

Medical interpreters have been studied, conceptualized and understood primarily based on generalist interpreter norms from specializations that are not specific to medical interpreting (conference, legal, community, lay bilinguals). Since medical and legal interpreting are specializations within community interpreting, norms and standards for community interpreting cannot be specific to the specialized needs of healthcare, for example. Some interpreters, specially the Canadian participants, who are guided by their National Community Interpreting Standards, have been practicing without a specific standard for healthcare interpreting. This creates a professional identity problem of forcing them to adopt a broader community interpreting standard with conflicting goals and objectives. On one side are the goals and objectives of all community interpreters, regardless of the context, mostly limited to their linguistic role. On the other side, there are the healthcare goals and objectives of the specialization itself, such as: 1) to provide culturally and linguistically competent healthcare services, or 2) to improve patient-provider therapeutic rapport, or 3) to manage conflict between the parties. These goals and objectives, specific to healthcare interpreting, are not mentioned in the Canadian National Community Interpreting Standards.

Further study is needed regarding the limitations of a professional standard that does not address the specific needs of the healthcare industry. It is difficult to exert one's specialized professional identity, autonomy and agency in the healthcare setting and in interpreted communicative events by following a traditional generalist model. A model of invisibility or limitation to a linguistic focus or a semi-generalist model of interpreting in many different community settings simply does not serve medical interpreters well. The differences of opinion regarding how much intervention is adequate will remain as in all professional circles. Practitioners have different approaches, in any specialization, as in any profession.

Based on this study, a very small minority in the field (two out of four hundred and fifty-eight) believes that interpreters should not intervene at all. However, thorough analysis of the vast research and standards reviewed regarding this subject point to medical interpreters as visible participants who mediate culture and language. The study demonstrated that at the same time that they are preoccupied with the difficult linguistic tasks of interpreting, they are also engaged in several other non-linguistic tasks, such as enhancing the therapeutic rapport or managing conflict through their mediation.

Some may fear that a visible participatory interventionist model will yield too much power to the medical interpreter. However, the data produced by this study demonstrates that interpreters are very cognizant of their professional limitations as mediators. Mediation work requires a high level of soft skills, control, and an emphasis on the relationship of those one is attempting to mediate for. Participants seemed very cognizant of the dangers of becoming the center of attention. These include their responsibilities to impartiality, neutrality, maintenance of communication flow, and the understanding that this is but one of their tasks. Participants reported a high level of professional commitment to enhance the patient-provider therapeutic rapport over their individual rapport with either the patient or the provider.

Limiting the scope of work of medical interpreters to only interpret language or focus on interpreting does a disservice to the provision and to promoting culturally competent care. Every standards of practice discusses the need to convey cultural nuances, even the Canadian standard. So the question is not whether interpreters should convey cultural nuances, but how, when and to what extent they should provide intercultural mediation services. Interpreters may need to improve how they convey their professional role as mediators and become better promoters of their own work within the organizations they work for. Interpreter introductions that describe the role of the interpreter to provide cultural and linguistic mediation may more clearly establish and negotiate the expertise and role boundaries of each party. On the other hand, introductions that simply state 'I am here to interpret everything you say between Spanish and English' will actually convey the medical interpreter as a technical language converter, and nothing more.

7.3.2 Client education is an important responsibility of any profession.

Many interpreters stated several providers do not understand their work. It is important to note that professionals in any field have a professional responsibility to engage in client education. The education of all healthcare providers, as well as the administrators of healthcare organizations on how their work affects patient care, is actually the responsibility of many stakeholders, including the medical interpreter. Since medical interpreting is a relatively new profession in healthcare, it is imperative to incorporate client education as an important and integral component of one's interpreting practice. This is the only way interpreters will garner greater support for this essential role in providing culturally competent healthcare. Interpreter managers and contracting agencies that provide medical interpreting services are in fact responsible, alongside with interpreters, to provide such client education. However, these stakeholders sometimes also need educating, specially if they are not familiar with the intricacies of each interpreting specialization or if they were never practitioners themselves.

Ultimately, since the interpreter is in close contact with several providers on a daily basis, in numerous communicative events, it is ultimately the interpreter who will have the greatest opportunities and teaching moments. Research has shown that individuals learn best when they are able to understand the implication of their learning to their work. This occurs best when experiencing the issue to be learned. Therefore, the most appropriate teaching moments for a provider on how to work with an interpreter is when the provider is faced with the reality of working with that interpreter, and nobody should be better equipped than the interpreter to explain their role, set the standards and guidelines of how to best work in a way that engenders collaboration and not competition or communication control issues. The profession's responsibility to provide effective client education has not been emphasized in codes of conduct or the standards of practice. Client education is a skill that is more developed in Sign language interpreting than in Spoken language interpreting. There is a need for interpreters to become better educated on this important aspect of their careers. Without this more sophisticated education, they will not be able to effectively explain their cultural role and demands in healthcare and how that affects culturally competent care to the parties that most need to hear it.

Healthcare providers are not the only direct users or consumers of healthcare interpreting. Patients are also consumers and therefore require client education just as much as healthcare providers. Their lack of knowledge about the role of the professional interpreter to provide accurate communication sometimes results in patients waiving their right or accepting to work with a family member or friend who is not trained in medical interpreting, and much less versed in medical terminology. Patients, as well as providers, are not aware of the nuances of language and culture, and cannot assess a person's ability to interpret accurately because they do not understand the other language to be able to know if the interpretation is accurate or not. Often times, those who are called to assist do the best they can, and are also unaware of the amount of information they omit, add, or distort. As interpreters are taught and improve their client education towards patients, patients will desire and be better equipped to demand professional interpreting services for their own patient safety. They will also feel more comfortable in interpreted communicative events, and know what they can and cannot ask the interpreter to do for them.

7.4 Recommendations for Researchers

This study is based on the premise that practitioners are the ultimate experts of their craft. Few studies have focused on the medical interpreters' perspectives about their work and expertise, as most have been interested in the linguistic or sociological aspects of the interpreters' work through field observation and/or discourse analysis. Medical interpreting is a relatively new specialization. Therefore majority of researchers in the field are not necessarily practicing or past medical interpreters. Healthcare providers, sociologists, and language professionals (linguists, and/or interpreters in other specializations) have been the ones publishing most of the research on medical interpreting. Therefore, these are studies of other professionals looking into what medical interpreters do from their own professional perspective, be it sociological, anthropological, or linguistic. Researchers need to better define who the interpreter practitioners are in their research. If a specific research is about the interpreting being performed by professional as well as laypersons in a particular hospital, and these activities are reported as one and the same activity, then this research can only claim to study the activity of interpretation and not the profession. The profession can only be studied when engaging with professional interpreters. Unfortunately, there are still many hospitals still relying on volunteers or family members, or bilingual healthcare providers who were not trained in interpreting. Therefore, this becomes an important distinction, as it affects whether the research is applicable to study of the healthcare interpreting *profession* or if the research is applicable to report on the *activity* of interpreting. The field needs more studies that have specified qualifiers of those who are defined as professional interpreters. The same is true regarding the distinction of healthcare interpreters or general interpreters who occasionally interpret in healthcare. Their opinions and perspective about healthcare interpreting will not be the same. Further study is needed to compare the professional opinions of interpreters working in different specializations.

There is great value of studying the verbal reports of interpreters, vs. observing what they actually do or interpret, when attempting to better understand their professional identity and working paradigms. This study shed light to the cognitive processes taking place regarding the demands participants faced regarding addressing cultural issues in healthcare. It also shed light into the communicative and healthcare reasons why interpreters feel they must act as intercultural mediators. The reason is not always cultural and according to the study, the reasons were mostly medical. This study gave medical interpreters a voice about interpreting culture. Studying what they had to say enhanced the collective understanding about their current views of their scope of work with regards to culture. Some studies have discussed the tasks that interpreters engage in beyond linguistic interpreting. One such study, entitled *The Community Interpreter's Task, Self-Perception and Provider Views*, included several tasks, including the task of explaining culture, and shows below how 32 interpreters agreed with an expanded scope of work (Pöchhacker, 1998, p.112).

Table 47

Does your TASK as an interpreter ALSO include:

Task in addition to interpreting task	Level of Agreement of 16 Spoken language interpreters	Level of Agreement of 16 Sign language interpreters
Simplifying language	75%	75%
Explaining Terms	75%	81%
Summarizing	94%	38%
Omitting to save time	44%	7%
Explaining culture	81%	80%
Clarifying directly	100%	88%
Alerting to miscommunication	94%	73%
Asking and informing	44%	56%
Filling in forms	63%	88%

The Community Interpreter's Task, Self-Perception and Provider Views
(p.112)

This task study was not limited to medical interpreting, and yet reports interpreters engaging in a much broader scope of work than linguistic interpreting as a conduit. Practitioners, researchers, and educators may need to rely more on the reality of the work of practitioners, to better understand the specialized work of meeting the communicative and intercultural demands of their environments as interpreters. Further research on the practice from the interpreter's perspective will help advance the field and generate greater mutual understanding and agreement between the professionals that practice interpreting.

7.5 Recommendations for the Healthcare System

The interpreters' work affects how diverse patients utilize the healthcare system. For example, the participant that explained to the patient that in Japan prescriptions expire is ensuring the patient knows this information to get his prescription in time. The level of healthcare environment support that interpreters are given to perform their cultural work will impact the provision of culturally and linguistically competent services. As stated earlier, the behavior of other parties or stakeholders (e.g., employers, educators, providers, or patients) affect the interpreters' behavior in the interpreted session. This behavior is also affected by the healthcare institution's culture and the message the institution gives to its employees regarding cultural competency, its culturally diverse patients, and intercultural mediation. A respondent exemplifies this concept in the following statement: *"My place of employment encourages interpreters to bring up any cultural beliefs that may interfere with treatment or understanding."*

7.5.1 Medical interpreters are cultural competency agents.

As stated by our participants, cultural issues do at times impair the communication between provider and patient. Not addressing cultural issues may actually affect the quality of care received. However, this study uncovered another reason that seems to be a strong driver for intercultural mediation: the impairment of the therapeutic rapport between individuals due to the presence of some level of cultural cognitive dissonance. Participants often intervened and/or engaged in intercultural tasks within and outside of the interpreted communicative event, aimed at enhancing the patient-provider therapeutic rapport, which affects patient trust, satisfaction, and compliance. Healthcare organizations will benefit from embracing interpreters as cultural competency agents.

Some argue that these two professions (intercultural mediators and medical interpreters) should remain separate. In some countries intercultural mediators interpret, and are mostly interpreters who also mediate. In other cases, they do not interpret, working only as mediators. Should a provider and a patient rely on two individuals present in a medical encounter? Should one to be the intercultural mediator to address the cultural gap and the other act as the interpreter to address the linguistic gap? Perhaps those who believe that medical interpreting and cultural mediation are complementary but different professions may prefer that providers be given two professionals to work with in intercultural communication for the most effective care. One professional would be there to provide cultural consultations and the medical interpreter would be limited to provide the medical interpretation without addressing culture. However, this would be difficult to implement and redundant since medical interpreter already has to facilitate 'intercultural' communication and convey culture within their scope of work. Let's think of the case of a hospital with a cultural mediator/consultant present or on call. In any interpreted communicative event, it would have to be the medical interpreter who would need to draw attention to a cultural issue that may require the cultural consultant to be called in to the session. Culture and language are intertwined in a way that cannot be easily separated. It may be that to meet the healthcare needs of patients and providers, practicality dictates that one person perform both roles, just as some nurses are dual role interpreters.

Many intercultural mediators have interpreting within their scope of work. It goes without saying that ideally they need to be trained adequately in both skills. If they are well trained in both skills, why should intercultural mediators who are trained to interpret not be allowed to interpret? Likewise, if they are trained in both skills, why should interpreters not be allowed to provide intercultural mediation? The training in intercultural mediation is important, and this study has shown that interpreters need more training. However, perhaps this is ultimately an employer's decision. Contracted interpreters may also have greater limitations to their work since they generally do not know the providers they are going to work with. Interpreting agencies that limit the interpreter's ability to mediate culture may be doing this more to avoid problems with their healthcare provider clients, rather than due to any professional standard or ethic limiting the interpreter's ability to do so. Further study is needed in this area to see if in the future the terms intercultural mediator, healthcare interpreter, and medical interpreter will continue to be interchangeable.

7.5.2 Intercultural interpreter mediators may become the norm.

New terms and professions may emerge, such as *intercultural interpreter mediator* to better describe a professional that is adequately trained and tested in both intercultural interpretation as well as intercultural mediation. In essence an intercultural interpreter mediator would be an individual who has gained the appropriate knowledge and skills to interpret medical information accurately *and* to mediate culture and language adequately. Interpreting medical language accurately and mediating intercultural communication are ultimately separate areas of domain, skills, and abilities. Currently interpreters are mostly being trained and tested on the domain of interpreting medical information adequately, without enough focus on the complexities of meaningful and intercultural communication facilitation. Better-trained medical interpreters who are able to address the cultural gap between providers and patients may be more beneficial to healthcare organizations that wish to decrease the disparity of and improve the healthcare outcomes of their culturally diverse patients. While many may believe that the data show that interpreters already possess these skills and abilities, unless training backs these skills, their intercultural mediation skills will not be validated and officially recognized. Likewise, without training and testing, it will be impossible to know which interpreters have mastered intercultural mediation skills and who have not. It is difficult to practice a profession as a mediator and yet be seen and treated even within your own field as a conduit. The move from technical professional to practice professional has already occurred in the Sign language field largely due to the DC-Schema, while in the Spoken language field it is just starting to occur.

7.5.3 Medical interpreters are integration agents.

The contracting and employment of professional medical interpreters results in improved care, greater patient satisfaction, and lower expenses for the medical system (Flores, 2005). The solution lies in the recruitment of trained medical interpreters as an integral part of the team of healthcare professionals (Seidelman & Bachner, 2010). Situations involving intercultural exchanges of information about risks and benefits of treatment depend on accurate and culturally appropriate interpretation of medical and health concepts. The requirement that patients achieve a level of understanding before agreeing to a proposed treatment ultimately may require intermediaries to reconcile fundamentally different and sometimes incompatible concepts of illness and healing (Kaufert, Lavallée, Koolage, & O'Neil, 1996).

Navigating a foreign healthcare system, with its own rules and idiosyncrasies, may be difficult for a patient who does not speak the language of care. The cultural task of explaining to patients how the system works in the country of care is of great benefit to patients for a more equitable level of navigation use. Several of the cases provided to the study by participants involved the task of the interpreter explaining how the local system worked to the patient. One example was to help the patient with compliance (e.g., fill your prescription within the next 4 days as it will expire in Japan). Another example was related to way finding (e.g., inform the patient that he needed to go to their employer and not the hospital). These are examples of how medical interpreters can aid the patients and ultimately the healthcare system to avoid redundancies or misuse.

These interpreters are providing information about the services offered in the organizations they work for, just as a nurse or an administrator. It has nothing to do with providing medical advice. The responsibility of assisting patients to navigate the system, including way finding, belongs to all healthcare professionals, and that includes medical interpreters. Those who are against interpreters providing service information claim that the interpreter may provide erroneous information. Any employee may provide erroneous information. Professional interpreters should be assumed to only inform patients of information they know. Patients will request information of all who they come into contact. Interpreters need to respond or redirect the patient to the individual who may have the information the patient is seeking. Relaying information to patients needs to be seen as a beneficial activity by the interpreter to the healthcare system and most importantly to the patient.

Should interpreters provide way finding, referrals, or other healthcare services, when part of the hospital staff? Why is this controversial to some in the field of interpreting? This is the view of those limited to thinking of interpreters as conduits, failing to recognize or understand their work outside the interpreted communicative event. When asked questions related to healthcare delivery that they know the answer to, why should interpreters seek another healthcare professional to explain something they already know because they also work there? It seems that looking for another healthcare professional with the same information and then interpreting that information is duplicative and redundant. When interpreters are fully seen as healthcare professionals, then perhaps there will be no push back for the medical interpreter, as a healthcare professional, to provide information to patients regarding the navigation of the healthcare system.

This can only be done, obviously by those interpreters who work within an institution, remotely or in person.

A medical interpreter who is an independent contractor, who does not know the organizational environment she is working for, will not be able to provide any information about the organization and would surely seek another healthcare professional with the information and interpret for the patient. It is up to each healthcare organization to decide how to utilize their interpreters for the greatest benefit to the organization, so long as it does not go against their code of ethics or standards of practice.

7.6 Limitations of Research

This research has several limitations. The number of interview participants ($n=18$) and focus group participants ($n=16$) was not large, and as such was a limitation of this study. The research plan incorporated an online survey ($n=423$) and accepted one essay in lieu of an interview in order to address this limitation. This also enabled the research to count on some quantitative data to test it against the qualitative data, and also to provide the research study with more qualitative responses and a larger number of participants.

The country of practice was another limitation. The participants worked in twenty-five countries, with the majority worked in the United States (65.2%). This means that the data is skewed to a certain point to the views and practices exercised in the United States. However, the United States is the country with the most developed medical interpreting profession in the world (the only country with national medical interpreter certification), and the largest medical interpreter population. Therefore, this study may reflect the distribution of interpreters in the world to a certain extent. The methodology should have included the translation of the survey into at least five languages. However, budgetary constraints prevented this, and therefore also limited the participants to those who had a sufficient level of written proficiency in English to answer the questionnaire.

Last, the study explores perceptions versus practice, in order to investigate what the practitioners had to say about their work, and not rely on the researcher's interpretation of the work observed. The reader has the added advantage of hearing interpreters' voices and opinions about their work in their own words. Both thought and action have to be studied when exploring a certain aspect of a professional practice. It involves thought processes, decision-making processes, and other tasks that may not be seen, yet can be exposed in a self-reported study.

7.7 Further Research Needed

This study focused on the medical interpreters' perspectives. More research is needed to explore the other stakeholders' perspectives. This includes providers, patients, and healthcare administrators. Their perspectives will shed light on how the different expectations of each participant can be harmonized to standardize this issue further. Better cooperation and collaboration will ensue if all parties understand the limitations and considerations of the other party at hand. A study that involves all stakeholders engaging in this discussion together could also bring very valuable research for the field. Last, research on cultural differences in healthcare could focus on how educational and religious differences affect intercultural communication in healthcare. This was a first study on the practice of addressing cultural issue, and as such could not go in-depth into exploring each of those aspects separately. Further research into each of those aspects will deepen the collective understanding of the subject matter. Another area of interest could relate to which specific aspects of culture are being addressed in medical interpreter training. The majority of medical interpreters shared the view that they did not receive enough training in this area. Some also conceded that there are difficulties of teaching this subject, usually learned through tacit learning, in the classroom. Research on the amount of time and subtopics educators are devoting to addressing culture would be enlightening in a field where there are no regulations on the education of medical interpreters. In the US, only voluntary educational standards exist via the accreditation program of the Commission for Medical Interpreter Education. Lastly, research is needed on how different modalities of interpreting (remote versus face-to-face, staff versus contractor) affect interpreting culture.

Chapter Eight

CONCLUSION

Cultural differences in intercultural communication are often a barrier to high-quality healthcare. Providing culturally and linguistically appropriate services is part of eliminating health disparities, minimizing risk, and increasing patient safety. Medical interpreters have an important role in the provision of culturally competent care. They described acting as linguistic and cultural mediators between providers and patients in a study about addressing cultural issues in healthcare. The previous chapter delineated concrete recommendations for various stakeholders to better support the work of healthcare interpreters in this area.

8.1 Summary of Findings

This study explored the perspectives and professional opinions of professional medical interpreters, regarding addressing culture, with the premise that practitioners are the primary experts regarding their own practice. This study utilized a mixed qualitative-quantitative methodology with four data sources. The literature review showcased the invisibility model (interpreters as conduits with little or no professional agency in the interpreted session) to be losing ground to a more visible model of active participation (where the interpreter has and utilizes their professional agency to facilitate and mediate language and culture). Interpreters expressed the need to exercise agency to be able address cultural issues.

Most of the research reviewed also showcased medical interpreters as active participants and as interlocutors (Angelelli 2004; Bot 2005; Hsieh 2006; Pöchhacker & Shlesinger 2003).

Interviewed participants were asked to provide examples of situations in which they addressed a cultural issue. This generated 32 case studies, analyzed in the results chapter. Other questions involved discussing the advantages, disadvantages, challenges, timing, stressors, and education related to interpreting culture. Participants described the primary advantages to interpreting culture as the ability to improve the provider-patient rapport and ensure understanding for effective meaningful communication, essential for patient safety. They also cited that the added benefits of making the patient feel at ease, included and respected, increasing patient trust, and allowing the delivery of services to be provided in a linguistically and culturally competent manner. They described how their interventions gave the provider an opportunity to adapt the service to the individual patient's cultural preferences, and thus improve patience satisfaction and compliance. Most importantly, participants actually claimed it improved health outcomes in a very objective and measurable way. More study is needed in this area. Participants discussed how addressing cultural issues improve the provider-patient therapeutic rapport, a core objective of their work mentioned in every intercultural intervention. They claimed that patient trust and patient compliance are directly related to this rapport, improved as a result of their interventions. Some of the focus group participants insisted that addressing cultural issues is a patient safety issue, not a cultural sensitivity issue, and that their shared responsibility with the provider for patient safety overrides any other concerns they may have in their work.

Even from a linguistic point of view, they discussed that addressing cultural issues was not an option, but a necessity in order to convey culturally nuances, embedded in messages, and essential for accurate interpretation. They also discussed how they are the only ones in the triadic encounter with the linguistic and some cultural knowledge of both parties. They seemed very cognizant of the importance of being neutral and impartial mediators, aware of and attempting to control their own cultural biases to enter the triadic discussion.

What were the primary challenges? The lack of time in the provision of healthcare was mentioned as the first of two primary challenges. Medical sessions that require consecutive interpretation typically require twice the time, since every utterance needs to be restated in two languages. However, interpreted sessions are rarely given more time, causing stress to providers and interpreters alike, as stated by participants. This is a real healthcare delivery issue that showcases that minority language patients are basically being allocated half the time than other patients, which may compromise quality of care to linguistically diverse patients. Since the same typical conversation cannot be had in half the time, providers have to cut the conversation and typical dialogue into a more streamlined one that addresses what cannot be skipped. Provider and interpreter feel rushed, which is a strong demand or challenge for the interpreter. This seems to put pressure on interpreters only to intervene and address cultural issues when it is absolutely necessary. Participants sometimes decided against providing intercultural mediation due to the shared healthcare objective with the provider of making good time While there may be variations of this issue depending on the country of practice, research is needed on this important issue, as time constraints directly affect the content of communication as well as time required for the provider to provide a diagnosis or treatment plan. This time constraint may be emblematic of a lower level of care being provided to culturally and linguistically diverse patients. Interpreters and providers have no control over allocation of time for patients, so they are given the challenge to get their healthcare goals met in practically half the time. That may be another reason why interpreters cut their introductions short and have no time for any pre-session or post session.

The second greatest difficulty reported is the fact that addressing cultural issues itself may go against the provider's view of the work of the interpreter. According to participants, some providers attempt to impose their control causing tension in the encounter, and one participant even described her difficulty with providers to even allow her to introduce herself to the other parties of the encounter. Provider interaction was described as a source of stress for some medical interpreters. More interestingly, it showcases that according to participants, they are not always able to act as they wish professionally.

Providers with little understanding of cultural humility or cultural competency are unaware of the interpreter's cultural role. They are also unaware of the cultural gap between themselves and their culturally diverse patient, and that this gap affects not only understanding but also patient satisfaction, compliance, and trust. These providers see the interpreter mostly as a mouthpiece that will 'repeat' everything the patient states. They really do think the interpreter is repeating the same words in a different language. They are not bilingual so they are not aware that interpreters interpret messages and concepts that may not be present in the other language or culture. In addition to uninformed providers, there were the providers who had difficulty in sharing the control of the communication flow with interpreters. These providers are not used to working with interpreters as facilitators or mediators, and resent the presence of a third party in their encounters with patients. Thus, they attempt to minimize the interpreter role in order to remain in control of the communication. This makes for a very difficult interpreted communicative event, where the collective communicative space is void of trust from the provider to the interpreter. Interpreters have to adapt to these scenarios and may be frustrated by a limited scope that does not allow them to perform their jobs in accordance to their standards of practice and code of ethics.

Addressing culture often means intervention, and that also goes against the interpreter's linguistic objective to maintain a natural and seamless flow of communication. Any intervention breaks this flow, so interpreters do not interrupt unless they feel it is an issue that merits discussion, rightly so. Due to this factor, interpreters have to evaluate and assess each situation quickly, sometimes at the same time they are interpreting. Regardless, the primary parties in the discussion, the provider and the patient, according to participants, are the ones who drive the discussion, with the interpreter primary stance being a neutral, yet an active linguistic and cultural mediator with subtle tasks and messages to encourage the engagement of the parties in the interpreted session. Outside of interpreted encounters, interpreters do not have the same time constraints and do not have to worry about maintaining the flow of communication. In pre or post sessions with providers or patients, or team meetings, participants described providing intercultural tasks in the form of cultural assessment of the patient, for example. At other times, they described their efforts of explaining culture, or providing unsolicited, but necessary cultural education to the provider or patient, among other activities.

8.2 New Theoretical Frameworks

Chapter Six showcased new formulations about healthcare interpreting. The data of this research led to the development of new theoretical frameworks to better understand the cultural work of the interpreter in the healthcare environment. They describe evolving principles specific to this professional specialization. The first of such frameworks relates to the indirect relationship between the cultural competency of the provider or healthcare organization and the need for intercultural intervention. One of the challenges for participants seems to be the fact that some providers do not understand well enough the interpreter's roles in healthcare. Reported institutional support varied greatly, and was cited as having a direct effect in the interpreters' ability to do their cultural work appropriately. This was a source of frustration for some participants. Participants stated that the provider and organization's level of cultural competency affected their ability to intervene and ensure optimal care. The lower the cultural competency of the provider or institution, the higher the need for intervention. However, due to the lack of cultural competency of the provider or the institution, these was also the most difficult interventions, if allowed at all.

Participants described their strategies, which included specific tips and techniques utilized to address culture. In order to address cultural issues in a professional, impartial, and neutral manner, they discussed how they need to constantly be cognizant of non-verbal cues, identify cultural issues in order to know when or even if there is a need or possibility to intervene. They also described how some of the interventions had other goals in mind other than clarification or accurate communication. Sometimes they intervened to avoid a negative reaction that could impair the patient – provider therapeutic rapport. At other times they did not intervene, or chose to intervene before or after the session, due to constraints of time or due to not wishing to interrupt the flow of communication or distract participants from the core medical issue at hand. In either of these cases, the reasons for intervening, or not, went beyond preventing miscommunication. Participants described cultural and communication mediation activities that portrayed a multi-faced professional identity beyond linguistic interpreting. In addition to being linguistic interpreters and intercultural communication professionals, they also expressed the views and objectives towards patients common to other healthcare professionals.

The second new theoretical framework developed from the data involves identifying three domains of professional identity and scopes of practice within the qualitative data. The intercultural activities reported were catalogued and categorized to belong to three professional domains or what here are called *macro roles* 1) medical/healthcare, 2) intercultural communication, and 3) linguistic interpreting.

The first macro role involves their professional identity, knowledge and skills of the healthcare environment, protocols, and objectives, embedded in all healthcare professionals; clinicians and ancillary staff alike. These included cultural concerns and actions directed to improve patient provider rapport, patient safety, compliance, trust, and satisfaction, among others. The intercultural communication macro role involves the professional identity, knowledge, and skills of all the issues that may affect intercultural communication. As intercultural communication mediators, interpreters reported their concerns and actions directed to improve patient and provider understanding, communication goals, explaining cultural concepts, addressing cognitive dissonance, and among others. The third macro role involves the professional identity, knowledge, and skills of linguistic interpreting. These included concerns and actions related to language and interpreting accurately into the target language, the medical and non-medical messages between providers and patients. These activities included sight translation, note taking, consecutive and simultaneous interpreting, as well as linguistic clarification activities required to ensure an interpretation that is accurate and faithful to the source message.

These macro roles may take place concurrently with each other. The study verified that medical interpreters are engaged in scanning for cultural issues at all times, concurrent with interpreting language, and not as a separate role or activity. The intercultural activities described may address the cultural issue overtly with a cultural intervention, or not. More research is needed in this area of multitasking, engaging in multiple roles, and role overload. In other words, interpreters do not stop interpreting each time they need to address a cultural issue. Intervention is but one of the intercultural activities of medical interpreters. They may address it within their linguistic interpretation, or prefer to address it before or after the interpreted session, or choose not to address it at all.

Medical interpreters are therefore engaging in interpreting culture in more ways than established in previous research. Participants described cultural assessment and decision-making processes that were unobservable to the parties involved, as well as observable behaviors and actions regarding intercultural mediation. They also shared obstacles, objectives and activities within their cultural work as medical interpreters that shed light into the thought processes and decisions medical interpreters make in their daily work. Data analysis showcased that some of these perceptions regarding interpreting culture are tied to the demands of the healthcare environment. Interestingly, when discussing their work, the participants' foremost focus was not on perfect linguistic interpretation, but on the health of the patient and the medical outcome. The healthcare environment demands for efficient and quality patient care are real, and participants claim to own these healthcare-related demands as part of their responsibility as medical or healthcare interpreters.

8.3 Interpreters Are Members of the Healthcare Team

This cultural work is characterized by a relatively high degree of skills and effort to reduce the complexity of the intercultural communicative events they are engaged in. The results challenge the current linguistic paradigm, as 99.56% of participants of this study reported the perspectives of active participants with contributions beyond linguistic mediation. Interpreters reported professional objectives that are healthcare related: to provide culturally competent care; to enhance the patient-provider therapeutic rapport; to be part of the healthcare team, and to improve patient health outcomes. The participants' focus on the patient's safety and health above all other linguistic considerations raises a question about which ethical paradigm interpreters are most loyal to, the interpreting ethics or medical ethical principles of do no harm, for example. Interpreter ethics may be trumped by medical ethics when both ethical paradigms are in conflict. Further study is needed on how medical ethics affects the decisions of medical interpreters.

Perhaps of the three macro roles, the healthcare professional macro role is the least understood, as most in the field (interpreters, including educators, employers, and researchers) are linguists who focus on interpreting and communication. The healthcare macro role is only shared by those working mostly in the healthcare field and not as consultants but as employees who are an integral part of the human resources of a healthcare organization. This macro role embodies the 'medical' in medical interpreting, and it incorporates much more than medical terminology.

8.4 Healthcare Interpreting, a Specialization in Development

Medical interpreting has been called an *emerging* profession since the 1970s. This specialization may now be called *in development* and will soon become one of the more mature specializations in the field, following the specializations of conference interpreting and legal interpreting. One may argue that the level of development of the specialization varies from country to country. This is true of all specializations. Medical interpreters need continue to better understand their professional standards as these relate to the practical realities of their work. Greater continuous updating of the guidelines will engender greater consistency in their work across regions and countries. As seen by Appendix F, different countries are calling interpreters different titles, and some countries have not developed the healthcare specialization to the extent that other countries have. All standards of practice reviewed included conveying cultural nuances as part of the interpreter's scope of work, albeit to different levels.

There is only one international standard specifically for medical interpreters (IMIA & EDC, 2007), which has been translated into several languages. However, since the specialization is not as developed in some countries, this particular standard may not be well known in these countries. It lists most of these non-linguistic conversion activities reported in the study. It is noteworthy to mention that the international standard used the DACUM process, an occupational analysis development model that observed practitioners in their environment, before developing the standards. All the other standards were not grounded in such a specific occupational research method. As more professional medical interpreters become interpreter trainers, employers, and educators, the practitioner perspective may start to change the older status quo of the invisibility paradigm. As this specialization matures and more literature is available showcasing the reality of a professional medical interpreter's work, a deeper understanding of the interpreter's unique healthcare focused scope of practice will appear. More study on the non-linguistic work of interpreters is needed. For example, studies of the interpreter's interactions with patients and providers outside the interpreted communicative event would help shed light on these other aspects of the interpreter's work.

8.5 General Standards Do Not Address Medical Interpreting Practice

Standards and ethics cannot be blindly transferred (Angelelli, 2000) from one specialization to the other. For example, the code of ethics of legal interpreters is specific to the legal setting and is not congruent with the goals of medical interpreters (National Association of Judiciary Interpreters Code of Conduct, 2011). Also, standards or guidelines for community interpreting are general to all community interpreting specializations, and as such these standards cannot address the intrinsic needs and unique demands of the healthcare interpreting specialization. These community standards need to address the needs of all related specializations at the same time, generalizing guidelines for all of the specializations, negating the specific unique demands of a particular specialization. This may be a reason why the Canadian standard for community interpreting is the most limiting with regards to intercultural mediation, since its guidelines need to serve interpreters working in the legal system. Court interpreters, for example, practice in two specific settings. One setting involves interpretation in legal proceedings, such as depositions, trials, or arraignments. This setting requires interpretation that is more closely aligned to conference interpreting, as it is not dialogic. The other setting involves interpreting dialogues between lawyers or other legal professions and their clients or defendants. These interactions more closely reflect medical interpreting, as these are dialogic communicative events where the parties are trying to understand each other. Meaningful communication is important in the second setting, while the judicial requirements of the legal system do not require meaningful communication in the first.

This study included only healthcare interpreters, and demonstrated high congruency of the perspectives of 458 interpreters who work in 25 countries. Whereas specific country-to-country comparisons were not made, all comparisons made, on a variety of variables, did not establish a significant variance in regards to the interpreter perspectives about interpreting culture. The only comparisons that showcased a slight variance demonstrated that Canadian interpreters are more conservative in addressing cultural issues when compared to all others, and Sign language interpreters were slightly more liberal in addressing cultural issues when compared to all others.

8.6 Medical Interpreters as Cultural and Linguistic Mediators

Participants portrayed a multi-faceted profession, acting as cultural and linguistic mediators with much more to offer besides language conversion, a complex professional activity in itself. This study does not attempt or wish to diminish the linguistic importance of the work of interpreters. However, it focuses on showcasing the equally important intercultural work of interpreters. It was often been considered as secondary task, for several reasons. First, it is not observed to take place at all times, as many stakeholders only recognize and see the intercultural work of an interpreter when the interpreter overtly stops interpreting to address a cultural issue explicitly in the interpreted communicative event. The data clearly show that the interpreters' intercultural tasks go beyond intervention and are therefore more intrinsic and prevalent to their work than previously seen.

The other reason is that most have not connected intercultural tasks to quality healthcare. However, interpreters reported that their intercultural actions were related to patient outcomes, and not just to provide friendly or culturally sensitive care to culturally diverse patients. The intercultural work reported is claimed to improve the quality of care, and healthcare outcomes, and just as the research has connected language access to improved quality care, patient safety and compliance, research has also connected cultural access to quality care, patient safety and compliance. This work is also more closely linked to the interpreters' healthcare macro role, with goals and objectives that are healthcare oriented, due to the demand of providing culturally competent care in the healthcare setting to decrease healthcare disparities.

8.7 Policies Needed to Address Intercultural Mediation Services

Better institutional policies and standards for the cultural aspect of the work of medical interpreters are urgently needed. Various stakeholders may benefit to learn that medical interpreters are not merely linguists who repeat medical terminology in two languages. Interpreters themselves may need to promote themselves as cultural and linguistic mediation professionals who are essential to the delivery of culturally competent healthcare.

Many educational programs teach general interpreting only, without addressing the needs of the healthcare market. For example, educators using more traditional general conceptualizations of the role of the interpreter and may wish to update their trainings and bring practicing medical interpreters to their trainings as the experts to explain the healthcare environment's demands and realities. There were a substantial number of participants of this study, practicing medical interpreters, who had not received any training at all in the patient(s) culture(s) (55.2%) nor on medical culture (43.24%). This showcases the need for greater specialization education, and for higher quality training in this specific area of intercultural mediation, as the majority of medical interpreters brought up the need for more training in cultural issues. Incorporating more in-depth standards of practice training will also improve interpreter education to address the work demand realities that participants reported on. According to the data, some interpreters in the field may not be aware of what the standards of practice state about interpreting culture.

Hospitals would benefit to develop policies to support the medical interpreter as an intercultural mediator. They can resolve to work with healthcare interpreters as *cultural competency agents* for the patients they serve. Organizational support related to the interpreter's intercultural work might relieve the stress and discomfort interpreters feel when interpreting culture in less culturally competent environments. It is important to note that the environment and parties an interpreter works with affects their ability to interpret culture and provide culturally competent care. Some interpreters stated that it is more difficult to interpret culture when providing telephone interpretation vs. on site interpretation due to the inability to see all non-verbal cues. Since the research did not identify remote from on-site interpreters, it is difficult to ascertain if these were outliers or a majority concern. More research is needed in this area, specifically comparing how interpreters are meeting the provider and patient's intercultural communication needs over the phone or via videoconferencing or other means.

The trend in some countries has been to move from on site interpreting delivery models to remote interpreting services and this has raised concerns for the quality of care in certain situations where remote interpreting is impossible, impractical, or simply not advisable for optimal communication. Healthcare organizations are becoming more cognizant of when on site interpreting is more appropriate and when remote interpreting is more appropriate. However, practical concerns of cost, efficiency, and coordination, are pushing some organizations to use mostly the remote modality, sometimes to the detriment of the quality of patient care. Healthcare organizations need to understand that cultural mediation is a highly contextualized activity and that majority language patients will need a certain number of medical interpreters on site to appropriately meet their cultural and linguistic needs. Thankfully video interpreting is now starting to replace telephone interpreting, adding a visual component to the interpreted communicative event. Research on comparing these three modalities exists, but mostly from the companies that provide the services, and not independent researchers in the field.

The traditional transparent, passive, neutral, linguistically focused, and detached approach may not be applicable to the highly contextualized and unique needs of the healthcare setting. As the profession evolves, a number of researchers will specifically look at the interpreter work from the context of culturally competent healthcare services. This research revealed that interpreters are acting as intercultural mediators within the healthcare sector to different degrees, and with multiple and often-simultaneous roles previously described in the literature review: as *welcomers, integration agents, community agents, bilingual professionals, cultural informants,* and *educators,* among others. The broader scope of work described by participants speaks to the need for a greater understanding of their healthcare specialization.

8.8 Medical Interpreters Need to be Acknowledged as Cultural Experts

Most medical interpreters do not hold an intercultural specializations or an anthropology degree. However, that fact seems irrelevant when acknowledging that their intercultural mediation work as it is being provided, within and outside the interpreted communicative events, seems to be essential in the provision of culturally competent health.

These premises can be applied worldwide since cultural competency is a global concept. Their cultural contributions to healthcare need to be fully recognized, better understood, and better supported.

As the practitioners in the field addressing the realities of the healthcare environments they work in, medical interpreters are the ultimate experts in intercultural communication, which involves interpreting culture. The voice of the practitioner may become a powerful tool to improve cultural competency for linguistically diverse patients, and ultimately for all patients. *It may be helpful for interculturalists to lead the profession in this area* (Pineda, 2010). As the providers and organizations interact with interpreters, they will grow in their understanding of cultural competency, via the sensitivity, assessments, interventions, education, and advocacy of interpreters as *cultural competency agents* (Souza, 2016).

This study aimed to explore and recognize this intercultural work as an important facet of the medical interpreting specialization, and acknowledge the participants' great contributions to the provision of quality healthcare services to culturally diverse patients and providers. They reported a highly contextual and holistic view of their intercultural work that did not compartmentalize themselves as linguists, or as cultural mediators per se, or advocates, but rather as intercultural and linguistic mediators who were primarily concerned with the patient's health outcomes. They acted in such ways as to improve, redirect, clarify, and moderate the provider-patient rapport with the patient safety and health outcome objectives in mind. Their complex and important role in healthcare needs to go beyond the traditional views that have characterized interpreters as invisible passive conduits of medical information, who limit themselves to interpreting messages from patients and providers back and forth.

This is important most of all because the reported data contributes to a better understanding of specifically how the interpreters' intercultural work affects the quality of care they believe is given to culturally and linguistically diverse patients. The medical interpreter seems to be as engaged in and be committed to the provision of quality medical care as all other healthcare professionals are. Interpreters use their linguistic, communication, and intercultural knowledge and skills to affect the medical interactions they are part of, and as such directly affect the quality of medical care provided.

8.9 Medical Interpreters' Essential Role in Culturally Competent Healthcare

It is ironic that a profession that gives a voice to patients and providers has not had a prominent voice in research, and with all the stakeholders they interact with (i.e., educators, researchers, employers, healthcare organizations, providers, patients, public) regarding their medical interpreting expertise. Their voices need to be heard as practitioners that bring much more to the table than the accurate interpretation of messages into another language in healthcare. Their professional intercultural input, at any moment, is not only useful, but is essential to the provision of culturally competent and patient-centered healthcare services. As the voice of the practitioner is heard louder and louder, a better understanding, recognition, and support of their full scope of work will evolve. Medical interpreters will distinguish themselves as a unique specialization in their own right, with certain characteristics, leeway and objectives that are uncommon to all other interpreter specializations. All medical interpreters need this recognition, even if validated through further education and testing on the subject. The need for this role is real and their cultural work simply responds to the healthcare demands they face and the needs of the culturally diverse patients they serve. This broader view of the interpreter's work benefits all professionals in healthcare to become better enabled to serve their clients, ultimately all for the good and safety of the culturally diverse patient.

REFERENCES

American Arbitration Association. (1994). Model standards of conduct for mediators. Retrieved from https://adr.org/aaa/ShowPDF?doc=ADRSTG_010409

Anderson, R. (1996) Magic, science and health. The aims and the achievements of medical anthropology. Fort Worth: Harcourt Brace.

Angelelli, C. V. (2000) Interpretation as a Communicative Event: A Look through Hymes' Lenses. Meta: Translators' Journal, Vol. 45, No. 4; 580-592

Angelelli, C. V. (2002) Deconstructing the invisible interpreter: A critical study of the interpersonal role of the interpreter in a cultural linguistic communicative event (Doctoral dissertation). Retrieved from ProQuest Digital Dissertation. (AAT 3026766).

Angelelli, C. V. (2004) *Medical interpreting and Cross-cultural communication.* Cambridge/UK: Cambridge University Press.

Angelelli, C. V. (2004a). Revisiting the interpreter's role. A study of conference, court, and medical interpreters in Canada, Mexico, and the United States. Amsterdam/Netherlands: John Benjamins Publishing.

Arocha, I. S. (2007) *Beyond the Conduit Role*, International Conference on Interpreting in Legal, Health, and Social Service Settings, CL-5, Parramatta, Sydney, Australia, April 11-15, 2007.

Arocha, I. S. (2009) A Healthy Battle, *The Linguist*, December/January, Vol/48 No/6: 12-13.

Arocha, I. S. (2010). National Certification Marks Progress of Medical Interpreting Profession. *Japanese Journal of Telemedicine and Telecare.* Vol. 6 (1), 2010:43-46

Arocha, I. S. (2012). Occupational and Environmental Health, Encyclopedia of Immigrant Health, Hidelberg/Germany; Springer Publishing.

Arocha, I. S., Bendana, L. (2013). Interpreting Culture. *Multilingual Computing, Inc.* Selkirk Mountains, North Idaho.

Arocha, I. S., Joyce, L. (2013). Patient Safety, Professionalization, and Reimbursement as Primary Drivers for National Medical Interpreter Certification in the United States. *The International Journal for Translation & Interpreting Research* Vol. 5 No 1 (2013): 127-142.

Arocha, I. S. (2013). International Accreditation Standards for Medical Interpreter Educational Programs. [Presentation on March 20, at Iryo Tsuyajushi Kyogikai, Haruno Tokubetsu Seminar [Japan Association of Medical Interpreter (JAMI) Spring Special Seminar], Osaka, Japan.

Arocha, O. & Moore, D. Y. (2011). The New Joint Commission Standards for Patient-Centered Communication [Report]. White Paper. Language Line Services.

ASTM International. (1996) F2089-14 Standard Practice for Language Interpreting, personal print copy.

ASTM International. (2015). F2089-15 Standard Practice for Language Interpreting. Retrieved from http://www.astm.org/search/fullsite-search.html?query=general%20interpreting&

Atwood, A.A., Gray, D. (1985). Interpreting: The Culture of Artful Mediation. Proceedings of the 1985 RID Convention

Avery, M. P. (2001). *The role of the healthcare interpreter, an evolving dialogue.* Retrieved from www.ncihc.org/NCIHC%20Working%20 Paper%20-%20Role%20of%

Bancroft, M. (2005). The interpreter's world tour: An environmental scan of standards of practice for interpreters. Retrieved from http://www.ncihc. org/assets/documents/publications/NCIHC%20Environmental%20 Scan.pdf

Battle, M. (1998). *Areas of Power.* Clinical Interpreter Training Program Manual, Harvard Community Healthcare Plan, Cambridge, MA.

Bennett, M. J. (1993). Towards ethnorelativism: A developmental model of intercultural sensitivity. In R. M. Paige (Ed.), *Education for the intercultural experience* (2nd ed., pp. 21-71). Intercultural Press: Yarmouth, ME.

Bloom, M., Hanson, H., Frires, G., & South, V. (1966). The use of interpreters in interviewing. *Mental Hygiene, 50*(2), 214-217.

Bontempo, K. & Malcolm, K. (2012). An Ounce of Prevention Is Worth a Pound of Cure. In L. Swabey & K. Malcolm (eds.) In Our Hands: Educating Healthcare Interpreters. Washington: Gallaudet University Press.

Bolden, G. B. (2000). Toward understanding practices for medical interpreting: Interpreters' involvement in history taking. *Discourse Studies, 2*, 387-417.

Bot, H. (2003). The myth of the uninvolved interpreter interpreting in mental health and the development of a three-person psychology. *Benjamins Translation Library, 46*, 27-36.

California Healthcare Interpreters Association. (2002). *California Standards for Healthcare Interpreters: Ethical principles, protocols, and guidance on roles.* Retrieved from http://www.interpreterschia.org/standards/standards_home.htm

Commission for Medical Interpreter Education. (2014). Accreditation standards for medical interpreter education. Retrieved from http://www.imiaweb.org/uploads/pages/580.pdf

Common Sense Advisory. (2010). *Interpreting marketplace study.* Retrieved from http://www.commonsenseadvisory.com/Portals/_default/Knowledgebase/ArticleImages/100617_R_Interpreting_Marketplace_Preview.pdf

Cross, T., Bazron, B., Dennis, K., & Isaacs, M. (1989). *Towards a culturally competent system of care (vol. 1).* CASSP Technical Assistance Center. Center for Child Health and Mental Health Policy, Georgetown University Child Development Center: Washington, DC.

Cross Cultural Healthcare Program. (1999). *Bridging the gap interpreter handbook.* Seattle, WA: Cross Cultural Healthcare Program.

Cultural Awareness Inventory. (2015). Retrieved from http://culturalcompetenceassociates.com/cultural-awareness-inventory/

CultureSmart. (2006). The Essential Piece™: 45-Hour Multilingual Training in Medical Interpretation for Bilingual Healthcare Staff, CultureSmart Inc., Quincy, MA.

Davidson, B. (2000). The interpreter as institutional gatekeeper: The social-linguistic role of interpreters in Spanish-English medical discourse. *Journal of Sociolinguistics, 4*(3), 379-405.

Davidson, B. (2001). Questions in cross-linguistic medical encounters: The role of the hospital's interpreter. *Anthropological Quarterly, 74*(4), 170-178

Dean, R. K. (2009). Challenges in interpreting addressed by demand control schema analysis. In B. E. Cartwright (Ed.), *Encounters with reality: 1,001 interpreter scenarios* (pp. 307 – 316). Alexandria, VA: RID Press.

Dean, R. K., & Pollard, R. Q. (2001). The application of demand control theory to sign language interpreting: Implications for stress and interpreter training. *Journal of Deaf Studies and Deaf Education* *6*(1), 1-14.

Dysart-Gale, D. (2005). Communication models, professionalization and the work of medical interpreters. *Health Communication. 17*, 91-103.

Education Development Center. (2001). New certification tool developed for medical interpreters. Retrieved from https://www.edc.org/newsroom/articles/new_certification_tool_developed_medical_interpreters

Elderkin-Thompson, V., Silver, R. C., & Waitzkin, H. (2001). When nurses double as interpreters: a study of Spanish-speaking patients in a US primary care setting. *Social Science & Medicine, 52*(9), 1343-1358.

Ericsson, K. A., & Simon, H. A. (1993). *Protocol analysis.* Retrieved from http://ammonwiemers.com/IdetPortfolio/articles/Assessment/Protocol%20Analysis%20--%20Verbal%20Reports%20as%20Data.pdf

Flores, G. (2005). The impact of medical interpreter services on the quality of healthcare: A systematic review. *Medical Care Research Review, 62*(3): 255-99.

Flores, G., Abreu, M., Barone, C. P., Bachur, R., & Lin, H. (2012). Errors of medical interpretation and their potential clinical consequences: A comparison of professional vs. ad hoc vs. no interpreters. *Annals of Emergency Medicine, 60*(5), 545–553.

Flores, G., Lawes, B., Mayo, S., Zukerman, B., Breau, M., Medina, L., & Hardt, E. J. (2003). Errors in medical interpretation and their potential clinical consequences in pediatric encounters. *Pediatrics, 111*, 6-14.

Forman, W. (2002). The bias of neutrality: The role of interpreters in healthcare settings. *Vision: A Journal of Nursing, 8*(14): 20–22.

Fortier, J. (2014). *Improving healthcare for foreigners in Japan.* Retrieved from http://www.slideshare.net/JuliaPueblaFortier/jp-fortier-presentation-jane-conference

Gentile, A., Ozolins, U., & Vasilakakos, M. (1996). *Liaison interpreting: A handbook.* Melbourne University: Melbourne, Australia.

Haffner, L. (1992). Translation is not enough. Interpreting in a medical setting. *Western Journal of Medicine, 157*(3), 255.

Hale, S. (2007). Community interpreting: Research and Practice in Applied Linguistics. Hampshire: Palgrave MacMillan.

Hale, S. (2012). Are we there yet? Taking stock of what we are up to and where we are heading. Jill Blewett Memorial Lecture. Keynote address delivered at the Jubilation of 25 2012 Biennial AUSIT Conference. Sydney, Australia 1-3 December 2012.

Hale, S., & Gibbons, J. (1999). Varying realities: Patterned changes in the interpreter's representation of courtroom and external realities. *Applied Linguistics, 20*(2), 203-220.

Hall, E. T. (1989). *Beyond culture*. Doubleday: New York.

Hammer, M.R. (2012). The Intercultural Development Inventory (IDI): A New Frontier in Assessment and Development of Intercultural Competence. In M. Vande Berg, M., Paige, R. M., & Lou, K. (Eds.) (Ch. 5,115-136). *Student learning abroad: What our students are learning, what they're not, and what we can do about it*. Sterling, VA: Stylus.

Hannouna, Y. (2012). The need for adequate community interpreting services in healthcare multilingual settings: A case study in Al-Ain, UAE. *Translation and Interpreting Studies, 7*(1), 72-95.

Haslett, J. (producer) & Grainger-Monsen, M. (director). (2003). Worlds apart: A four-part series on Intercultural healthcare [film]. United States: Fanlight Productions.

Hatton, D. C., & Webb, T. (1993). Information transmission in bilingual, bicultural contexts: a field study of community health nurses and interpreters. *Journal of Community Health Nursing, 10*(3), 137-147.

Healthcare Interpretation Network. (2007). National Standard Guide for Community Interpreting Services. Retrieved from http://accessalliance.ca/wp-content/uploads/2015/03/NationalStandardGuideForCommunityInterpretingServices.pdf

Health Service Executive. (2012). *National Intercultural Health Strategy 2007-2012*. Retrieved from http://www.hse.ie/eng/services/Publications/SocialInclusion/National_Intercultural_Health_Strategy_2007_-_2012.pdf

Hellenic Open University. (2015). *Research report on intercultural mediation for immigrants in Europe*. Retrieved from http://mediation-time.eu/images/%CE%9F1_synthesis_report_EN.pdf

Hernandez, P. M., Piedra, L. M., & Goldberg, A. (2010). Brokering language and culture: Can ad hoc interpreters fill the language service gap at community health centers? *Social Work in Public Health, 25*, 387-407.

Hsieh, E. (2001). *To be or not to be: Discrepancies between the ideology and the practice of interpreters*. Paper presented at the annual conference of the National Communication Association, Atlanta, GA.

Hsieh, E. (2003). *The importance of liaison interpreting in the theoretical development of translation studies*. Retrieved from http://faculty-staff.ou.edu/H/Elaine.K.Hsieh-1/download/Hsieh2003-2.pdf

Hsieh, E. (2006). Conflicts in how interpreters manage their roles in provider-patient interactions. *Social Science & Medicine, 62*, 721-730.

Hsieh, E. (2008). "I am not a robot!" Interpreters' views of their roles in healthcare settings. Qualitative Health Research, 18, 1367-1383.

Hsieh, E. (2009). Bilingual health communication. *Communicating to manage health and illness,* 135.

Hook, J.N. (2013). Cultural Humility: Measuring openness to culturally diverse clients. *Journal of Counseling Psychology,* (60)3, 353-366.

Hung, H. (2002). *Neutrality and impartiality in mediation.* ADR Bulletin: Vol 5, Article 7, ePublications@bond. Available at http://epublications. bond.edu.au/adr/vol5/iss3/7

International Organization for Standardization. (2014). Guidelines for community interpreting. Retrieved from https://www.iso.org/obp/ ui/#iso:std:iso:13611:ed-1:v1:en

International Medical Interpreters Association & Education Development Center. (2007). *Standards of practice.* Retrieved from http://www. imiaweb.org/uploads/pages/102.pdf

International Medical Interpreters Association. (2008). *Salary survey.* Retrieved from http://imiaweb.org/about/salarysurvey2008.asp

International Medical Interpreters Association. (2013). *Glossary of definitions.* Retrieved from http://www.imiaweb.org/medical-resources/ default.asp

Jacobs, S. (2002). Maintaining neutrality in dispute mediation: Managing disagreement while managing not to disagree. *Journal of Pragmatics,* 34, 1403-1426.

Jalbert, M. (1998). Travailler avec un interprète en consultation psychiatrique. *Prisme, 8*(3), 94-111.

Jerusalem Intercultural Center Competence Team. (2007). *Cultural competence in healthcare organizations in Israel: A concise guide.* Retrieved from http://jicc.org.il/documents/publications/Concise-Guide-cultural-competence-healthcare-Israel-English-Version-April-2015.pdf

Jezewski, M. A. (1990). Culture brokering in migrant farmworker health care. *Western Journal of Nursing Research, 12*(4), 497-513.

Joint Commission on Accreditation of Healthcare Organizations. (2007). What did the doctor say?: Improving health literacy to protect patient safety. Retrieved from http://www.jointcommission.org/assets/1/18/ improving_health_literacy.pdf

Karasek Jr., R. A. (1979). Job demands, job decision latitude, and mental strain: Implications for job redesign. *Administrative Science Quarterly,* 7, 285-308.

Karasek, R., & Theorell, T. (1990). *Healthy Work:* Stress. *Productivity, and the Reconstruction of Working Life.* Basic Book: New York.

Kaufert, J. M. (1999). Cultural mediation in cancer diagnosis and end of life decision-making: The experience of Aboriginal patients in Canada. *Anthropology & Medicine, 6*(3), 405-421.

Kaufert, J., Kaufert, P. L., Koolage, O, N. (1986). Advocacy, media, and native medical interpreters. In R. Paine (ed.),.*Advocacy and anthropology, first encounters.* University of Newfoundland: Institute of Social and Economic Research.

Kaufert, J. M., & Koolage, W. W. (1984). Role conflict among 'culture brokers: The experience of native Canadian medical interpreters. *Social Science Medicine, 18*(3), 283-286.

Kaufert, J., Lavallée, M., Koolage, W., & O'Neil, J. (1996). Culture and informed consent: The role of Aboriginal interpreters in patient advocacy in urban hospitals. *Issues in the North, 1*(34), 89.

Kelleher, J. (2014). *U.S. DOJ sides against Hawaii in English only lawsuit.* Retrieved from http://health.hawaii.gov/ola/files/2014/05/Issue-25-Spring-2014-final.pdf

Kelly, C., & Meyers, J. (2014). *Cross Cultural Adaptability Inventory.* Retrieved from http://ccaiassess.com/

Kirmayer, L. J., Groleau, D., Guzder, J., Blake, C., & Jarvis, E. (2014). Cultural consultation: A model of mental health service for multicultural societies. *Focus, 48*(3):145-153.

Kleinman, A. (1980). *Patients and healers in the context of culture.* University of California Press, Los Angeles. 1980.

Kleinman, A., Eisenberg, L., & Good, B. (1978). Culture, illness, and care: Clinical lessons from anthropologic and Intercultural research. *Annals of Internal Medicine, 88*(2), 251-258.

Kondo, M. (1990). What conference interpreters should not be expected to do. *The Interpreters' Newsletter, 3,* 1591-4127.

Labun, E. (1999). Shared brokering: the development of a nurse/interpreter partnership. Journal of Immigrant Health, Oct; (4): 215-222

Larrison, C. R., Velez-Ortiz, D., Hernandez, P. M., Piedra, L. M., & Goldberg, A. (2010). Brokering language and culture: can ad hoc interpreters fill the language service gap at community health centers? *Social Work in Public Health, 25*(3-4), 387-407.

Leanza, Y. (2003). Education, pédiatrie et cultures. *Du sens de l'activité professionnelle pour des pédiatres dans leur travail de prévention auprès de familles migrantes* (unpublished doctoral dissertation). University of Geneva, Geneva, Switzerland.

Leanza, Y. (2005). Roles of community interpreters in pediatrics as seen by interpreters, physicians and researchers. *Interpreting, 7*, 167-192.

Loenhoff, J. (2011). Tacit Knowledge in Intercultural Communication, *Intercultural Communication Studies* XX: 1, 57-64.

Li, K. (2002). Modélisation chimico-mécanique du comportement des bétons affectés par la réaction d'alcali-silice et expertise numérique des ouvrages d'art dégradés (Doctoral dissertation, Ecole des Ponts ParisTech).

Maiese, M. (2005). Neutrality. Beyond Intractability, *The Beyond Intractability Project*, The Conflict Information Consortium, University of Colorado, www.beyondintractability.org

Mason, I., & Ren, W. (2012). Power in face-to-face interpreting events. *Translation and Interpreting Studies, 7*(2), 234-253.

Messias, D. K. H., McDowell, L., & Estrada, R. D. (2009). Language interpreting as social justice work: perspectives of formal and informal healthcare interpreters. *Advances in Nursing Science, 32*(2), 128-143.

MFH Project Group. (2004). *Amsterdam Declaration Towards Migrant Friendly Hospitals*. Retrieved from http://www.mfh-eu.net/public/files/european_recommendations/mfh_amsterdam_declaration_english.pdf

Mikkelson, H. (2008). Evolving views of the court interpreter's role: Between Scylla and Charybdis.
Benjamin Translation Library, 76, 81.

National Association of Certified Mediators. (2015). *Frequently asked questions*. Retrieved from http://www.mediatorcertification.org/faq.html

National Association of Judiciary Interpreters & Translators. (2011). Code of ethics. Retrieved from http://www.najit.org/about/NAJITCodeofEthicsFINAL.pdf

National Council on Interpreting in Health Care. (2005). *National code of ethics and standards of practice*. Retrieved from http://www.ncihc.org/assets/documents/publications/NCIHC%20National%20Standards%20of%20Practice.pdf

National Council on Interpreting in Health Care. (2011). *National standards for healthcare interpreter training programs*. Retrieved from http://www.ncihc.org/assets/documents/publications/National_Standards_5-09-11.pdf

New South Whales Healthcare Interpreter Services (2014). Interpreting in healthcare: Guidelines for healthcare interpreters. Retrieved from file:///C:/Users/Laura/Downloads/HCIS%20Brochure.pdf

Norris, W. M., Wenrich, M.D., Nielsen, E. L., Treece, P. D., Jackson, J. C., & Curtis, J. R. (2005). Communication about end-of-life care between language-discordant patients and clinicians: Insights from medical interpreters. *Journal of Palliative Medicine, 8*(5), 1016-1023.

Norström, E., Fioretos, I., & Gustafsson, K. (2012). Working conditions of community interpreters in Sweden: Opportunities and shortcomings. *Interpreting, 14*(2), 242-260.

Oviatt, S. L., & Cohen, P. R. (1992). Spoken language in interpreted telephone dialogues. *Computer Speech & Language, 6*(3), 277-302.

Pérez-González, L. (2012). Translation, interpreting and the genealogy of conflict. *Journal of Language and Politics, 11*(2), 169-184.

Phelan, M. (2010). Interpreting in Northern Ireland. *Translation Ireland, 18*(2), 99-107.

Phelan, M., & Martín, M. (2010). Interpreters and cultural mediators– different but complementary roles. *Translocations, 6*(1).

Pineda, K.R. (2010). Intercultural Communication in Healthcare Interpreting: An Exploration of Possibilities. Master of Arts Thesis Paper. University of the Pacific, Stockholm, California.

Pinker, S. (1995). The language instinct: The new science of language and mind (Vol. 7529). Penguin UK: London.

Pistillo, G. (2003). *The interpreter as cultural mediator.* Retrieved from http://www.immigrantinstitutet.se/immi.se/intercultural/nr6/pistillo.pdf

Pöchhacker, F. (1995). Simultaneous interpreting: A functionalist perspective. *Hermes, Journal of Linguistics, 14,* 31-53.

Pöchhacker, F. (1995). Interpreting Research. D. Gile (ed.), *"Those Who Do...":A Profile of Research(ers) in Interpreting.* (p.47-64). Philadelphia: John Benjamins Publishing Company.

Pöchhacker, F. (1998). Selected papers from the Second International Conference on Interpreting in legal, health and social service settings, *The community interpreter's task, the critical link 2: Interpreters in the community,* Vancouver, BC, Canada.

Pöllabauer, S. (2004). Interpreting in asylum hearings. *Interpreting, 6*(2), 143-180.

Putsch, R. W. (1985). Intercultural communication, the special case of interpreters in healthcare. *Journal of American Medical Association, 254*(23):3344-3348.

Price-Wise, G. (2015). An Intoxicating Error: Mistranslation, Medical Malpractice, and Prejudice. BookBaby Book Publishing.

Quan, K. (2010). The High Costs of Language Barriers in Medical Malpractice. *School of Public Health,* University of California.

Queiroz, M. (2014). Panorama da interpretação em contextos médicos no Brasil: perspectivas. Tradterm *Revista do Centro Interdepartamental de Tradução e Terminología*, FFLCH, USP, São Paulo/Brasil. v. 23

Rao, A. A., & Sridhar, G. R. (2007). Quality of care: Assessment. *Lipids in health and disease, 6*(1), 12.

Raval, H. (2005). Being heard and understood in the context of seeking asylum and refuge: Communicating with the help of bilingual co-workers. *Clinical Child Psychology and Psychiatry, 10*(2), 197-217.

Rice, M. F. (2005). A framework for understanding the need for cultural competency in public administration (Vol. 578). Bush School Working Paper.

Roy, C. B. (1999). *Interpreting as a discourse process.* Oxford University Press: London.

Rudvin, M. (2007). Professionalism and ethics in community interpreting: The impact of individualist vs. collective group identity. *Interpreting, 9*(1), 47-69.

Sadikov, O. N. (1981). Pravovoe regulirovanie mazhdunarodnykh perevozok.

Sapir, E. (1929). The status of linguistics as a science *Language, 5*(4), 207-214. doi:10.2307/409588

Sapir, E., & Mandelbaum, D. G. (Eds.). (1986). *Selected writings of Edward Sapir in language, culture and personality.* Berkeley: University of California Press.

Segal, J. Z. (2007). "Compliance" to "concordance": A critical view. *Journal of Medical Humanities, 28*(2), 81-96.

Seidelman, R. Bachner, Y.G. (2010). That I won't translate! Experiences of a family medical interpreter in a multicultural environment. *Mount Sinai Journal of Medicine, 77*(4), 389-393.

Sengupta, I. (1996). Cultural Competency in Health and Human Services, Training of Trainers Manual, Cross Cultural Health Care Program.

Shirinzadeh, S.A., Majadi, T.S.T. (2015). Translators as Cultural Mediators in Transmitting Cultural Differences, Procedia – *Social and Behavioral Sciences,* 208:167-174.

Solomon, M. Z. (1997). From what's neutral to what's meaningful: reflections on a study of medical interpreters. *Journal of Clinical Ethics, 8*(1):88-93.

Souza, I. E. T de V. (2016). Interpreting Culture: Exploring The Perspectives of Professional Practitioners, Doctoral Thesis Paper. Osaka University, Osaka, Japan.

Straniero, S. F. (2007). La mediazione linguistica nella conversazione spettacolo. Trieste: EUT

Takimoto, M. (2006). Interpreters' role perceptions in business dialogue interpreting situations. *Monash University Linguistics Papers, 5*(1), 47-57.

Theodosiou, A., Aspioti, M. (2015). European Intercultural Mediation Report. Retrieved from http://mediation-time.eu/images/ 01_synthesis_report_EN.pdf

Tracy, K. (2002). Everyday talk: Building and reflecting identities. New York: Guilford.

Uvarov, V.D. (1981). Paradoksy rolevogo povedenija u~astnikov situacii perevoda. *Tetradi Perevodcika, 18*, 13-16.

Valero-Garcés, C. (2008). Chapter 8. Hospital interpreting practice in the classroom and the workplace. In C. Valero-Garcés and A. Martin (eds.), *Crossing borders in community interpreting: Definitions and dilemmas* (pp.18165-185). Philadelphia: John Benjamins Publishing Company.

Van De Mieroop, D., Bevilacqua, G., & Hove, L. V. (2012). Negotiating discursive norms: Community interpreting in a Belgian rest home. *Interpreting, 14*(1), 23-54.

Verrept, H. (2008). Chapter 9. Intercultural mediation: An answer to health care disparities? In C. Valero-Garcés and A. Martin (eds.), *Crossing borders in community interpreting: Definitions and dilemmas* (pp.187-201). Philadelphia: John Benjamins Publishing Company.

U.S. Agency for Healthcare Research and Quality. (2015). TeamSTEPPS: Strategies and tools to enhance performance and patient safety. September 2015. Retrieved from http://www.ahrq.gov/professionals/ education/curriculum-tools/teamstepps/index.html

U.S. Department of Health and Human Services, Office of Minority Services. (2001). *National Standards for Culturally and Linguistically Appropriate Services in Health Care.* Retrieved from http:// minorityhealth.hhs.gov/assets/pdf/checked/finalreport.pdf

Uvarov V.D. (1981): "Paradoksy rolevogo povedenija u~astnikov situacii perevoda", *Tetradi Perevodcika*, 18, pp.13-16.

Wadensjö, C. (1998). *Interpreting as interaction.* Routledge: London.

Weber, O. & Molina, M. (2003). Le point de vue des médiateurs culturels/ interprètes. In P. Guex & P. Singy (Eds.), *Quand la médecine à besoin d'interprètes.* Genève: Médecine & Hygiène, 85–112.

Wenger, A. F. (1995). Cultural context, health and health care decision making. *Journal of Transcultural Nursing, 7*(1), 3–14.

Whorf, B. L. (1939). The relation of habitual thought and behavior to language. *ETC: A Review of General Semantics*, 197-215.

Wilcox, S., & Shaffer, B. (2005). Towards a cognitive model of interpreting. *Benjamins Translation Library, 63*, 27.

Witter-Merithew, C. S. C., & Nicodemus, C. I. (2012). Toward the international development of interpreter specialization: An examination of two case studies. *Journal of Interpretation, 20*(1), 8.

Woloshin, S., Bickell, N. A., Schwartz, L. M., Gany, F., & Welch, H. G. (1995). Language barriers in medicine in the United States. *Journal of the American Medical Association, 273*(9), 724-728.

Wolters Kluwers Health: Lippincot, Williams, and Wilkins. (2015). *Trained medical interpreters can reduce errors in care for patients with limited English proficiency.* Retrieved from www.sciencedaily.com/releases/2015/10/151015132312.htm

World Association of Sign Language Interpreters. (2013). *Code of Ethics for Community Interpreters.* Retrieved from http://wasli.org/wp-content/uploads/2013/10/80_coe-svt.pdf

Zimányi, K. (2009). A diagrammatic approach to redefining the role of the interpreter based on a case study in forensic psychology. *Translation & Interpreting, 1*(2), 55-70.

Appendix A

CULTURALLY AND LINGUISTICALLY APPROPRIATE SERVICES (CLAS) STANDARDS (UNITED STATES)

Principal Standard:

1. Provide effective, equitable, understandable, and respectful quality care and services that are responsive to diverse cultural health beliefs and practices, preferred languages, health literacy, and other communication needs.

Governance, Leadership and Workforce:

2. Advance and sustain organizational governance and leadership that promotes CLAS and health equity through policy, practices, and allocated resources.
3. Recruit, promote, and support a culturally and linguistically diverse governance, leadership, and workforce that are responsive to the population in the service area.
4. Educate and train governance, leadership, and workforce in culturally and linguistically appropriate policies and practices on an ongoing basis.

Communication and Language Assistance:

5. Offer language assistance to individuals who have limited English proficiency and/or other communication needs, at no cost to them, to facilitate timely access to all healthcare and services.
6. Inform all individuals of the availability of language assistance services clearly and in their preferred language, verbally and in writing.
7. Ensure the competence of individuals providing language assistance, recognizing that the use of untrained individuals and/or minors as interpreters should be avoided.
8. Provide easy-to-understand print and multimedia materials and signage in the languages commonly used by the populations in the service area.

Engagement, Continuous. Improvement, and Accountability:

9. Establish culturally and linguistically appropriate goals, policies, and management accountability, and infuse them throughout the organization's planning and operations.
10. Conduct ongoing assessments of the organization's CLAS-related activities and integrate CLAS-related measures into measurement and continuous, quality improvement activities.
11. Collect and maintain accurate and reliable demographic data to monitor and evaluate the impact of CLAS on health equity and outcomes and to inform service delivery.
12. Conduct regular assessments of community health assets and needs and use the results to plan and implement services that respond to the cultural and linguistic diversity of populations in the service area.
13. Partner with the community to design, implement, and evaluate policies, practices, and services to ensure cultural and linguistic appropriateness.
14. Create conflict and grievance resolution processes that are culturally and linguistically appropriate to identify, prevent, and resolve conflicts or complaints.
15. Communicate the organization's progress in implementing and sustaining CLAS to all stakeholders, constituents, and the general public.

Appendix B

INFORMED CONSENT FORM

This informed consent is for the medical interpreters (MIs) who are going to be asked about their perspectives on interpreting culture in the healthcare setting between providers and patients who do not share the same language and culture.

1. INFORMATION OF THE RESEARCHER
    1-1 Name: Izabel E. T. de V. Souza, M.Ed, CMI-Spanish
    1-2 Affiliation: Graduate School of Human Sciences, Osaka University, Japan
    1-3 Title: Interpreting Culture: Exploring the Perspectives of Professional Medical Interpreters

2. INTRODUCTION
    This research is for the doctoral dissertation of Ms. Souza, Ph.D candidate with Graduate School of Human Sciences, Osaka University, Japan. You are invited to take part in this research. Details of the research are described as follows:

    2-1 Purpose: To understand MIs perspectives acting as a cultural bridge in the healthcare setting between providers and patients who do not share the same language and culture. (Timing, Challenges, Advantages, Disadvantages, Strategies, Specific Cases)

2-2 Type of the Research: This research will involve you in a survey and/or an interview with the researcher who records and transcribes it for your reading. The questions are primarily related to your views about interpreting culture in ha healthcare setting and your name will not be shared.

3. PARTICIPANT SELECTION
Professional medical interpreters will be selected for a survey and/ or for interviews.

4. VOLUNTARY PARTICIPATION
Your participation in this research is entirely voluntary. It is your choice whether to participate or not. You may change your mind after decision of participation and you can stop participation at any time before, during and even after the interview.

5. PROCEDURE
After you accept participation, I will ask you to have an interview and allow me to record it so later it will be transcribed and read by you before my analysis. During the analysis or transcription process, you might be asked some questions or additional information through emails.

6. RISKS AND DISCOMFORTS
There is a risk that you may share some personal or confidential information by chance. If this happened to you in your judgment, you are able to correct or delete it during your reading of transcribed texts.

7. CONFIDENTIALITY
This research will protect your identification and will be anonymous. No personal information will be shared.

8. BENEFITS
There might be no immediate benefit to you, but your generous participation will help explore the views of practitioners on interpreting culture in their work as medical interpreters. I expect that my findings of this research will be used for future progress of the teaching and standardization of the cultural interface component of the medical interpreters work. Your observations and

comments will provide valuable insight from which to establish future professional standards on this topic.

9. WHO TO CONTACT

   If you have any question about this research, please call Ms. Izabel Souza at +1-305-781-2427 (USA) or email at izabeletdvs@gmail. com

   If you have any question or concern about your rights as a research participant, please call Dr. Yasuhide Nakamura, Graduate School of Human Sciences, Osaka University at +81 6 6878 8064.

10. CONSENT STATEMENT

    I have read all the information provided above. I have been given the opportunity to ask questions and all the questions have been answered to my satisfaction. I have been provided a copy of this form for my records and I agree to participate in this research.

_____   _____

Signature of Participant   Signature of Researcher

Print Name of Participant   IZABEL E. T. de V. Souza

Date: Date:

Appendix C

LIST OF HEALTHCARE ORGANIZATIONS STUDY PARTICIPANTS WORK IN

ABC Hospital

Access Alliance Language Services

Alhambra Hospital

Access Alliance

Access Alliance Community Health Centre

Access Alliance Languages Services

Access Alliance Multicultural Health and Community Services (AAMHCS);

Language Bank

Alliance for African Assistance

AnMed Health

Auckland District Health Board

AUSL Bologna

Berkshire Health Systems

Berkshire Medical Center

Beth Israel Deaconess Medical Center

Blue Cross Blue Shield

Bon Secours Hospital

Boston Medical Center

Brockton Neighborhood Health Centre

Cambridge Health Alliance

Cancer Treatment Center of America

Cape Cod Healthcare

Caremore

Carolinas Health

Banfield

Barnet Primary Healthcare

Barton Health

Barton Health Systems

Barton Memorial Hospital

Baylor University Medical Center

Children's Hospital Seattle

Children's Hospital Boston

Children's Hospital of Philadelphia

Everett Clinic

Cigna

Cincinnati Children's Hospital

Cincinnati Children's Hospital Medical Center

Cleveland Clinic

Cobb and Douglas county Health Department

Columbia Pediatrics

Community Outreach Program for the Deaf

Connecting Cultures, Inc.

Cyracom International Inc.

Dean Clinic (Madison, Wisconsin)

Denver Health

DHHS

DHSH

DSHS Washington State

East Carolina University Brody School of Medicine

Carolinas Healthcare System

Cedar Sinai medical center

Central Mass AHEC

Certified International Interpreting

Certified Language International (CLI)

Cyracom, Inc.

First Choice

Florida Hospital

Franciscan group

Frederick Memorial Healthcare

Free Clinic in Washington State

Garden and Associates

Glenwood Medical Associates

Global Village Interpreting and Cultural Solutions

Global Village Language

Grady Health System

Greenville memorial hospital

Grossmont Hospital. San Diego. CA,

Hanna Interpreting Services

Harborview Medical Center, Seattle, WA

Harris Health System

Harris Health System

Harvard Vanguard

Henry Ford Health System

Hershey Penn State Medical Center

HM Hospitals

El Dorado County Health Department

Hokkaido University Hospital

Eye Associates of New Mexico

InDemand Interpreting

Interpreting Agencies: Cyracom

Japan Association of Medical Interpreters (JAMI)

John Peter Smith Hospital

Kaiser Permanente

KentuckyOne Health

Kin-ikyo Sapporo Hospital

Lahey Clinic

Lahey Hospital and Medical Center

Lancaster General Health

Lancaster General Health

Language Line Services

Language Line Solutions

LGH

Lifebridge

Los Angeles County Department of Health Services

LRC

LSA

Maine Medical Center

MD Anderson Hospital, Houston TX

Memorial Hermann Healthcare System

Peace Health

Hospital Mammoth

Hospital Santa Catalina

Humana

Mercy Gilbert Medical Center

Methodist LeBonheur Healthcare

Metro South Health - Princess Alexandra Hospital

Mid-Hudson Forensic Psychiatric Center

Moffitt Cancer Center

Mt. Auburn Hospital, Cambridge, MA

Multicare

National Institute of Social Security (Italy)

New York Presbyterian Hospital

NHS UK

NIH

NMC

Northern Virginia AHEC

NSW Health

OHSU

Online Interpreters

Oregon Health and Science University

ORMC

Orthopedic International Hospital

Reading Medical Center

Regions Hospital

Roswell Park Cancer Institute

Pacific Interpreters PATH

St. Michael's Hospital

Peace Health Hospital

Pfizer

Phoenix Children's Hospital

Piedmont Hospital

Presbyterian Medical Group

Providence

Public Health Department (Nash, Martin, Washington, Tyrrell Counties)

Public Health Department (Madison and Dane county)

Pure Language Services

Royal Adelaide Hospital

Saint Vincent Hospital

Samitivej Hospital

Santa Rosa Memorial Hospital

Sapporo Medical Interpreters' Group

Seattle Cancer Care Alliance

Seattle Cancer Care Alliance, Seattle

Seattle King County Department of Public Health

Skagit Regional Health, Mount Vernon, WA, U.S.A

Southwest Healthcare Management

Spectrum Health

St. Joseph Hospital

University of Tsukuba Hospital

University of Wisconsin Hospitals and Clinics

U.S. Army

St. Peter's Health Partners

Steward Health (Good Samaritan Medical Center)

Swedish Medical Center

Tacoma General Hospital

Telelanguage

Temple University Health System, Philadelphia

The Academy of Languages

The Human Rights Clinic in Yaffo

Tramonte Dental Implants - Milan, Italy

UCSD Medical Center

UHN (includes various hospitals)

ULS

United Healthcare

University Health Network

University of California San Francisco Medical Center

University of Colorado Health system

University of Maryland Medical Center

University of Miami/Jackson Memorial Hospital

University of Michigan Health System

University of Nebraska Medical Center

University of New Mexico Hospitals

Yale New Haven Hospital

U.S. Healthworks

UT M D Anderson Cancer
Center

UW Health

UW Hospitals and Clinics

UW Medicine

Valley Medical Hospital

Vetsmart (Animal
Ohpthalmology Clinic)

Via All Languages at North
York Hospital

Vidant Medical Center

Waitemata District Health
Board

Walla Walla Community College

Washoe County Medical
Reserve Corps Volunteer

WC

Western Kentucky University

Wheaton Franciscan
Healthcare- All Saints

World Health Organization
(WHO)

Wishard Health Services

WNC Medical Society

Companies that promoted the study:

Linguistic Systems, Inc.

Culture Advantage

Go Fluently

M2 Language Consultants, LLC

COMMGAP

ICA Language Services

Certified Languages International

Culture Advantage

ECData

Masterword Services

Appendix D

INTERPRETING CULTURE INTERVIEW INSTRUMENT:

Exploring the Medical Interpreter Perspective

Date:
Time Started: Time Ended: Duration (minutes):
Country:

Before we start I want to define three terms so that we all under the same
understanding regarding the main concepts behind this research study.

Culture Clarifier, Interface, Mediator and Broker:
when the interpreter acts as a bridge between two cultures.

Cultural issue:
a belief or practice in health practices or in general that might affect
intercultural communication.

Cultural intervention:
when an interpreter has intervene in order to address an cultural issue that
is prior, during, or after a clinical encounter.

DEMOGRAPHIC SECTION

Name:

Age: ☐18 - 24 ☐25 - 34 ☐35 - 44 ☐45 - 54 ☐55 – 64
☐65 – 74 ☐75 or older

Gender: ☐Male ☐Female

Institution(s) for which you work: (3 max)
1.
2.
3.

Working Language(s):
1.
2.
3.

Email:

Years working as a medical interpreter:
☐0- 5 ☐6-10 ☐11-15 ☐15-20 ☐over 20 years

Average ours of training received to work as a medical interpreter:

☐under 8 ☐8-20 ☐21-40 ☐41-60 ☐101-200 ☐201 – 400
☐over 400

Certified? ☐Yes ☐No

RESEARCH QUESTIONS

First of all do you believe that professional interpreters must address the cultural issues that affect a clinical encounter that they are interpreting for? ☐Yes ☐No (If no, discontinue interview after asking why)

1. When interpreting in healthcare, in what types of situations do you need to intervene to explore a cultural issue that might be affecting communication?
   a. Please give me an example or two of such situation.
   b. Is there anything you wish to add regarding situations that require you to intervene due to a cultural issue?

2. In your daily work, how often do you have to stop interpreting to intervene due to a cultural issue that arises? (Very often, occasionally, it depends) Please explain.
3. What are the advantages of addressing cultural issues?
4. What are the disadvantages of addressing cultural issues?
5. What are the challenges addressing cultural issues?
6. What are the strategies that you have used when intervening due to cultural issues?
7. If you were trained, do you think you received enough training on how to handle cultural differences between providers and patients when you were trained to work as a medical interpreter? What would you like to see educational programs do to better train future medical interpreters?
8. How stressful is it for you to intervene or interrupt a session you are interpreting for and why?
9. Is there anything that you would like to add regarding interpreting culture between a provider and a patient who do not share the same language and culture?

Appendix E

25 COUNTRIES PARTICIPANTS WORK IN

1. Argentina
2. Armenia
3. Australia
4. Azerbaijan
5. Brazil
6. Canada
7. China
8. France
9. Germany
10. India
11. Italy
12. Iraq
13. Israel
14. Japan
15. Mexico
16. New Zealand
17. Nicaragua
18. Russia
19. Spain
20. Sudan
21. Tamil (Srilanka)
22. Thailand

23. Turkey
24. United Kingdom
25. United States

Note: 2 participants listed Puerto Rico as their country. At the moment of publication, Puerto Rico is officially a state of the United States and is not a contested territory, so it was not included on this list.

Appendix F

RESEARCH REPORT ON INTERCULTURAL MEDIATION FOR IMMIGRANTS IN EUROPE (P. 26-27)

As the report states, "The encounter with the field of intercultural mediation is fairly chaotic due to the variety of terms used. Of course the use of different terms reflects the different genealogies of the phenomenon detected in each country and the different roles assumed. Yet, despite differences it is important to note that two elements are of major importance in understanding the reality of intercultural mediation: on the one hand the **practice of interpretation** as reflected in the frequency of the term "interpreter" employed in the terminology and on the other the importance attributed to the **cultural context**, as reflected in terms such as community, intercultural, sociocultural etc." (Theodosiu &Aspioti, 2015).

The list below presents some of the terms used across the countries surveyed to describe intercultural mediators. As you will see, some countries use the term interpreter while others use the term mediator, supporter, counselor, and facilitator.

Austria
- Cultural interpreter
- Community interpreter

Belgium
- Intercultural mediator
- Family supporters
- Social interpreting

France
- Interpreter in the social sector
- Social and cultural mediators

The Netherlands
- Interpreter
- Ethnic minority healthcare counselor

Germany
- Mediation and Arbitration - Alternative Dispute Resolution (ADR)
- Mediation
- Integration facilitator

Greece
- Interpreter
- Intercultural mediator

Italy
- Social interpreter
- Communication facilitator
- Linguistic mediator

Portugal
- Sociocultural mediator
- Mediator
- Community mediator
- Intercultural mediator

Spain
- Intercultural mediator

Switzerland
- Intercultural interpreter
- Intercultural mediator